W9-DDC-481

DISCARD

# SACRED ASSEMBLIES AND CIVIC ENGAGEMENT

# SACRED ASSEMBLIES AND CIVIC ENGAGEMENT

*How Religion Matters for America's*

*Newest Immigrants*

FRED KNISS

PAUL D. NUMRICH

RUTGERS UNIVERSITY PRESS

*New Brunswick, New Jersey, and London*

Library of Congress Cataloging-in-Publication Data

Kniss, Fred Lamar, 1956–

Sacred assemblies and civic engagement : how religion matters for America's newest immi-grants / Fred Kniss, Paul D. Numrich.

     p.    cm.

Includes bibliographical references and index.

ISBN 978-0-8135-4170-9 (hardcover : alk. paper)—ISBN 978-0-8135-4171-6 (pbk. : alk. paper)

   1. Chicago Metropolitan Area (Ill.)—Religion. 2. Immigrants—Illinois—Chicago Metro-politan Area—Religious life. 3. Religion and culture—Illinois—Chicago Metropolitan Area. 4. Immigrants—Illinois—Chicago Metropolitan Area—Social conditions. 5. Social participa-tion—Illinois—Chicago Metropolitan Area. I. Numrich, Paul David, 1952- II. Title.

  BL2527.C482K55 2007

  200.86′9120977311—dc22

                         2006039171

A British Cataloging-in-Publication record for this book is available from the British Library.

Visit our Web site: http://rutgerspress.rutgers.edu

Manufactured in the United States of America

*From Fred*
*To Stephen, Michael, and Alexis, with thanks for all the pride and joy*

*From Paul*
*To my wife, Christine, and my late mentors, Kenneth V. Mull and Edmund F. Perry, who each made this book possible in unique ways*

# Contents

# Acknowledgments

In this book, we report on the findings of the Religion, Immigration, and Civil Society in Chicago (RICSC) project. A project as large, complex, and time consuming as this one is not accomplished without the assistance and support of many individuals, groups, and organizations. We are grateful to each of them, and we herewith absolve them all of complicity in any shortcomings.

From its germination as an idea in 1999, and throughout the fieldwork and interviewing from 2000 to 2003, the project benefited from the generous financial support of The Pew Charitable Trusts and its Gateway Cities Initiative. Along with funding, we were fortunate to have the moral and intellectual support of Kimon Sargeant, the program officer at The Pew Charitable Trusts who encouraged and challenged us. Also, from the very beginning, R. Stephen Warner served as our principal advisor in the research design and data collection stages. We benefited from his continuing interest and support as we moved toward publication.

We received able university support of all our research and writing activities. The Office of Social Science Research at the University of Illinois at Chicago, and especially its director, John Gardiner, provided space and support as the project was being conceptualized. From 2000 onward, when the project was housed in Loyola University Chicago's McNamara Center for the Social Study of Religion, Loyola's Office of University Research Services provided additional financial and administrative support. Special thanks to William Yost and David Crumrine, who gave generously of their time and expertise. Professors Judith Wittner and Richard Block provided specialized training for our researchers early in the project. Throughout, our research enjoyed the collegiality of and engaging conversations with Lowell Livezey and the University of Illinois at Chicago's Religion in Urban America Program, with whom Numrich was also affiliated. We are grateful to the faculty of Loyola's Department of Sociology, chaired by Peter Whalley during most of the project's duration, for providing a stimulating and collegial environment, helping us to develop our thinking, and, no doubt, avoid embarrassing mistakes. We are especially grateful to department staff members Patty Robertson and Rosa Negussie, who were supportive in too many ways to enumerate.

Two postdoctoral researchers worked closely with us through most of the study. Randal Hepner did yeoman's work as project manager, and Tracy Thibodeau provided important technical and ethnographic skills. We are also immensely grateful for the insights and hard work of numerous graduate assistants in sociology at Loyola. At various stages all of the following committed significant time and energy to data collection, entry, and/or analysis: Andrew Fraker, Aneta Galary, Jennifer Helton, Nori Henk, Katrina Hoop, Matt Logelin, Kersten Bayt Priest, Juan Carlos Rivera, Sarah Schott, Saher Selod, Lisa Speicher, Farha Ternikar, Travis Vande Berg, and Dmitro Volkov. Laurie Stoll assisted us in the final stages of manuscript production, especially with constructing the index. We are pleased and proud that Ternikar, Vande Berg, and Volkov incorporated project data into their doctoral dissertations.

We pulled together a distinguished body of project advisors, some of whom were able to meet in Chicago for early discussions about the direction and significance of the research: Joseph Ahne, Thomas Baima, Edith Blumhofer, John Boivin, Elias Kyprianos Bouboutsis, Peter Friedman, Carolyn DeSwarte Gifford, Steven Gold, Marcia Hermansen, Asayo Horibe, Asad Husain, Arvin Juan, Edward Kantowicz, Kwang Chung Kim, Prem Lalvani, James H. Lewis, Lowell Livezey, Jessica Nem, Robert Orsi, Jane I. Smith, Anthony Stevens-Arroyo, Thomas Tweed, Elfriede Wedam, and Raymond B. Williams. As noted above, Steve Warner served as our principal project advisor, to whom we often turned for counsel and support.

Upon completion of our initial fieldwork and interviewing, we held a conference at Loyola to present our preliminary findings. We especially appreciate the formal responses given by Steve Warner, Raymond Williams, and Dirk Ficca at that conference, as well as the positive feedback we received from those representatives of our research sites in attendance. We also ran a monthlong professional photographic exhibit entitled "Faith and Fellowship: Building Chicago's New Immigrant Communities," featuring the photographic art of Zbigniew Bzdak and Jerry Berndt. Randal Hepner was instrumental in conceiving and organizing this exhibit, which offered remarkable visual testimonies to the religious experiences we were attempting to understand.

We treasured our rare opportunities to compare notes with our sister Gateway Cities projects, especially the gathering of principal investigators in Washington, D.C., in early 2002. Special thanks to Jose Casanova, Helen Rose Ebaugh, and Donald Miller, who consulted with us during visits to Loyola. Helen Rose Ebaugh, in particular, offered a very helpful critique of early text from this book. Jose Casanova and Aristide Zolberg graciously invited us to participate in the New York project's conference in May of 2002.

Many other colleagues engaged our work helpfully. In particular, we thank Wilbur Zelinsky, the Chicago Area Group for the Study of Religious Communities, and the participants in the Sociology Department faculty colloquium at Northwestern University. We are grateful to participants in sessions at several national and regional scholarly conferences (American Academy of Religion, American Sociological Association, Association for the Sociology of Religion, Midwest Sociological Society, and Society for the Scientific Study of Religion).

The peer review process is a wonderful mechanism for clarifying thought and prose, and we have taken advantage of it in this and earlier publications. Peter Kivisto, an external reviewer for Rutgers, provided us with insightful advice on improving the manuscript. Our Rutgers editors, Kristi Long and Adi Hovav, have our deep gratitude for their scholarly guidance and unmerited patience. Portions of the theoretical framework presented in chapters 3 and 4 previously appeared in Kniss's essay in *Handbook of the Sociology of Religion*, edited by Michele Dillon and published by Cambridge University Press (Kniss 2003). Portions of chapter 6 appear in Numrich's essay in *The Child in American Religions*, edited by Don Browning and Bonnie Miller-McLemore and published by Rutgers University Press (Numrich, forthcoming c). Parts of chapter 8 previously appeared in "Immigrant Congregational Names in Chicago: Religious and Civic Considerations," an article in the journal *Names* (Numrich and Kniss 2005).

Those closest to us invested nearly as much in this project as we did. Paul gives special thanks to Christine Numrich, who accompanies him in his scholarly odyssey with patience and appreciation; to Nathan and Rachel Numrich for strategic technical aid; and to Melissia Harrell and Sean Michael Gaddy for their understanding during the early years of vocational transition. Fred thanks his family: Rosalyn, his constant companion for the past twenty-seven years; his sons, Michael and Stephen, who provide frequent joy and continual adventure; and his daughter-in-law, Alexis, who added to the joy and adventure by joining the family while this book was in process. Only our families know how much we put them through during our project, but they also know (we hope) how much we love them.

Finally, we thank the congregations and people who allowed us to visit, to talk, and to pry. Without them, our conclusions would be speculative at best. We hope we have captured something of how religion matters for them and, through them, for American society as a whole.

# SACRED ASSEMBLIES AND CIVIC ENGAGEMENT

# 1    *Introduction*

> *It is intriguing that the history of sociology through the early decades of the 20th century is simultaneously the history of the social scientific study of religion. About the time of Durkheim's death in 1917 and Weber's in 1920, the two fields began to diverge. . . . Given the heightened public awareness of religion as a result of current events, and the greater attention to the topic by social scientists in a number of subdisciplines, the time is ripe for catapulting the social scientific study of religion back into the mainstream of our disciplines.*
>
> —Helen Rose Ebaugh (2002)

## A Virtual Tour of America's New Cultural and Religious Diversity

America's cultural landscape is undergoing a dramatic transformation. Changes in U.S. immigration laws since 1965 have given new meaning to the notion of American pluralism.[1] The 1990s became the greatest decade of American immigration. The number of foreign-born residents and their children, what scholars call the first and second immigrant generations, recently reached fifty-six million, the highest level in U.S. history. As the country prepared for the turn of the millennium, it pondered the implications of its "rapid move toward a multiracial, multiethnic society, fueled in part by 1 million immigrants each year, [which was] likely to continue into the next century" (Westphal 1999).

This new cultural diversity brings a new level of religious diversity to a society touted from the beginning for the "manyness" of its religions (Albanese 1999; Gaustad and Schmidt 2004). In his introduction to *Gatherings in Diaspora*, sociologist R. Stephen Warner sums up the current multireligious state of the Union: "Although Christians, in their staggering variety, are still by far the largest religious group in the United States, millions of adherents of other religions—Islam, Hinduism, Buddhism, and more—have joined Jews to expand the boundaries of American religious pluralism to an extent unimaginable only forty years ago. At the same time, Christians from Asia, the Middle East, and Latin America are de-Europeanizing American Christianity" (Warner and Wittner 1998, 4). Even those who criticize common estimates of non-Christian populations in the United States as inflated admit that America is more religiously diverse than ever before.[2]

America's new diversity is concentrated in its largest metropolitan centers— 70 percent of foreign-born residents live in six states—but it certainly is not limited to them. Harvard University's Pluralism Project is mapping religious diversity in Maine, Mississippi, Kansas, the Miami Valley in Ohio, and elsewhere across the country. Southeast Asian Buddhists have settled the bayous of southwestern Louisiana (Bankston 1997); Indian immigrants have built Wisconsin's first Hindu temple in the woods of Pewaukee, west of Milwaukee (*Indian Reporter,* September 15, 2000); and Postville, Iowa, boasts residents from twenty-nine countries, many employed by the town's kosher slaughterhouse (Bloom 2000; Mihalopoulos 2003). Whatever the hard demographic statistics may be, America as a whole has clearly turned a perceptual corner of cultural identity. It takes only one group of resettled African Muslim refugees, one non-Christian religious center, or one new ethnic expression of Christianity to shift local self-perception, while media coverage of national trends affects perceptions even in the hinterlands.

In the chapters to follow, we will take a look close-up at how religion and the new religious diversity affects the civic engagement of new immigrants in a particular urban region—the Chicago metropolitan area. We begin very locally at our own campus, Loyola University Chicago. A quick tour of Loyola's neighborhood, beginning at the corner of Devon Avenue and Broadway on Chicago's north side, brings America's new cultural and religious landscape into focus. Traveling west on Devon a couple of miles, we pass a Nigerian Apostolic church, a Japanese Protestant congregation, a storefront Hindu temple, a walkup Sikh *gurdwara,* a Muslim mosque or two, and several Hasidic Jewish synagogues. Going south on Broadway a few blocks, we encounter a Bosnian cultural center, an Ismaili Shi'ite mosque, two Vietnamese Buddhist centers, a Haitian Church of God in Christ, and a Roman Catholic parish that serves Spanish-speaking immigrants. The local public high school claims that more than sixty languages are spoken in the homes of its students; a nearby Catholic elementary school has more than fifty. Numerous ethnic businesses add to the teeming cultural mix of this "windshield survey" of Loyola's neighborhood, Rogers Park.

Admittedly, Rogers Park is one of the most diverse neighborhoods in the city. But this new diversity is increasingly visible throughout metropolitan Chicago. According to the 2000 census, nearly 20 percent of Cook County's population is foreign-born (up from 14 percent in 1990), while nearly 9 percent entered the United States within the past decade (almost double the 1990 percentage). More than 30 percent of the county speaks a language other than English at home (up from 23 percent in 1990). The six-county metropolitan region as a whole saw a 52 percent increase in its Asian population between 1990 and 2000, which now totals nearly 400,000 (a conservative estimate). The region is home to fifty immigrant

New religious diversity. Ling Shen Ching Tze Buddhist Temple is housed in a remodeled former Presbyterian church building. Photo by Jerry Berndt.

Muslim mosques, more than thirty immigrant Buddhist temples, and more than two dozen Hindu temples. Countless Latin American, Asian, and African immigrant congregations diversify Chicago-area Christianity in new ways, while a continuing influx of European immigrants complicates the ethnic makeup of the longstanding Roman Catholic and Orthodox Christian communities.

Rogers Park, Chicago, the nation. The new cultural and religious landscape has caught the attention of scholars and other observers. Most significantly for our purposes, many have begun to take religion seriously in understanding recent immigration trends and their implications for American society.

## Taking Religion Even More Seriously

This book contributes to the emerging scholarly conversation regarding recent American immigrant religions, especially the social science side of the conversation. Since the early 1990s, more and more observers have sought to redress the neglect of religion in the larger field of recent American immigration studies.[3] However, despite significant progress in this agenda, a legacy of past inadequacies still haunts the scholarship.

In 1993, two sociologists of religion identified the lacuna in recent work on American immigration. In making his case for the New Ethnic and Immigrant Congregations Project, R. Stephen Warner (1993a) characterized the extant literature on recent immigrant religious institutions as "appallingly sparse." Peter

Kivisto (1993, 104) observed that "for some [recent immigrant] groups the religious dimension is a virtually untapped topic. Even for those groups that have received scholarly attention, the current corpus is quite small." Five years later, Stewart Lawrence (1998) found the literature still underdeveloped, since "only a handful of scholars in this field treat immigrant churches and religiosity as their *sole* object of study." As late as 2000, Warner (2000b, 267) maintained that research was "just now beginning" on the topic of new immigrant religions in America.

Several observers have explained this neglect of religion in recent American immigration studies. In his 1997 presidential address to the Association for the Sociology of Religion, Warner (1998a) examined barriers associated with census, survey poll, and institutional roll sources, which provide more—and more reliable—data on income, education, occupation, and the like than on religiosity and religious identities. But beyond such data-based obstacles, Warner also identified ideological biases, such as Marxian prejudices and secularization and declension theories of religion, that permeate various scholarly disciplines.

Ethnic historian David Yoo (1999, 11) wonders, "Given the pivotal opening that religion provides into the lives of Asian Americans, it is puzzling that religion has been largely omitted from narratives of American history and Asian American studies." Yoo suggests that Asian Americanists may have difficulty "interpreting religion," or may simply lack interest in it given their Marxian antireligionism and disdain for American imperialism in Asia (8–9). Yoo argues that "a reconceptualization of the field is necessary so that the serious treatment of religion becomes the interpretive rule rather than the exception" (10).

Sociologist Helen Rose Ebaugh (2002) explored religion's marginalization in the social sciences in her 2001 presidential address to the Society for the Scientific Study of Religion, excerpted in our opening epigraph (cf. Kivisto 1993). Ebaugh explained that "over the past sixty or so years the study of religion has, in fact, been largely absent from mainstream social science" due to uncritical acceptance of a secularization thesis that predicted religion's inevitable demise in modern societies (386–387). Ebaugh and fellow sociologist Janet Chafetz (2000b, 15) offer the following broad indictment: "In our opinion, the anti-religion bias that keeps immigration scholars from focusing on this topic . . . characterizes the social sciences in general." As Ebaugh (2002, 388) points out, "Because religion involves transcendent, non-empirical realities in the lives of people, it is frequently seen as outside the purview of the objective, value-free world of science, despite the fact that religious variables are central in explanations of human behavior." It appears easier for social scientists to understand an immigrant congregation, for example, as the institutional locus of ethnic, social, and economic (read: "empirical") dynamics, rather than as an association that perceives itself to be "the living embodiment of universal and timeless truths," to borrow a phrase from sociologist Carolyn Chen (2002, 220). In his 2003 presidential address to the

Society for the Scientific Study of Religion, sociologist Robert Wuthnow (2004, 162) expressed his disdain for "the kind of social science that not only tries to float above these truth claims as a methodological strategy, but also implicitly assumes that such truth claims matter so little that religious communities can be treated like so many social clubs or athletic teams."

Historians have also criticized the lack of attention to the intersection of religion and immigration in American historical studies. In his seminal essay, "Religion and Ethnicity in America," Timothy Smith (1978, 1169) argued that ethnic association in the United States by religious identity far outstripped association by other identities, yet this fact was obscured, in large part, by "the preoccupation of historians and sociologists with the secular aspects of ethnicity and nationality." Jon Gjerde (1986, 682) criticized historians for portraying the immigrant church as merely "a place where the mother tongue was spoken and customs were familiar." Jay Dolan (1988, 65–66) documented the "meager" attention to immigration by historians of American religion, concluding that "to continue such neglect is inexcusable."

Recent scholarship has responded to these and other criticisms. Thanks to substantial work by the Gateway Cities research initiative of the Pew Charitable Trusts (Sargeant 1998; Warner 1998c; Warner and Wittner 1998),[4] and by many independent scholars (e.g., Kwon, Kim, and Warner 2001; Min and Kim 2002; Yoo 1999), research on American immigrant religions has reached a plateau of new knowledge. The larger field of immigration studies can no longer ignore religion. Even so, the legacy of the past still plagues scholarship, especially in work influenced by the social sciences. While we applaud the new attention to religion in American immigration, we also advocate that this attention become more sophisticated. In other words, it is time to take religion even more seriously.

## Conducting a Comprehensive Examination of Core Religious Ideas, Practices, and Identities

It is insufficient to claim—as many implicitly do—that religion's role in recent immigration has been taken seriously merely by choosing congregations (or other religious associations) as the unit of scholarly investigation. Of course, by definition, religion provides the primary organizing principle of associational life for a congregation. Its transcendent locus of meaning is the value added of a congregation, distinguishing it from secular associations (cf. Christerson and Emerson 2003, 179; Wuthnow 2004, 162). Yet case studies of immigrant congregations often fail to give an adequate accounting of a congregation's distinctiveness. The usual description of the congregation's role in the lives of its immigrant constituents could apply to any immigrant organization, religious or not. The church/mosque/synagogue/temple serves as a venue for cultural reproduction, ethnic identity construction, communal fellowship, and immigrant adaptation to the host society, like other immigrant organizations. Perhaps the congregation is judged more effective or inclusive in fulfilling these functions than other immigrant organizations, but too often the specifically religious character of the congregation is not comprehensively articulated. The literature recognizes the complexity of the interrelationship between ethnicity and religion in such associations, yet the religious side of the equation usually receives short shrift (cf. Chong 1998, 275; S. Lawrence 1998; Smith 1978). Of course, without direct comparative investigation of religious versus secular immigrant associations, the characteristically religious nature of religious associations remains somewhat speculative, but not inordinately or unhelpfully so.

The first fruit of the Pew Gateway Cities research initiative, the book *Religion and the New Immigrants* from phase one of the Religion, Ethnicity, and New Immigrants Research (RENIR) project in Houston (Ebaugh and Chafetz 2000b), moved scholarship forward significantly. *Religion and the New Immigrants* describes many of the religious ideas, practices, and identities that characterize its thirteen congregational case studies. Still, the book tends to underanalyze these topics. They do not show up as a separate category in the thematic section of the book (part 3), which focuses on immigrant adaptations, social services, and ethnic reproduction. The last topic comprises three full chapters (19, 20, 21), with only six pages devoted to the intertwining of ethnic and religious identities (401–406). Religious aspects are sometimes explicitly or implicitly bracketed out of the analytical discussion. For instance, chapter 17 explores "how immigrant religious institutions structure themselves and what formal services they provide for their members *over and above serving as places of worship and religious education*" (347, emphasis added). The book's concluding chapter includes a helpful historical comparison of classical and recent immigrant congregations, yet religion qua religion does not appear in lists of divisive issues or factors affecting congregational evolution. A sixfold typology of immigrant congregations is offered, based on ethnicity (mono- and multi-), without considering how religious identities can inform ethnicity and create key fault lines within ethnic communities.

Paying more sophisticated attention to religion in recent American immigration also means avoiding overly simple or broad generalizations, especially about religious identities. Religious groups and organizations certainly belong to broad historical heritages and draw from large religious traditions, and so it is appropriate for scholars to talk about Buddhists, Christians, Muslims, etc., and to make meaningful distinctions among them. However, religious groups and organizations are also motivated by their particular expressions of the wide streams in which they stand. Temples or churches are never merely generically Buddhist or Christian, for instance. They also embody specific types of Buddhism or Christianity. Recent scholarship often remains at a general level of analysis and needs to spend more time with the particulars. It is important to know, for instance, that a Chinese temple is "Buddhist," but it is even more important to know the details of its "reformed Buddhist" identity (Yang and Ebaugh 2001). Likewise, what does it mean, in particular, that an Argentine church is "Plymouth Brethren" (Ebaugh and Chafetz 2000b)?

Bruce Lawrence (2002) criticizes scholars whose analysis of immigrant religions remains abstract and uncontextualized, which he calls Religion One, where labels such as "Buddhism," "Hinduism," or "Islam" come off as timeless and essential categories. Lawrence advocates a more sophisticated treatment of the complexities of immigrant religions, a Religion Two analysis that considers ethnic, racial, class, and other social variations within and among religious categories. We agree, adding yet another layer of complexity to Lawrence's admonition—scholars must pay careful attention to *religious* differentiation within immigrant religions.

### Treating Religion as an Independent Variable

Commenting on the effects of residual ideological biases on young scholars, Warner (1998a, 202) says, "Adoption of such ideas appears to require that students turn religion analytically from an active, independent, emergent factor to a defensive, dependent, doomed one" (cf. Warner 2000b). Yoo (1999, 9) argues that religion, like race, is "an independent variable [that] merits serious study in its own right as a force that shapes, transforms, and unifies as well as divides Asian American communities." We agree that the predominant direction of the causality or influence arrow in research must be reversed.

The tendency to portray immigrant congregations in dependent rather than independent terms has contributed to the underappreciation of religion generally. Both classical and recent immigration research focuses largely on the internal dynamics of immigrant congregations as they respond to the powerful pressures of migration and Americanization. Thus we may learn something about transformations and adaptations of imported religious ideas, practices, and identities in the American context, but less about how those religious ideas, practices, and identities affect members' activities outside of the congregation and shape the congregation's organizational ecology. Adequate analysis of organizational ecologies is especially rare in recent scholarship and typically traces only networks within a congregation's denomination or religious lineage, rather than broader congregational interactions—for instance, with outside religious groups, society generally, or governmental bodies. In *Gatherings in Diaspora* (Warner and Wittner 1998), only Karen Chai's study of a Korean Protestant church presents a full organizational ecology; in *Religion and the New Immigrants* (Ebaugh and Chafetz 2000b), only Fenggang Yang's study of a Chinese reformed Buddhist temple and Maria Gasi's study of a Greek Orthodox church do likewise. Even *Religion across Borders,* the RENIR project's second book, which features a transnational analysis, limits itself to the internal workings of religious networks (Ebaugh and Chafetz 2002, 181, 183). Of course, some immigrant congregations may have relatively weak organizational ecologies, but that is also a researchable topic.

In treating religion as an independent causal force, much can be learned from the scholarly discipline of the history of religions or comparative religion (e.g., Kitagawa 1967; Sharpe 1975; Smart 1984, 2000). This discipline is known for what Ninian Smart (2000) calls an "empathetic" appreciation of religion as experienced from the standpoint of religious insiders, with a keen vigilance against anything smacking of reductionism—that is, "reducing" religious phenomena to non-religious factors, thus "explaining them away." This discipline's Achilles heel is the opposite of recent social science—namely, too much fondness for religion, even to the point of being charged with confessionalism and crypto-theology (Wiebe 1984, 1998; cf. Reat 1983). Still, its close, empathetic attention to religious phenomena could explain why Warner (2000b) judged history of religions least culpable of all the scholarly disciplines in neglecting religion in the recent immigration.

Much also can be learned from the field of American congregational studies, which pays careful attention to the religious content of congregational life (e.g., Ammerman 1997, 2001; Ammerman et al. 1998; Becker 1999; Roozen, McKinney, and Carroll 1984). Often lost in the attention given to immigrant congregations is the simple fact that they are congregations, and therefore share much in common with nonimmigrant congregations. Of course immigrant identity adds a special dimension to the experience and behavior of a congregation, but in many ways such a congregation looks and acts like any other sacred assembly.

Scholars of recent American immigrant religions have indeed reached a plateau of new knowledge, but they must now move on to a more sophisticated exploration of their research topic. This book challenges both the larger field of recent American immigration studies to take religion more seriously and the social sciences to reconsider the questions regarding religion and society that were so central in their founding. Our advocacy for paying more sophisticated attention to religion in the scholarly study of recent immigration is not motivated by any normative theological or ethical agendas (for examples, see Herberg 1955; Prorok 1994; Stout 1975). Religion qua religion deserves close scholarly attention because of its potential motivating force in the lives of religious individuals, groups, and organizations, often on a par with, sometimes exceeding, other variables favored by scholars. We will not, however, make too much of religion. We recognize that religion does not matter to all immigrants (cf. B. Lawrence 2002, 94–99), and that other variables sometimes matter more than religion in explaining immigrant perspectives and behaviors.

Our intention in this book is to explore how religion matters as a force in the civic engagement patterns of America's newest immigrant groups. This was our mandate as part of the Gateway Cities research initiative, which funded our Religion, Immigration, and Civil Society in Chicago Project (2000–2003), along with projects in Houston, Los Angeles, Miami, New York, San Francisco, and Washington, D.C. The Pew Charitable Trusts directed us to "document how religion contributes to or impedes the civic incorporation of new immigrants," without prejudicing us as to how to define "civic incorporation" (Sargeant 1998). Whereas significant scholarship has since been done on the civic engagement patterns of American congregations generally (e.g., Ammerman 2005; Chaves 2004; Schwadel 2005), this topic has garnered far less attention from scholars of immigrant congregations due to a preoccupation with internal organizational dynamics (Chen 2002; Ecklund 2005). Our main analytical advantage in researching the civic engagement patterns of immigrant congregations stems from our broad multireligious research pool and our attention to the particularities of religious ideas, practices, and identities.

## How We Took Religion Seriously

In order to show how religion qua religion matters for recent immigrants, we need to examine particular elements of religion itself—elements that may be shared by all religions, but that also exhibit significant variation within and between particular religious groups. We chose three such religious variables—sectarianism, moral authority, and moral projects—to incorporate into our research design. Our choices were not arbitrary. Based partly on our own earlier research (e.g., Kniss 1997, 2003), we had reason to believe that these particular religious factors would have a significant impact on a religious group's civic engagement patterns. The three factors we chose to highlight are themselves informed by doctrines, symbols, rituals, scriptures, sacred stories, and other constitutive phenomena of religious heritage. In turn, these three affect the social life and civic engagement of immigrant groups.

The first religious factor is the degree of *sectarianism* in the particular groups we observed. How much are they in tension (often intentionally so) with the larger society, with co-immigrants, and/or with co-religionists? Serendipitously, several of the religious sites we selected for the project turned out to be fairly sectarian forms of their broader religious tradition. This allowed us to make comparisons between sectarian and more mainstream religious ideas, practices, and identities.

The second religious variable concerns how a religion conceives of *moral authority*. Is authority primarily located in a collective tradition, often embodied in a shared text or in a religious hierarchy, or does moral authority belong to autonomous individual agents who depend on their reason and experience in the application of religious ideas and values or in pursuit of moral projects? Catholics, evangelical Protestants, Orthodox Christians, Jews, and Muslims tend to fall on the collective end of this continuum, while liberal Protestants, Hindus, and Buddhists are, in general, more individualistic in how they conceive of moral authority.

The third variable concerns how a religion defines its most central *moral projects*. Are these primarily collectivist, concerned with community-building, social justice, or structural issues, or are they primarily individualist, concerned with reforming and empowering individual believers? In general, Catholic, liberal

Protestant, and Muslim communities fall toward the collectivist end of this continuum, while Hindus, Buddhists, and evangelical Protestants fall toward the individualist end. The Orthodox Christian and Lubavitch Hasidic Jewish communities are more complex cases, but they seem to fall closer to the individualist end than do some of their religious cousins.

Of course, these generalizations need to be treated in much more detail and with more nuance, a task we will take up in the following chapters. As noted above, treating groups as uncontextualized or generic Hindus or Buddhists may obscure important aspects of their experience. Certainly none of the Hindu or Buddhist temples we studied could be considered simply generic—nor could the Catholic or Protestant congregations, for that matter. Each of the major religious traditions has given birth to regional and local variants that, while sharing many core ideas or values, also exhibit important variations in how they define their moral projects or how they exercise moral authority. Focusing on these religious factors is important; but if we are truly to take religion seriously, then we must be cognizant of both the general similarities and the particular variations within religious traditions as well as between them.

In addition to religious information, we collected data on several areas of social life where we thought we could observe the impact of these religious factors on civic engagement. We studied immigrant experiences with occupation, education, marriage, and language, all major topics in the recent literature. We consider each of these areas in turn in part 2.

Finally, for our dependent variables we looked for two kinds of civic engagement. By "civic engagement" we mean the public action of individuals and groups as they interact with and participate in the organizations, associations, and institutions of society, especially in three arenas: government, the economy, and civil society (see Ehrenberg 1999). In the U.S. context, the last arena has been dominated by a host of voluntary associations, especially religious ones.

The first type of civic engagement is "citizenship" broadly defined. Here we are interested not only in how individuals might behave politically as citizens, but also in how immigrant individuals act as members of a variety of broader publics, whether that might be in the workplace, the PTA, or other community involvements. Our second type of civic engagement, "organizational ecology," concerns how the group in question engages institutionally with other groups or organizations. While we focused most of our attention on local organizational linkages, the content and character of these local networks are obviously influenced by the congregation's ecological ties at the national and transnational levels as well. Part 3 considers these two types of civic engagement and how they are influenced by religious factors and institutional contexts.

We find Mark Chaves's (2004, 8) general assessment of American congregations to be applicable to recent immigrant congregations as well—namely, that they "mainly gather people to engage in the cultural activity of expressing and transmitting religious meanings." Chaves specifies the content of this cultural activity as ritual events, religious education, and the sacred arts, which in turn shape congregational interactions with society. He singles out the importance of the arts: "If we look for the secular arena of American social life in which congregations are most a part, we will find it in the arts, not in social services or politics." We agree with Chaves's last statement about the noteworthy absence of overt social and political initiatives in American congregations, whether immigrant or indigenous. Our broadly construed notion of citizenship, as described above, intends to capture less obvious, but equally important, forms of civic engagement found in recent immigrant congregations.

To collect the data needed for addressing these questions, we did ethnographic fieldwork and extensive interviewing at sixteen immigrant congregations in the Chicago metropolitan region. Unlike many of the Pew-funded Gateway Cities projects, we organized our data collection by religion, rather than by ethnicity or country of origin. We did this because we wanted to keep religious factors front and center as our core independent variables. Based on the size and historical significance of their respective communities for Chicago, we chose Roman Catholic, Protestant, Orthodox Christian, Jewish, Muslim, Hindu, and Buddhist congregations that served immigrants from a variety of ethnic backgrounds.

For each of the religious groups, we compiled (as much as possible) comprehensive lists of congregations where at least 20 percent of the participants were post-1965 immigrants or their children.[5] From each list, we identified potential research sites that would enable us to do systematic comparisons within and between both religion and ethnicity. That is, for each religious tradition, we attempted to select sites representing at least two different ethnicities; for each ethnicity, we selected sites from at least two different religions. Unfortunately for scholars, the world does not organize itself into neat grids, and our grid was no exception. For example, in the case of Judaism, few congregations met the 20 percent rule. Despite a good-faith attempt, we could find no Conservative or Reform synagogues that had 20 percent or more recent immigrant members. So, for Judaism, we limited ourselves to a Lubavitch Hasidic congregation with a predominantly Russian membership.

Clearly, this was not a random sample of congregations. Our selections were theoretically driven, based on the ethnic and religious comparisons we wished to make. After winnowing our lists to those sites with the religious and ethnic characteristics we sought, we made our final selections based on our ability to gain access for our researchers and on our interest in including both urban and suburban locations, conservative and liberal tendencies, and variation in class composition of congregations. A brief description of each research site is provided in an appendix. The accompanying map (fig. 1.1) orients the sites in the greater Chicago area. Although our research sites were not selected randomly, we are

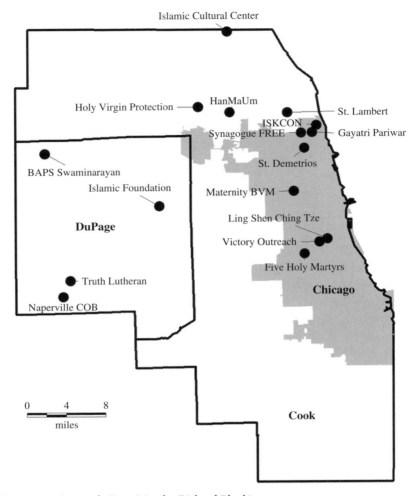

Figure 1.1    Research Sites (Map by Richard Block)

confident that they represent the most important religious, ethnic, geographic, and demographic variations that affect the question of religion and civic engagement for new immigrants.

At each research site, we collected a variety of data via ethnographic fieldwork, documentary analysis, and face-to-face formal interviews. For the sake of accuracy, we tape-recorded and transcribed all interviews. In compliance with our human-subjects research protocols regarding confidentiality, we do not identify interviewees by name, personal characteristics, or specific position in the congregation. At times we have made editorial changes to verbatim quotes for the sake of clarity, but without making substantive changes in content or meaning. At the outset of our project we secured written consent from authorized representatives to research their congregations and, although we offered the option of disguising the congregation's identity, all of our research sites were willing to be named in our publications. To find out more about the congregations' ecological ties, we also conducted telephone surveys of organizations connected to our congregations. Under our guidance, most of the data collection was carried out by an able team of graduate student research assistants and postdoctoral researchers.

From the start of the project, teamwork was the order of the day. Site selection, interview protocols, codebooks, and analytical designs were all developed collaboratively. For each site, we assigned one primary researcher who did most of the fieldwork and interviewing. Occasionally, especially when gender was an important issue, we assigned two researchers to a site, one male and one female. The primary researcher, however, was often assisted by other researchers on the project. Further, researchers transcribed and coded data from all research sites, not just their own. At regular team meetings, we discussed our latest work together and planned our next steps.

Thus, the primary researchers in each site conducted their research with the larger comparative project in view, and with at least a rudimentary knowledge of what was being found at other sites. This enhanced their ability to pursue particular issues in the interviews and greatly enriched the data we collected. It also meant that graduate assistants were more than hired hands but were semi-autonomous analysts in their own right. Our decision to give research assistants a freer hand than is sometimes the case in large projects bore fruit in a number of dissertations, theses, and papers, in addition to the present book. It also enriched our own thinking, as we were able to test our emerging arguments in conversation with a team of other creative and interested scholars.

The organization of our book follows the basic analytical design that informed our data collection. Unlike much of the previous work on recent immigrants, we will not offer a series of detailed congregational case studies. Rather, we will address themes and questions based on data drawn from comparative case analysis. We believe this thematic approach will allow us to address more systematically the gaps we have noted in previous research. In part 1, we will explore three religious variables that significantly shape how these communities engage public life in the United States—sectarianism, moral authority, and moral projects. In part 2, we will analyze several institutional contexts within which such civic engagement takes place—occupation, education, marriage, and language. Finally, in part 3, we will identify various patterns of civic engagement by examining organizational ecologies and citizenship issues and offer an explanation of how and why those patterns emerge. A concluding chapter summarizes our findings and highlights the larger implications of the civic engagement patterns of immigrant religious groups, both for continuing scholarship and for the nation's future.

## How Religion Matters: Some Examples

How do religious ideas, practices, and identities influence the civic engagement patterns of immigrant congregations? Here are a few examples that will be elaborated in later chapters.

### Disaster Response

Early in our research project, in January 2001, a devastating earthquake struck the Gujarat region of India. Nearly sixteen million people were directly affected, while official death tolls exceeded twenty thousand. Which of our research sites in Chicago would respond? How? To what extent? And why?

The BAPS Swaminarayan Hindu temple stood out for the magnitude and efficiency of its response, as it tapped into a massive relief effort mounted by its international parent network. This might surprise the uninformed observer. Local newspaper coverage listed contact information for just two organizations, the well-known international relief organization CARE and BAPS.

No one familiar with the legacy of Swaminarayan Hinduism was surprised, however. Since its inception in nineteenth-century Gujarat, this sectarian Hindu group has been renowned for a moral project that emphasizes the link between individual regeneration and social improvement. Just days after the earthquake, the chief minister of Gujarat issued a public commendation of the BAPS relief efforts.

### Marital Preferences

Who marries whom in immigrant religious circles and why? What religious beliefs shape marital preferences? And what significance does marriage have for evolving ethnic/racial and religious group identities in the United States? Consider two sectarian Hindu groups.

BAPS Swaminarayan identity includes a strong ethnic component. BAPS Hindus are predominantly Gujaratis and prefer both religiously and ethnically endogamous marriage. Marrying a person from another Hindu lineage or region of India is acceptable if that person converts to Swaminarayan Hinduism. This indicates a willingness to extend the group's ethnic boundaries beyond a regional Gujarati identity and portends a more panethnic Indian identity in the group's future.

On the other hand, ISKCON Hinduism draws from doctrines that undermine all ethnic/racial distinctions. People are not their bodies, they are spirit-souls. Whether Gujaratis, Indians of another regional identity, or white Americans, the goal in marriage is to join two people in a spiritual, Krishna Conscious relationship. Whereas BAPS Swaminarayans, and perhaps most Indian Hindu groups, will likely contribute to the formation of pan-Indian ethnicities through their marriage preferences in the United States, groups like ISKCON will likely break out of Indian ethnic/racial boundaries. Likewise, South Asian Christians and Muslims will likely expand their ethnic boundaries as their marriage preferences tap into their larger, respective multiethnic/racial groupings in the United States.

### Political Action

"Here we are all equal/Aqui todos somos iguales," said the English/Spanish T-shirts. AMNESTY NOW for undocumented immigrants, proclaimed the fliers. God bless the workers in their search for justice and dignity, the priest prayed.

The event: a community rally about day laborer exploitation. The audience: Hispanics, whites, African Americans, a coalition of religious and community groups, and two day-labor companies on the hot seat. The venue: the auditorium at Maternity BVM Roman Catholic Church.

Why here? The Catholic social justice heritage. Wrote Pope John Paul II in his 1981 encyclical, *Laborem Exercens (On Human Work),* "Every possible effort should be made to ensure that it [emigration] may bring benefit to the emigrant's personal, family and social life, both for the country to which he goes and the country which he leaves." May emigration bring benefit, not exploitation. "The most important thing is that the person working away from his native land, whether as a permanent emigrant or as a seasonal worker, should not be *placed at a disadvantage* in comparison with the other workers in that society in the matter of working rights. Emigration in search of work must in no way become an opportunity for financial or social exploitation." How is social justice to be accomplished? With a collectivist moral project: "In this area much depends on just legislation, in particular with regard to the rights of workers."

### Going to School

When we think of parochial school education in immigrant circles, Lutherans and Catholics spring to mind. Which of America's newest immigrant religious groups are taking up the parochial education banner today? Why? And with what implications for American society as a whole?

The answer to the first question is Muslims, to an extent far greater than the next largest groups, Buddhists and Hindus. As to the second question, the motivations for parochial education are much the same in the Muslim case as in the earlier Lutheran and Catholic cases—namely, to maintain group religious identity and to provide children a moral education superior to that offered by the public schools.

And the implications for American society? Won't this lead to religious enclavism and balkanization? On the contrary, we see great potential for bridging between Islamic parochial schools and the larger society, as when Islamic Foundation School participates in the cooperative Muslim Scouts of Greater Chicago program, interweaving Islamic and Scouting philosophies in order to nurture upstanding Muslim-American citizens.

*Names Say a Lot*

An immigrant congregation must choose an official or legal name, no trivial decision despite the fact that scholars have paid virtually no attention to the decision-making process involved. One might expect a preponderance of Old World ethnic or national identity markers in immigrant congregational names, bespeaking an enclave mentality. Yet surprisingly few such names can be found, and those usually balance their names with American national terms, like the Nigerian Islamic Association of United States of America, an immigrant mosque in Chicago.

At the same time, religious terminology abounds in immigrant congregational names. This, too, is no trivial fact, although it might seem so at first glance. Immigrant congregations identify the heart of their identity and purpose in their names—they are sacred assemblies first and foremost, even though they also perform many nonreligious functions.

This points to the heart of the narrative to follow. America's newest immigrants have established sacred assemblies through which they engage the larger society in a variety of ways with multiple civic consequences. How do religious ideas, practices, and identities help to shape immigrant congregations' civic engagement patterns? How religion matters in this is a matter worthy of serious consideration.

# PART ONE

## RELIGION MATTERS

# 2

## Purity and Protest

> The sect adheres to the ideal of the "ecclesia pura"
> (hence the name "Puritans"), the visible community
> of saints, from whose midst the black sheep are
> removed so that they will not offend God's eyes. . . .
> [It] cannot be anything but a purely voluntary associ-
> ation if it wants to retain its true religious identity
> and its effectiveness.
>
> —Max Weber (1914)

There was a wistful look on the face of Jay Desai, a prominent lay leader of the BAPS Shree Swaminarayan Mandir in Bartlett, Illinois. "I wish more community groups or families from outside the temple would make use of this space," he said, "but most outsiders don't want to accommodate our restrictions." We were standing in a dining/ballroom space beneath the main meeting hall of the *haveli*, a large community center building that also served as temporary worship space while the *mandir* (temple) was under construction. The haveli was roughly the size of half a football field, with wonderful kitchen facilities and well-appointed restrooms and other ancillary rooms able to accommodate a wide range of events. Mr. Desai was the public relations officer of the temple, a gregarious man who, along with other temple leaders, had built friendly relations with neighboring residents and churches in Bartlett. He had also helped to forge strong, mutually supportive connections to local politicians and suburban DuPage County Republican party leaders.

So, why, given all this openness to the outside, were the BAPS folks unable to attract more groups into their space? Desai was probably correct to single out the restrictions imposed by BAPS Swaminarayan religious obligations. Restrictions against physical contact between the sexes turned away wedding parties that may have wanted to include dancing. Restrictions against alcohol and tobacco also put a crimp on celebrations. Strict vegetarianism and restrictions against the use of onions and garlic (staples in most Indian cuisine) discouraged non-BAPS Indian groups from making use of the kitchen facilities.

Women worshipping at BAPS Swaminarayan temple. BAPS has strict gender segregation rules within the temple. Photo by Jerry Berndt.

Sectarianism is an analytical concept that social scientists have used to understand these sorts of strict religious lifestyle regulations (and other religious phenomena) that separate a group from outsiders. Religious organizational typologies that contrast sects to churches, denominations, or cults have been widely used in the sociology of religion. But the BAPS Swaminarayan community is also a good illustration of the complexities and variations within the category of "sect." While the congregants who identify with this temple are intentional and explicit in distinguishing themselves from other religions (and especially other Hindus) in their religious and social practices, they are also intentionally welcoming of guests (both religious and secular) who do not share their views, and they are active in building and expanding relationships to civil society and modernity in general. They have forged strong relationships within the local political system, and local dignitaries regularly attend their holiday celebrations.

They also embrace modernity in ways that are not often associated with sectarianism (which scholars frequently consider a return to pristine tradition). Their temple has the latest in high-tech Internet and satellite technology that allows them to engage in real-time communication with BAPS temples and religious leaders around the world. Their members are successful in a multitude of professions, especially in the medical, legal, and computer fields. They have alliances with professional associations like the Indian Pharmacists of Chicago, who participated materially in the earthquake relief efforts described in the introduction.

Among the groups we studied, the BAPS Swaminarayan temple is not alone in holding sectarian views. In fact, more than a third of the congregations we researched could fairly be called sectarian. But how their sectarianism is instantiated varies among the different groups. Sectarianism can occur along multiple dimensions that set a group in tension with a variety of others. Depending on how sectarianism is practiced, it can create separation from some groups or with regard to some activities, while at the same time permitting or even facilitating relationships with others. If we are to understand how religious sectarianism shapes immigrant civic engagement, we need to take these complexities into account. Particular kinds of sectarianism will produce particular patterns of engagement and will preclude others.

## Sectarianism as an Analytic Concept

What do we mean when we say that more than a third of our research sites were sectarian? There is no simple answer to this question. The concept of sectarianism has been widely used (and contested) ever since the Weber/Troeltsch church–sect typology entered the sociological canon more than eighty years ago (Troeltsch 1931; Weber 1922). In its original form, the typology described two Weberian ideal types of religious organization. Churches were large, accommodative, inclusive institutions that were closely allied with the state. Church membership was bestowed by birth. Sects were small, resistant, exclusive religious organizations that existed in tension with the state and its church. They were an attempt to return to the original pristine religious ideals of the tradition. Members joined sects by choice (conversion) rather than by birth.

H. Richard Niebuhr (1929) added "denomination" to the typology to account for large accommodative religious institutions in a context of pluralism like that found in the United States. Following Niebuhr and continuing into the 1970s, a sociology of religion cottage industry emerged around the elaboration and specification of these typologies. Various lists of defining characteristics and subtypologies emerged and competed with one another for acceptance by scholars. For example, Wilson (1959), expanding on earlier work by Becker (1932) and Yinger (1946), identified four sect subtypes—conversionist, revolutionist, pietist, and Gnostic.[1] Most significantly, "cult" was added to the set of ideal types (see especially Stark and Bainbridge 1979) to denote sectlike religious movements that were new religions rather than returns to a "pure" tradition.[2] Johnson (1963), one of the earliest critics of typological elaboration, took the opposite tack and suggested boiling all the elaborations down to one essential variable—the degree of tension between the religious group and the social environment.

We will combine these two strategies. That is, like Johnson, we will boil down, focusing on two essential characteristics of sectarianism as a religious type. We share Johnson's view that the degree of tension with the surrounding religious and social environment is a key component of sectarianism. This, in fact, is what makes the sectarianism concept so useful for a study of religion and civic engagement. We will also, however, elaborate that conception based on our empirical observations of recent immigrant religions. One of the problems with the detailed typological elaborations in the earlier literature was that they tended to be based on the experience of Western Christianity and were especially influenced by observations of religion in the United States. This raises the question of whether or not theories of sectarianism are even applicable to non-Western religions.[3] If we are to use sectarianism as one of our comparative dimensions in the analysis to follow, we need to consider this problem at the outset.

If we examine the various specifications and elaborations of the sectarianism concept that have been handed down to us from previous scholarship, we find that there are two key components that most conceptualizations share. We might call them "purity" and "protest." The first refers to sectarian groups' core interest in preserving the purity of the religious tradition. Sectarian groups usually form as a schism from a larger religious tradition that is seen as having become apostate—that is, having wandered too far from its original ideals. This focus on purity produces the second characteristic—the tendency to take a prophetic stance (in the Weberian sense of the term) over against co-religionists and/or against the larger outside world. Sectarians view themselves as a faithful remnant, an example to others who have lost their way. They may vary in the intensity with which they confront or proselytize outsiders, but they all share an explicit protest stance, an intentional "over-againstness" in relation to some significant "other."

When we reduce the concept of sectarianism to these two essential components, it is equally applicable to Western and non-Western religious traditions. The sectarian Hindu and Buddhist congregations that we studied see themselves as embodying a fundamental, "truly true" pure form of their religion, as do the Hasidic synagogue and the Pentecostal church. All the sectarian groups in our study defined themselves explicitly in contrast to a larger religious tradition or an outside world that had failed in some fundamental way. And, to return to our central theme, how a sectarian group defines that distinction will have a powerful impact on its civic engagement. It will identify its enemies and, perhaps more important, its allies.

The last point begs the most important questions for applying the concept of sectarianism to an analysis of civic engagement. Purity with regard to what? Protest against what? In defining the pure tradition, some groups may focus on issues of individual morality, such as dietary or sexual practices. Others may focus on theological conceptions or hierarchies of religious or familial authority. The substance of what it is that needs to be purified will influence the content of a group's civic engagement. Likewise, the who or what against which a group defines itself will influence whom it engages and what kind of response it receives from the powers that be.

In the rest of this chapter, we will analyze sectarianism along two cross-cutting dimensions. The first regards the substantive type of sectarianism, the content of a group's notions of purity. Some groups highlight religious or theological purity. Others emphasize cultural purity, focusing on issues such as dress, diet, or language. Still others are concerned with social purity organized around gender or class-based identities.

Cutting across this substantive or qualitative dimension is the more quantitative dimension of the degree of tension between the group and others—that is, how much the group protests. Some groups are clearly sectarian, setting strong distinctions between themselves and others, while others are mainstream (churchlike, in Troeltsch/Weber terms), embracing the outside world and engaging it openly, or perhaps even seeing themselves as coterminous with the world. Others may be somewhere in the center of this continuum.

Both of these dimensions have consequences for civic engagement. The first defines friends and foes. Religious purity will tend to set a group against co-religionists or co-ethnics; cultural purity will create tensions with other ethnic or cultural groups; and social purity will create tensions with the broader society. The second dimension shapes the nature of the relationships between a religious community and others outside the group. Of course, the real life of the religious groups we studied is more complex and messier than these neat conceptual distinctions would imply. But these analytical dimensions of sectarianism are helpful in describing and understanding the experiences of new immigrant religious communities.

Serendipitously, our sixteen research sites had roughly equal numbers of mainstream and sectarian representatives of their larger religious traditions. Eight of the congregations were clearly mainstream groups, and five others were clearly sectarian. The remaining three were more ambiguous but could be considered mixed, in that they were clearly sectarian on some dimensions while remaining mainstream on others. We assigned these broad labels based on our field observations and interview data. Naturally, within each of these general categories there are more complex and subtle nuances of distinction that we will discuss further below. Of most interest here are the sectarian cases and the degrees of separation from their respective mainstreams. The sectarian and mixed cases were unevenly spread across our major religious traditions. Appendix B lists each of the research sites, along with brief descriptions of how and why we considered them sectarian or not.

## Varieties of Purity and Protest

As noted above, the substantive type of purity (religious, cultural, or social) that a sectarian group emphasizes will lead it to protest against particular sorts of other groups. The strength of a group's opposition to others will also vary along a continuum. In the discussion to follow, we will pay special attention to three continua of separation that can have an impact on civic engagement: congregations vis-à-vis co-religionists, vis-à-vis co-ethnics, and vis-à-vis the broader society. Relationships between immigrant congregations and others vary by degrees of separation ranging from affinity to hostility, from cohesion to tension.

## Religious Purity

Religious groups and organizations can be categorized as either mainstream or sectarian representatives of their larger religious tradition, depending on the rituals, doctrines, stories, texts, and other religious elements they maintain. Although the precise boundaries may not always be clear, it is usually not difficult to distinguish groups and organizations that occupy the core of a tradition's history from those that deviate significantly from that core by virtue of their distinctive religious elements. In partisan parlance, such distinctions are sometimes labeled orthodoxy versus heterodoxy. Mainstream/sectarian distinctions can be institutionalized into separate religious organizations, as among Protestant denominations and Hindu *sampradayas* (lineages), or can manifest within the same group, as between a traditional core and reformist or revivalist movements.

Participants in both mainstream and sectarian congregations spoke explicitly about the separation of marginal groups from the mainstream of a religious tradition. For example, Maternity BVM, a mainstream Catholic parish in a predominantly Puerto Rican neighborhood, discussed its relations with its Pentecostal neighbors. Pentecostalism, due to its distinctive charismatic rituals and doctrines, has been a relatively sectarian expression of Christianity throughout its century-long existence. Nearby Pentecostal storefront churches pose a challenge to Maternity BVM, according to one spokesperson, due to their systematic recruitment of Hispanic Catholics living in the neighborhood. This relationship is competitive, in contrast to the "friendly" relationship—our interviewee's characterization—Maternity BVM maintains with local mainline Protestant churches, leading to cooperative social justice projects like antigang initiatives. Separation from other Christian groups was also evident in our only Pentecostal research site. Victory Outreach had the sparsest organizational ecology of all of our sixteen sites. Pentecostal theological distance from mainstream Christianity tends to deter potential alliances, even in those social concerns dear to a particular Pentecostal group (Anderson 2004). The Victory Outreach congregation we studied emphasized antigang ministries, but unilaterally, not cooperatively with socially likeminded Christians or even other neighborhood organizations.

Interviewees contrasted our three Hindu sites, each belonging to a different guru-oriented sampradaya, to other local Hindu temples that offer more traditional, deity-oriented practices. One regular member of Gayatri Pariwar Mandir spoke about attending the BAPS Swaminarayan temple, both of which differ from the mainstream temples located in two Chicago suburbs: "I came to know about Swaminarayans after coming to this country, through this Gujurati friend of mine.

Before that time, in India, I had not heard of the Swaminarayans at all. That's why, if you go to [the temples in] Lemont or Aurora, you get a different perspective of Hindu religion from that point." This interviewee stressed the authenticity of the rituals and architecture of the Lemont and Aurora temples, explaining, "Everything that is done in the temple, is done according to the way it is done back in India."

### Religious Protest

Such claims of authenticity are common among immigrant religious groups, given their need to transplant and adapt homeland ways to a new context. But claims to authenticity can also become the basis for protest by sectarian groups, defining the tension between them and their co-religionists. Authenticity has different referents depending on a group's relative location in the mainstream or on the periphery of a religious tradition. A visiting dignitary to the Gayatri center in Chicago summarized that group's self-perception of its place within the larger Hindu tradition, describing Gayatri as "a sect that promotes family values and teachings from our scriptures . . . going back to the roots, a culture that's lasted five thousand years." Talk of recovering the roots of a religious tradition in this manner is a hallmark of sectarian ideology.

Ritual practices also serve to demarcate the boundaries between the margins and the mainstream of a religious tradition. We observed a ritual expression of Lubavitch distinctiveness on Devon Avenue in Chicago, one block from our research site, Synagogue FREE. The ritual, called *kapparot*, entails swinging a fowl around one's head while reciting certain religious verses. Lubavitch men swing roosters, the women hens. Some rabbinic authorities denounce this practice, and most Jews today substitute money for fowl, but Synagogue FREE supports it as an important expression of the distinctiveness of the Lubavitch movement vis-à-vis other Jewish groups.

When an immigrant congregation adopts a sectarian stance focusing on religious purity, that stance shapes its relationships with other groups in particular ways. Religious purity tends to set up fairly strong oppositional relationships to co-religionists. Purity-based protest is nearly always directed at alleged apostates from the "true" faith. For example, all three of our Hindu research sites are guru-oriented sects, but with their own particular notions of religious purity. Each of them sees "those other Hindus" as somehow missing the boat. This makes cooperation with other Hindus difficult, even when such cooperation might be expected. For example, after the 2001 earthquake in Gujarat and after the 9/11 tragedy in the United States, the BAPS Swaminarayan Mandir in Bartlett organized massive programs of relief aid. They cooperated with a number of regional corporations, foundations, and NGOs, but we found no evidence of cooperation with other Hindu groups.

Immigrant congregations do not themselves always have an internally homogeneous expression of their larger religious tradition. Mainstream and sectarian expressions can exist under the same congregational roof, which may cause divisions within the membership and can even lead to organizational schism. Congregational proliferation is well known among Korean Protestants, although specifically religious motivations have been underexamined (e.g., Kim 1988). Buddhist temples sometimes proliferate through religious schism, but they may also contain "parallel congregations" of ethnic and nonethnic adherents who understand and practice Buddhism in substantively distinct ways (Numrich 1996, 2000b). Such is the case with one of the Buddhist centers we studied. The HanMaUm Zen Center accommodates the religious needs of a small group of non-Korean meditators in addition to its majority of Korean immigrant members. ISKCON offers an interesting variation on the parallel-congregations phenomenon. At the ISKCON temple in Chicago, the early predominance of countercultural American adherents has given way to a parallelism between inner circle devotees and casual attendees, both groups predominantly Indian, but one (the devotees) more sectarian than the other (Vande Berg 2005; Vande Berg and Kniss, forthcoming).

Some immigrant mosques across the United States have experienced internal tensions over differing Islamic interpretations or practices. In one of our Muslim research sites, the Islamic Cultural Center of Greater Chicago, some thirty to forty families practice Sufism, a mystical form of Islam, placing them somewhat at odds with the majority of the mosque's members. As a key mosque leader explained to us, the interested members, all Bosnians, "want to participate in Sufi gatherings to see how that would affect their ritual life. And they tend to keep coming. They see that as beneficial." However, the Sufi seekers must keep their activities low key so as not to antagonize other members. These Sufis follow a branch of the Naqshbandi Order led by Shaykh Muhammad Nazim Adil al-Haqqani, a Sufi master (*shaykh*) from Cyprus. "Sufi Orders are known for their peacefulness," our informant explained, "and peaceful submission to God, and lovely relationships with Muslims and non-Muslims. So it's something that we need very much. It's something that Muslims in this country especially need, and unfortunately they are mostly ignorant about even the existence of Sufi teachings and Orders and masters because the mainstream version of Islam here is closer to a Wahhabi version than to a Sufi version. Sufi is maybe one extreme—positive, I would say, extreme. And Wahhabism is a negative extreme." (Wahhabism, an Islamic revivalist movement, was not a significant force in our research sites, but its perceived influence has been an issue in other Chicago area mosques [Ahmed-Ullah et al. 2004; Cainkar 1988, 212; Hack and Hantschel 2003].)

Religious protest may also run along generational lines in some congregations. It appears that most religiously active immigrants are more conservative than their American counterparts (Numrich 2007), a situation confirmed generally across our research sites. The American-born and/or American-raised generations, however, may not share the immigrant generation's conservatism. In one of our Protestant research sites, Naperville Church of the Brethren, the majority of the immigrant Indian members bring a conservative "missionary Brethren" identity with strong evangelical underpinnings into "liberal Brethren" territory in the midwestern United States. A liberal Brethren identity has characterized the congregation's non-Indian clergy and lay leadership during most of the period of Indian influx (1970s–present), and has been instilled in the second/1.5 generation of Indians raised in the congregation. The interplay of these (and other) religious identities affects both internal congregational dynamics and interactions with outside groups and organizations. The direction this congregation takes in the future will depend on which identities win over the second and subsequent generations of Indian members.

To be sure, tension with co-religionists based on religious purity exists on a continuum. The BAPS and ISKCON temples we studied make explicit religious distinctions between themselves and other Hindus. But Gayatri Pariwar Mandir is able to take a more ecumenical stance. At first glance, Gayatri appears to be a typical sectarian group. A small storefront temple in the South Asian neighborhood centered on Devon Avenue in Chicago, it is also part of a guru-oriented sect, but its religious distinctions relative to mainstream Hinduism are not as sharp as those of BAPS or ISKCON. As a result, Kusum Patel, the leader of the local Gayatri group, is able to function as a kind of chaplain for the Devon community, offering marriage and funeral services for a broad range of Hindu people in the neighborhood. She and her followers are often key organizers for inter-Hindu gatherings for festivals and other neighborhood events. Yet their religious peculiarities also keep them out of the mainstream. Few of their non-Gayatri neighbors attend the Mandir regularly for *pujas* (deity worship).

A focus on religious purity, however, does not necessarily produce tensions with co-ethnics of other religions or with the broader society. BAPS, for all its difficulty in relating to other Hindus, has a warm and supportive relationship with civic and political leaders in suburban DuPage County. They have fairly close relationships with the nearby Catholic parish, attending each other's events and sharing parking lots. As mentioned before, local Republican political leaders regularly attend their public celebrations, and they have been able to ally themselves with corporate and civic organizations in their social service initiatives.

In fact, given the importance of religious voluntary organizations in American civil society, emphasizing religious distinctiveness may serve as an advantage in civic engagement. Sectarian religious groups can stake their claim to a place at the long-standing table of U.S. religious pluralism. Religious distinctives are often not seen as threatening and may provoke friendly curiosity rather than opposition from others. This is particularly true when religions (for example, Hinduism or Buddhism) are seen as exotic. It may not hold quite so well when the religion in question is tied to threatening racial or political tensions, as in the case of Islam.

How religious purity affects relations with co-ethnics of other religions can vary quite a bit. Here, relationships and tensions in the country of origin may play an important role. For example, tensions between Muslims and Hindus in South Asia may produce similar tensions in the United States. Although day-to-day relations remain cordial in Indo-Pakistani neighborhoods like Devon Avenue, Buddhists and Hindus were conspicuously absent from Muslim-organized interfaith events in Chicago following 9/11. On the other hand, the Lubavitch synagogue we studied, although highly religiously sectarian, was able to forge alliances with other Jewish social service agencies serving Russian immigrants. Religious distinctions in this case were not a significant source of tension in the country of origin, where the Jewish ethnic community was a beleaguered minority and focused more on external concerns than on internal divisions.

## Cultural Purity

Sectarian religious groups may also focus on purity markers that are not explicitly religious ideas, practices, or rituals. Sometimes sectarian purity emphasizes religiously based ideals that many would label "cultural" rather than "religious." Such cultural purity may be focused on language, dress, or dietary practices—things often associated with ethnic identity, even though the practices may have religious roots or motivations. In selecting our research sites, we attempted to create a comparative grid within and between both religion and ethnicity. For each religious tradition, we sought sites representing at least two different ethnicities; for each ethnicity, we sought sites from at least two different religions. Although not systematically representative for practical reasons, our eventual site grid did reveal religiously motivated cleavages within ethnic groups.

Scholars of American immigration have long recognized the complex interrelationship between religious and ethnic identities (Abramson 1980; Hammond and Warner 1993; Smith 1978; Stout 1975). For some groups, ethnicity is shaped primarily by religious identity rather than by race or other distinguishing markers, such as the Mormons and Amish. To be Bosnian is to be Muslim, to use an example from our research sites, and the Islamic Cultural Center in Northbrook gives institutional expression to this fact. Although multiethnicity has been incorporated into the mosque's governance structure, the ICC includes on its campus a Bosnian-American Cultural Center and a Bosnian museum/library. The close connection between ethnicity and religion may also create divisions within broader ethnic or racial categories. For example, South Asian ethnics are internally divided by the differing cultural practices and identities associated with religion. In just over half of our research sites, religion produces or supports cultural practices that function as ethnic markers, or religious identities and nation-based ethnicity are significantly conflated.

The best example of this is the BAPS temple, where leaders articulate a mission that is both religious and cultural. In fact, they refer to their temple complex as a "cultural center." In addition to the religious rituals that one would expect, the center provides Gujarati language classes, Gujarati dance and drama productions, and after-school activities for children promoting Gujarati language and culture. Their long-term development plan includes the construction of a large visitor center for a non-Gujarati, non-Indian audience. (One leader described it as a kind of "BAPS Gujarati theme park.")

But Indians are not the only immigrant group to meld religious and cultural activities. On a smaller scale but with a similar mission, the Islamic Cultural Center, as noted above, also works explicitly to promote and preserve Bosnian culture in addition to its multiethnic Islamic religious activities. Likewise, St. Demetrios Greek Orthodox Church organizes activities and programs that preserve the Greek language and culture. Both of these sites have been successful in maintaining their ethno-religious identities for decades: ICC since its precursor Bosnian organizations going back to 1906, and St. Demetrios since its founding in 1928.

### Cultural Protest

The merger of religion and culture, even in the name of pluralism, is sectarian in its consequences, setting up sharp distinctions between the congregation and others. When a broadly defined ethnic group (e.g., South Asians) is itself religiously plural, cultural sectarianism is likely to produce distance or tension between subethnicities—hence, the BAPS temple's difficulties in cooperating with other Indian groups. When an ethnic group is virtually monoreligious— e.g., Bosnians (Muslim) or Greeks (Orthodox Christian)—the tensions are more likely to be with other ethnic groups of the same religious tradition. Thus, the Islamic Cultural Center has a long history of trying (often quite successfully) to negotiate the inclusion of non-Bosnian Muslims in its religious activities and in the leadership of the mosque.

In immigrant congregations where the fusion of ethnic and religious identities is not so strong, two dominant patterns or positions on the continuum of culture-based protest are evident. One is a low-tension pattern where a congregation may celebrate ethnicity as a complement to its core religious identity. This is often the case in congregations like the St. Lambert Catholic parish, which has considerable ethnic diversity in its membership. A celebratory approach to ethnicity fits well with American pluralist ideals and may lower the tension between a congregation and the broader society.

The second pattern appears in congregations where religion and ethnicity may be in tension. This is particularly the case for congregations that are a product of missionary efforts that may have set up an antipathy between "true" religion and secular (or even "pagan") culture in the country of origin. The obvious examples of this are the Asian Protestant congregations, but it is also typical of missionary sects in other religions. ISKCON, for example, promotes its "pure" religion in contrast to corrupt Hindu/Indian expressions. They speak of "Vedic" culture rather than "Indian," which they believe is tainted by Western influence (Vande Berg 2005). Tension between religion and ethnicity can lead congregations to focus on religious distinctives and to view culture as less important or even evil. This clashes with classic American liberalism on these matters and may make civic engagement more difficult.

For some groups, however, their religious ideals promote intercultural amity and cooperation, embracing cultural pluralism and highlighting broader common interests that enable cooperation. Some non-Christian congregations in our research pool have tapped into liberal ecumenical and interfaith networks, although these linkages do not always open direct channels to co-ethnic Christian groups. Both of the mosques in our study make significant interfaith investments. The current imam of the Islamic Cultural Center of Greater Chicago is an active member of the local clergy association. The other mosque, Islamic Foundation, has forged several interfaith connections, often hosting significant gatherings like Muslim-Catholic dialogues with the Chicago Archdiocese and a post-9/11 forum titled "An Evening of Religious Solidarity." The latter featured Dr. Robert H. Schuller, well-known pastor of the Crystal Cathedral in California, plus representatives of the Council for a Parliament of the World's Religions, the Chicago Board of Rabbis, and the Council of Religious Leaders of Metropolitan Chicago. Leaders of both mosques hold to a kind of Islamic modernism or progressivism that embraces diversity and finds common ground with likeminded liberal religionists—namely, mainstream Protestants-Catholics-Jews and modernist non-Christians.

It is apparent from the examples discussed thus far that focusing on cultural purity is most likely to create tensions within rather than between broad ethnic identities. Significant separation between subethnic groups can range from mere arm's-length recognition of religio-cultural differences to direct confrontation. At the low-tension end, on Devon Avenue in Chicago one can find Hindu vegetarian restaurants existing side-by-side with Muslim *halal* butcher shops. The direct confrontation between Hindus and Muslims that occurs in India, however, has thus far been relatively absent in the United States.

### Social Purity

Sectarianism may also take the form of religiously motivated separation between categories that are commonly thought of as "social," such as race, class, gender, and politics. Gender issues are particularly interesting, given their complexity and relevance for contemporary American society. Religious teachings often address gender relations and marriage/intermarriage practices more explicitly than they address race, class, or politics, so it is worth looking at gender in greater detail here.

Religious teachings about gender can serve to demarcate the mainstream and the margins of a religious tradition. For most major religions, leadership of the mainstream is male dominated. In such a context, female leadership may constitute a sectarian expression of the larger religious tradition, especially if it is presented as a "purer" or "truer" articulation of the tradition. This is the case with the HanMaUm Seon (Zen) movement of the popular Korean Buddhist nun, Dae Haeng Kun Sunim, whose center in suburban Chicago serves a predominantly Korean immigrant congregation. Female leadership of this movement, at all levels, distinguishes it from the larger Chogye Order of Korean Buddhism to which it belongs. Doctrinally, the HanMaUm movement is part of a growing feminist reconstruction within contemporary Buddhism (Gross 1993).

The examples of HanMaUm and Gayatri Pariwar Mandir, another female-headed congregation in our study, show that, contrary to common assumptions, sectarianism is not always conservative. In these cases, religiously based distinctive gender practices (e.g., female ordination) are progressive and, while they may produce tension with co-religionists, can actually facilitate social integration into contemporary U.S. society. In the case of Gayatri Pariwar Mandir, the leader, Kusum Patel, has been embraced by local and national Democratic Party leaders. Her district's congressperson (also a woman) has attended Gayatri events, and she also visited the Clinton White House. In 2000, she and network anchorman Tom Brokaw received the Walter Cronkite Faith and Freedom Award, a national award given by the Interfaith Alliance Foundation. This external legitimation of her leadership gives her clout in interfaith circles that is disproportionate to her congregation's size and its marginal status within the larger Hindu tradition.

On the other hand, very strict notions of gender purity can also indicate separation from the mainstream of a religious tradition, as in the ISKCON and Swaminarayan movements of Hinduism. The routine and near-total gender segregation found at ISKCON and Swaminarayan facilities contrasts with mainstream Hindu temples where the sexes and families mix freely. An ISKCON interviewee in Chicago explained the doctrinal motivations for keeping males and females apart in *ashrams* (religious retreat centers) and temples, speaking from his perspective as a male spiritual renunciate, or *brahmachari*.

> This whole order has been outlined by Krishna, and knowing that the female body can agitate young minds, they [the females] try to be as inconspicuous as possible, to not agitate any of the brahmacharis' minds. Because the brahmacharis' minds are supposed to be on Krishna, celibacy, etc. If he should change his mind, let's say they see each other across the table, love blooms, you know, first sight. He has to consider changing, like, okay, this saffron [referring to his orange-yellow robe] means celibacy. That's a clear symbol to any *makaji* [young single woman] out there, you know, Hey, don't flirt. Don't do anything 'cause, you know, she could get in this bad karma. It's a bad offense to sort of flirt with someone in saffron or behave in an improper way.

So if I should see, and I get agitated and I think, gee, I like, you know how you get flustered and all this. I must consider changing my ashram, which means change my clothes to white or colors other than saffron. And that means that's a signal saying, Hey, I'm available. I wouldn't mind getting married and you know—household [take on lay status].

Swaminarayan Hindus practice comparably strict gender segregation in their communal religious activities. As one informant from our BAPS research site explained, the relevant doctrine is that sexual desires are distractions on the path to God. Given that sexual attraction between men and women is a natural part of the mundane world, it is something that is out of bounds in sacred places like the temple.

### Social Protest

How immigrant congregations embody social distinctions such as gender has a particularly significant impact on relations with neighbors in the United States and the prospects for civic engagement. In the BAPS case just mentioned, gender segregation is not combined with other forms of social renunciation or separation. In fact, Swaminarayans are quite open and embracing of contemporary middle- and upper-class technologies and material consumption practices. Their views on gender are neither extreme enough nor visible enough in the public arena to alienate them from the suburban business and political leaders with whom they cooperate.

On the other hand, traditional Muslim values and practices regarding gender relations are carried into the public square in visible and consequential ways, setting up potentially significant social tensions. Public schools have been a particularly prominent battleground over gender. The dating practices in U.S. schools as well as participation in co-ed physical education classes and extracurricular activities are problematic for Muslim parents. One solution, applied in both mosques that we studied, is to establish a parochial school. This practice parallels the Catholic penchant for establishing parish schools in the classical immigration era, although Muslims have done this with less frequency to date than have Catholics.

The social categories of race and class also matter in the congregations we studied. At the low-tension end of the protest continuum, mainstream congregations frequently worked to overcome or bridge such boundaries. Given the long history and significance of race in the United States, this is a particularly important issue for immigrant congregations. Immigrants often cannot be placed unambiguously in either the "black" or "white" racial categories that organize American racial dynamics. It is in their interest both to downplay the importance of racial identities, and to gain entry into "white" identity. These are complicated and sometimes contradictory tasks.

We were able to observe these difficult negotiations at various times, but most particularly in the mosques following 9/11. Islam's theology and religious rhetoric provide ample resources for downplaying racial distinctions, and these were brought forcefully to bear as Muslim groups tried to distance themselves from terrorists and identify themselves as mainstream Americans. For example, Islamic Foundation, in the days following 9/11, organized an interfaith gathering held in its mosque that included on the platform a range of dignitaries from the Reverend Jesse Jackson, to a prominent Chicago Jewish rabbi, to representatives from the Catholic archdiocese and the local United Methodist conference.

Class distinctions appeared primarily in immigrant congregations' engagement with the U.S. economic and labor markets. Some religious groups, especially those who were fairly homogeneous with regard to class, used religious resources to pursue class interests. For sectarian groups, the pursuit of class interests can lead to withdrawal into class-based enclaves, where elite classes are viewed as apostate or even evil. Synagogue FREE, for example, showed some of this enclave mentality. For mainstream religions, however, as in the case of Maternity BVM, class homogeneity is more likely to promote engagement with social and political institutions such as labor unions, city hall, or even the U.S. Congress. Such engagement is legitimated by religious values that stress social justice as a religious duty. It may promote conflict with some groups (for example, with the state over amnesty for undocumented immigrants) or promote alliances with other groups in society that share their class interests.

In each of these examples, sectarianism organized around social issues of gender, race, or class has its greatest impact on relationships to the broader society. Social practices align religious communities with some groups in American civil society while distancing them from others. At times, social sectarianism may lead to significant withdrawal from public institutions (e.g., Muslims and education). At other times it may produce engagement (e.g., working-class Catholics and labor unions).

Sectarian social practices can also produce externally imposed separation. Especially in the case of groups like ISKCON, who combine social separation with highly visible cultural sectarianism, significant opposition may be instigated by outside groups. Such opposition from neighborhood groups was one factor in the ISKCON temple's move from Evanston to Chicago in 1979. Our interviewees also spoke of harassment at public civic events. One of our field researchers recorded the following observation of ISKCON activity on the Fourth of July at Taste of Chicago, a large public outdoor festival held every summer in Chicago's downtown Grant Park:

> On their second pass through the field, they came closer to where I was sitting and appeared to be handing either pamphlets or *prasada* [food dedicated to a deity], or both, to interested persons near the sidewalk. They were

loudly chanting "Hare Krishna . . ." which was upsetting many of the people nearby. I heard several people behind me yell derogatory comments at the devotees and others told them to "Shut up!" or "Sit the fuck down!" I heard one man next to me talk about how he wished the police would get rid of "these brainwashers." The women he was with said something in response, and he replied, "Yeah, they've all been brainwashed, and they're here to brainwash more people."

Clearly, sectarian distance from society can be a two-way street, where both newcomers and hosts contribute to their mutual opposition.

## Sectarianism and Civic Engagement

As the previous story shows, the intensity of sectarianism as well as its content has an impact on patterns of civic engagement. Sectarianism shapes the relationships a group has with others and influences which others are friends and which are foes. Sectarianism organized around religious purity is most likely to produce protest against co-religionists and, in some circumstances, co-ethnics. Sectarianism organized around cultural purity produces protest or tension primarily over against other ethnicities. And sectarianism organized around social purity sets up tension with particular groups and institutions in the broader society. In each case, tension with some groups may lead to amity with others. Based on these observations of the particularities of sectarian dynamics, there are several things we can say more generally about how sectarianism is related to civic engagement.

First, sectarianism defines friend and foe. It determines against whom its protests will be targeted, and this in turn shapes the response of the powers that be. Engagement with the powers that be highlights how closely sectarianism is connected to issues of power. Earlier church-sect theorists argued that sects provided shelter for the powerless from the powerful and were responses to status threats. While it is certainly true that powerful groups can afford to be accommodating and inclusive because their status is not likely to be threatened by openness to others, sectarianism also involves the intentional exercise of power. Sects are organizational forms, providing flesh and blood to prophetic stances over against some powerful other. Especially in the context of the United States, where sects have been a ubiquitous and legitimate part of the nation's history, sectarian religious forms may be attractive to groups trying to define their identity over against a larger world that is both attractive and threatening. How and why some groups take this route while some groups do not is an interesting question that needs further exploration.

Second, sectarianism, despite our common-sense notion of it, is not always traditional and conservative. Protest against the mainstream may take a progressive direction that promotes change rather than preservation. We can see this in the case of HanMaUm and Gayatri Pariwar Mandir, sectarian Buddhist and

Hindu groups who promote gender equality. In Christian traditions, liberation or feminist theologies can produce high tension between religious groups and the surrounding society that is distinctly progressive, even revolutionary, in its orientation.

Third, sectarianism may be part of the process of Americanization. Warner (1993b) has argued that the American religious system is "constitutively pluralist." Sectarian strategies can serve to strengthen the internal organization and resources of an immigrant religious group. Tomasi's (1975, 105) observation about immigrant Catholic parishes can be generalized to other immigrant congregations—namely, that they serve a quasi-sect function for their marginalized members who live "on the religious and social periphery of society." Given the historic and ongoing importance of religious voluntary associations as actors in civil society, it may well be that sectarianism is truly the American way. Religious identity is one legitimate basis for making claims in the public arena, and the stronger the identity, the stronger those claims may be. (And here we return to the close relation between sectarianism and power.)

Fourth, some forms of purity and protest may have a greater public impact than others. The U.S. tradition of religious pluralism and freedom means that protests over religious purity are likely to be viewed as an internal matter for religious groups and of no concern (other than prurient interest) to the public. Likewise, promoting cultural purity, at least within certain bounds, fits quite well into American pluralism. It may even be profitable. (The Amish found that out a long time ago.) This is particularly true where the cultural practices in question concern "safe" issues like dress or diet. Some cultural concerns, especially language, may have considerably more relevance for public life. Social purity, organized around issues of race, class, and gender, is the most likely to affect public civic engagement. These identities are not so easily embraced by American pluralism and, in fact, remain as significant arenas for social conflict. To the extent that immigrant religious groups are sectarian on grounds of social purity and protest, they involve themselves directly in contests in the public arena—contests in which they will need to take sides as friend or foe of specific other social groups.

Fifth, sectarianism is often intentional on the part of a religious group, but it may also be imposed from outside. Groups that are highly sectarian on all three grounds—religious, cultural, and social—are likely to be viewed as threatening, and not as likely to be embraced as part of the American pluralist mosaic. This is particularly evident in the case of ISKCON. Externally imposed sectarianism limits the possibilities of civic engagement, because a group's voice has been silenced or marginalized by those who control access to the conversation.

Taken together, these general insights on sectarian dynamics suggest that religiously based purity/protest is not invariably a distancing dynamic. Rather, sectarianism is a religious strategy that can be a valuable means for a group to establish itself and pursue its religious and secular interests in the U.S. context. The tensions that sectarianism sets up can be transcended in the public arena, at least for some types of purity and protest. More important, perhaps, the form and content of a group's sectarianism can identify and strengthen alliances with other groups in civil society, making engagement even more effective. In part 2, we will be able to look in more detail at how sectarianism operates in particular social arenas to produce particular kinds of civic engagement.

# 3 Locating the Moral Authority of Immigrant Congregations

*The less human beings who remain or come into contact with each other are bound together in relation to the same Gemeinschaft, the more they stand opposite each other as free agents of their wills and abilities. . . . [T]he less this will is dependent upon or influenced by a common will, the greater is the freedom.*

—Ferdinand Tönnies (1887)

The Kursk Icon, one of the most venerated icons in old Russia, was visiting the Holy Virgin Protection Cathedral in Des Plaines, a suburb northwest of Chicago. The parish is affiliated with the Russian Orthodox Church Outside of Russia (ROCOR), one of the largest (and most conservative) Russian Orthodox church organizations that emerged outside of Russia after the Russian Revolution. A group of the most devoted parishioners was gathered for a night vigil in the cathedral to pray and venerate the icon.

Father Paul, the parish priest, used the occasion to speak to the gathered faithful about the authority of the Russian Orthodox tradition and the congregation's place within it. He spoke of the history of the old state of Kievan Rus', the heartland of Russian, Belorussian, and Ukrainian Orthodox Christianity and culture. He referred to important historical figures, including Russian tsars, military leaders, martyrs, and saints, such as St. Seraphim, who had prayed before the icon. He noted that the icon should bring out the best in all the congregants, that it should lead them to contemplate their lives, acts, and souls, and, above all, to repent. "We must all repent," he said. "Some say that Russians in Russia have to repent, but we must all repent. . . . It is our transgressions and our forgetting about repentance that led to the loss of two other great icons. . . . Here in America, they say 'to take for granted,' but this is precisely what we must not do."

The visit of the Kursk Icon, along with Father Paul's interpretation of its meaning, illustrates how many (but not all) religions conceive of moral authority. Authority is located in a shared tradition, sometimes embodied in a text (or icon), sometimes in a religious hierarchy, sometimes in both. The appropriate stance for the believer in the face of such authority is repentance and obedience. This, of course, is not the only way religions understand moral authority. Some religions give moral primacy to an individual's reason and/or experience as he or she interprets and applies religious texts, insights, or inspiration.

## Defining Moral Authority

We draw the notion of moral authority from a heuristic map of the religious or moral order in the United States that one of us developed in previous projects (summarized in Kniss 2003). The heuristic map consists of two dimensions representing two central issues in any moral order. One is the locus of moral authority and the other is what constitutes the moral project. The moral authority dimension is concerned with the primary basis for ethical, aesthetic, or epistemological standards. It answers the question, Who or what determines the nature of good, beauty, and truth? The moral project dimension addresses the question of where moral action or influence should be targeted. What are a religion's primary moral projects? Or, put another way, if good, beauty, and truth are to be pursued, how is this to be done? There is something of a means-ends distinction between the two dimensions. That is, the issue of moral authority is concerned with the grounds for defining or evaluating ultimate ends, while the question of the moral project is concerned with means to those ends. The former is the basis for a group's central values, while the latter shapes religious and social action.

The poles on each dimension represent the tension between the individual and the collective that most analysts of American political culture have noted. On the first dimension, moral authority may derive from the individual's reason or experience, or it may be located in the collective tradition. On the second dimension, the primary moral project may be the maximization of individual utility or it may be the maximization of the (collective) public good, to use economic metaphors. Each of these dimensions represents a spectrum along which a wide variety of ideas and positions may occur. The two dimensions are crosscutting and interact in complex ways. Figure 3.1 (adapted from Kniss 2003) depicts the ideological map resulting from crossing the two dimensions. It places various religious groups in relation to each other and the broader religio-political culture in the United States.

At the individualist end of the moral authority dimension the foundation for ultimate values is grounded in an individual's reason or experience—or, more often, reason as applied to and filtered through a person's experience and perceptions. This view shares much with modernist epistemologies. Thus, the individualist conception of moral authority tends to downplay notions of traditional transcendent absolute authority. Religious authority structures are subject to criticism and legitimation based on reason/experience. Further, moral authority is applied relativistically, because reason is located in particular individuals in particular times and places. Determining what is good, beautiful, and true requires the application of reason to particular circumstances and will vary across contexts.

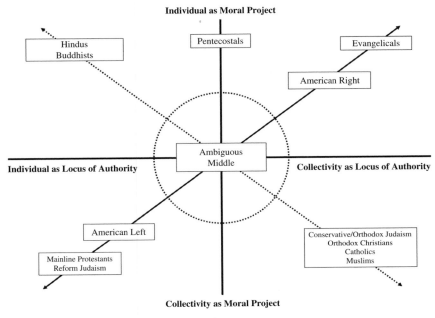

Figure 3.1    Moral Order Map (Adapted from Kniss 2003)

The individualist conception of moral authority affects how religions view human nature and society. Insofar as rationality is basic to human nature, human nature is basically good. Modern society, insofar as it is based on rational forms of social organization and technology, is also viewed optimistically. Based on a continuous application of reason to experience, individualists tend to value progress and welcome social or religious change—hence the correlation (but not equation) between individualism and progressive religion. Individualists' inherent trust in human nature and society produces an emphasis on individual freedom and civil liberties.

Within American religion, individualism, rooted as it was in modernism, engendered much religious and social conflict, especially in the fundamentalist/modernist controversies in the twentieth century. The individualist view of moral authority legitimized the rational criticism of ecclesiastical and biblical authority. As Hutchison (1982) pointed out, religious modernism held that religious ideas should be consciously adapted to modern culture, God is immanent in and revealed through human cultural development, and human society is progressively moving toward the realization of the Kingdom of God. Religious traditionalists, in the fundamentalist-modernist conflicts that were major drivers of American religious history in the past century, opposed the individualist/modernist view as an attack on fundamentals and a challenge to traditional authority (Marsden 1980; Hunter 1991).

At the collectivist end of the moral authority dimension (what Hunter [1991] labeled "traditionalism") religious worldviews hold that the authority to define ultimate values is grounded in the collective religious tradition. Where individualists view individual human agents as free actors, collectivists (or "traditionalists") see individuals as members of a collectivity, a social group defined by its relation to a higher authority—an authority that transcends the particularities of individual times and places, whether it is housed in a religious text or an ecclesiastical hierarchy.

Definitions of good, beauty, and truth, grounded in a transcendent ahistorical moral authority, tend to be viewed in absolute terms—less (or not at all) subject to criticism. Religious groups at the collectivist end of the moral authority dimension emphasize obedience to ecclesiastical and/or scriptural authority. Ethics are viewed in absolutist more than situational terms, and individuals are expected to forgo their own interests for the good of the collective. Since moral authority is transcendent and ahistorical, so are the values it defines. The goal of change, then, is not progress toward perfection, but recovery of traditional values. Modern culture is perceived not so much as a consequence of progress as a fall from paradise.

Collectivist views of moral authority, thanks to the elevation of collective tradition, certainly have strong affinities with conservative religion. But it would be a mistake to equate the two. Dillon (1999), for example, shows how progressive Catholics construct an identity that recognizes the authority of Catholic tradition, even while promoting change within it. Likewise, many progressive Muslims continue to emphasize and reinforce collective moral authority over individual self-interests.

Based on this conceptual distinction between the individual and the collective as the locus of moral authority, we divided our congregations into two broad categories. We categorized groups based on what we know of the broader religious traditions to which they belong. In the individualist category, we placed the Buddhist, Hindu, and mainline Protestant congregations. In the collectivist category, we placed the Catholic, Orthodox Christian, conservative Protestant, Jewish, and Muslim congregations.

## Individual Locus of Moral Authority

As noted, we placed Buddhists, Hindus, and mainline Protestant denominations in the individualist category with regard to the primary locus of moral authority. This case is the easiest to make for mainline Protestant congregations. Protestantism's origins, after all, were rooted in understandings of individuals as free moral agents. The "priesthood of all believers" is a fundamental Protestant notion, championed by Luther, but originating even earlier in pre-Reformation religious movements such as the Lollards.

The notion of individual moral agency had a comfortable affinity with the new Enlightenment epistemologies based on reason and empirical observation. By the time the United States was emerging as a nation, these Protestant/Enlightenment values had become so-called self-evident truths and were enshrined in the U.S. Declaration of Independence and, later, its Constitution. This gave mainline Protestantism the upper hand in defining core American cultural values and practices, even though, as Tocqueville (1831) and later observers noted (e.g., Baltzell 1964, 1979; Wuthnow 1987), there continued to be a dynamic tension between individualist and collectivist impulses in U.S. religious and political culture. As we shall see later, this tension is presently visible in immigrant mainline congregations, especially given their more evangelical missionary roots.

Buddhism and Hinduism also tend to place primary moral authority within the individual's reason and experience (perhaps with more stress on experience, especially compared to the Protestant emphasis on reason). The tendency of many Americans to view Asians and Asian religions as radically other may, at first glance, make Buddhism and Hinduism seem like strange bedfellows with mainline Protestants in the same moral authority category. But they do share some underlying assumptions in common, a commonality that may help explain why some Eastern religions have been attractive to middle- and upper-class converts in the United States.

The individual locus of moral authority manifests itself in various ways in Eastern religions. Since truth is context dependent rather than absolute, individuals are free to choose religious beliefs and practices—even from multiple religions—that give meaning and purpose to their particular circumstances. Thus, Chinese immigrants, without any sense of self-contradiction, may identify with Buddhism, Confucianism, and Taoism (Williams 1990).

The concept of karma, one of the core ideas of both Hinduism and Buddhism, is another manifestation of the individual as the primary locus of moral authority. Karma is a complex concept that is defined in different, even contradictory, ways in various Hindu and Buddhist sacred and philosophical texts (Sharot 2001). Essentially, it refers to the idea that individuals make moral choices when they act, and that these actions have consequences in this life and in future incarnations. Thus, an individual's karma is a condition, a product of moral choices made in previous lives and in this one. The karmic condition can be changed over the course of a lifetime through proper actions and ritual practices. Note that the moral authority and responsibility lie primarily with the individual who must choose how to act and must live with the consequences. There is not, as in the Russian Orthodox example above, the primary expectation that individuals are to grant authority and obedience to a religious hierarchy or sacred text. In fact, the multiplicity of sacred texts in the Hindu and Buddhist traditions do not speak with one voice in defining karma or other key religious concepts. Religious hierarchs such as priests and nuns are viewed as role models, virtuosos to be emulated rather than obeyed. They may teach others and lead in some ritual practices, but the choice of individuals to participate is made on the basis of particular individual interests and needs, and many ritual practices are carried out by individuals in their own homes or places of work.

Thus, as radically other as Hinduism and Buddhism may seem in American popular consciousness, they do share some fundamental assumptions with the mainline Protestantism that is at the root of so many core American cultural values—especially that individuals are free moral agents, with the autonomy to interpret and apply religious teachings in their own particular contexts, and to make moral choices in light of their particular individual understandings and situations. This affinity can be seen particularly well at Gayatri Pariwar Mandir, a small storefront Hindu temple on Devon Avenue, an area on the north side of Chicago heavily populated with Indian and Pakistani businesses and restaurants.

Not surprisingly, explicit talk of moral authority did not show up frequently in our interviews with leaders and laypeople at Gayatri Pariwar Mandir. Moral authority is a conceptual abstraction, but it is reflected in various ways in the life of the temple's participants, even if it is not articulated explicitly.

First, it can be seen in how people find their way to the temple. Unlike the collectivist traditions, people at the temple were unlikely to have been born into the particular Hindu tradition represented by the Gayatri temple. Interviewees gave us individualized accounts of how they chose to join the congregation. Their choices were based on both reason and experience. They spoke of their particular interests and needs that were met by the temple. For example, one interviewee spoke of difficulties in her family life after immigrating and the comfort and empowerment she experienced at the temple. "God always meets everybody's needs, you know? You come here . . . and it's like a holy place. When you come here, you take something out of here. You don't just come to temple. You take power. What is in here. The holy power goes with us." She didn't go to the temple out of a strong sense of collective identity or obligation. In fact, she also told us about regularly attending other temples for other purposes, such as Bhagavad Gita classes. And, although she was active in social services to others, she didn't seem to expect the temple to organize these activities in any programmatic or collective way. When we asked her whether people at Gayatri ever worked together to provide social services to others, she seemed puzzled. "Um, I don't know about here, but I'll do my own somewhere else. I do that."

Second, the individualist locus of moral authority can be seen in how the Gayatri temple articulates its mission. The Gayatri sect of Hinduism was founded by a guru, Pragyavtar Gurudev, and specially reveres the goddess Gayatri. It emphasizes use of the mind and intellect to commune with God and live rightly. Its official mission statement states that Gayatri is "a universal constructive movement for resurgence of a new era by educating people to think in righteous ways." The core of Gayatri ritual life is the Gayatri mantra, translated as, "Oh

God! Thou art the Giver of Life, Remover of pain and sorrow, The Bestower of happiness. Oh! Creator of the Universe, may we receive thy supreme sin-destroying light, may Thou guide our intellect in the right path. Illuminate our intellect to inspire us for good deeds." Although, like the BAPS Swaminarayan temple, most of the Gayatri followers are Gujarati, there is much less emphasis on celebrating and preserving Gujarati ethnicity. Rather, the focus is on spreading the message of the Gayatri mantra around the world.

The Gayatri focus on individual intellect and lay empowerment is reflected in how it carries out its corporate life from day to day. Kusum Patel, the woman who leads the temple and most of the ritual activity, is an important actor in the services, but not the central character in the way that a priest is in a Catholic or Orthodox Christian Mass. Worship rituals are often led by laypeople. Participants chant mantras together, but the mantras themselves reinforce the important role of individual intellect and personal experience of the divine as a moral guide. Nonritual activities, as well, have the same sense of being driven by the energies of lay volunteers. Interviewees spoke of their involvements in voluntaristic terms—pitching in and doing things because they needed to be done, not because they had been told to do them by some sort of religious authority or hierarchy.

Finally, an individualist view of the locus of moral authority is apparent in how leadership is practiced. Traditional religious hierarchy is not so important at Gayatri. Leadership is shared somewhat democratically and includes women as equals to men. In fact, the Devon Avenue temple is headed by a woman, and

Kusum Patel, leader of the Gayatri Pariwar Mandir. Photo by Jerry Berndt.

many of the lay leaders are women. Men are active participants in rituals, but frequently under the leadership of women. Kusum Patel, the founder and president of the temple, spoke of her role not so much as priestly mediating of the divine, but rather as orchestrating the mission of the Gayatri movement in Chicago and coordinating the activities of its members.

## Collective Locus of Moral Authority

Such a focus on individual moral authority is much less likely, if not unthinkable, in other religious traditions. Religions who locate moral authority in the collective tradition are much more likely to confer authoritative status on clergy or on sacred texts that embody the shared tradition. In the collectivist category, we place Roman Catholicism, Christian Orthodoxy, conservative Protestantism, Islam, and Judaism. Each of these religious groups gives primary authority to the collective tradition rather than individual reason or experience. Individual religious believers are expected to pass their reason and experience through the filter of collective authority, whether that authority is expressed in sacred texts or mediated by religious hierarchs.

Roman Catholics and Christian Orthodox groups give primacy to a centralized religious hierarchy. For Roman Catholics, even after the democratizing reforms of Vatican II, authoritative doctrinal and moral pronouncements issue from the Vatican, and individual Catholics are expected to accept them as normative. Orthodox Christianity follows a similar pattern, even though the relevant structures are organized by national or ethnic rather than global identities. Orthodox Christian churches hold a more communal view than Roman Catholics, in that authoritative doctrines must be accepted by the whole church rather than pronounced by a pope; but both traditions reflect a strong sense of the corporate authority of the church, implemented by a hierarchy of priests and prelates.

Orthodox Christian traditions give a somewhat more prominent role to individuals in their emphasis on mystical communion with the divine via icons and personal spiritual experience. But, even though the Holy Spirit may speak directly to the hearts of individual members, as one scholar points out, "a Christian is expected to compare [one's] experience with that of other members of the Church, especially with those men and women whose purity of heart and soundness of judgment have been testified to by the rest of the community in listing them among the recognized saints of the Church" (Zernov 1997, 86).

Conservative Protestant groups such as Evangelicals, Fundamentalists, and Pentecostals likewise hold to collective notions of the locus of moral authority. For them, however, the authoritative tradition is housed in an infallible sacred text. Collective authority may be more decentralized, given their typical congregational polity, but individuals are still expected to grant ultimate religious and moral authority to the Christian scriptures as interpreted and taught by the church. Various conservative Protestant denominations may quibble over the niceties of doctrine regarding scripture, and they may debate the precise language articulating scriptural authority, but they hold in common a view that biblical authority transcends the particularities of time and place. Truth is not primarily contextual, derived from reason and experience. It is revealed and transcendent—truth with a capital "T." This traditionalist, transcendent conception of authority as compared to the more contextual and relativist views of liberal Protestants is what underlies the contemporary "culture wars," according to Hunter (1991). Conservative Protestants in Pentecostal traditions, like Orthodox Christians, give a somewhat more prominent role to individual religious experience as a source of divine revelation; but, also like the Orthodox groups, if such revelations are to be authoritative, they need to be tested against the transcendent authority of scripture and with other Christians in the context of a church community.

Conservative Protestant groups do not have the elaborate, powerful, and authoritative religious hierarchies typical of Roman Catholic and Orthodox Christians (or even many mainline Protestant denominations), but the role of the clergy in embodying collective authority remains important. Clergy have special expertise in knowledge of the authoritative sacred text, and are empowered to teach authoritatively. Thus, ordained ministers often have significant religious authority and organizational power in a congregation or denomination, deriving both from their own particular charisma and from the authority bequeathed to them by their special expertise with authoritative texts.[1]

Muslims give the sacred text an even more prominent authoritative place in the religious tradition than do many conservative Protestants. Muslims believe that the Qur'an in its original Arabic was directly dictated by God to/through Muhammad. The Muslim community (*ummah*) is governed by Shari'ah, a system of law that elaborates and applies the commands of the Qur'an, providing the faithful with a comprehensive "path" (the literal meaning of Shari'ah) on which to walk both individually and communally. "Throughout history Islamic law has remained central to Muslim identity and practice, for it constitutes the ideal social blueprint for the believer who asks, 'What should I do?'" (Esposito 2002, 139). Over time and in different places around the world, various schools of law and practice have emerged. Some Islamic groups, especially among the Shi'ites, also developed more elaborate clerical and juridical hierarchies that embody and carry out the collective moral authority, such as issuing *fatwas* or legal opinions.

Finally, Judaism also comprises a community based on a system of law, the Torah, a divine revelation that is sacred and immutable. The Torah, and the rabbis and legal scholars who interpret and apply it, constitute the primary moral authority over Jewish life. The obligations and prohibitions of sacred law are seen as infusing all of life, even mundane acts. In the modern era, especially in the United States, various "denominations" of Judaism have emerged. Some more progressive groups (for example, Reform Judaism) give a greater role to an individual's particular application of reason and experience in religious life, but all Jewish denominations share a strong communal identity that is defined and governed by Torah. Hasidic Judaism is a particularly interesting case in this regard. Hasidism, while promoting strict traditional applications of the Torah in daily lifestyle practices, also elevates spiritual virtuosi, the *zaddikim*, who have mystical communication with God unmediated by the Torah. But, as Sharot (2001) points out, such mystic communion with the divine is not expected of the mass of ordinary followers of Hasidic traditions. Rather, their path to religious (or even this-worldly) goals is through devotion and submission to the zaddikim.

A strong communal identity and a collective locus of moral authority are exemplified in the Holy Virgin Protection Cathedral, mentioned earlier. As a Russian Orthodox parish, it melds religious and ethnic traditions (as do most nationally identified Orthodox Christian churches). The collective moral authority of the Russian Orthodox tradition is located in both the Russian and the Orthodox halves of this pairing.

The primacy of Russian identity is signified in a variety of ways. The Russian language is prominent in the congregation's life, and many of our interviews needed to be conducted in Russian. As we noted in the opening vignette, the veneration of icons also involves the veneration of Russian history. Praying before an icon brings the worshiper into communion with all the Russian saints and historical figures who have also prayed before the same icon. In the services, religious themes and Russian national themes were frequently intertwined. For example, in a service celebrating the Transfiguration, the archbishop gave a sermon in which he noted the parallel needs of individual transfiguration based on prayer and good deeds, and the transfiguration, as yet to come, of Russia after the Soviet rule.

But the members of Holy Virgin Protection were not only Russians; they were also Orthodox Christians. (In fact, the umbrella of Orthodoxy allowed the congregation to include some ethnic minorities, albeit ethnicities that shared a broader Slavic identity.) The moral authority of Orthodoxy, exercised primarily by the clerical hierarchy, was evident throughout our interviews. For example, one member described the role of the archbishop in the cathedral. "He is officially a superior . . . the one who is ultimately going to make the decisions. . . . People can make suggestions—the Church Council, I should say, can make their suggestions, but he has the final 'yes' or 'no' for whatever it might be." Congregants seemed very aware of the hierarchy in place at Holy Virgin Protection. Archbishop Vladyka headed the Chicago and Detroit Diocese of ROCOR, Father Paul was the head of the parish, and due deference was paid to them. Other parish officers such as deacons or council members were clearly below them in the hierarchy of authority. As another member told us: "The church is what the priest manages to make it. Everything depends on the priest." He went on to explain that the priest was a connector, someone who was involved in each person's life, who knew each member and connected members to each other. "This is, in principle, the idea of '*Sobornost*,' to get people together." (*Sobornost*, usually translated as "unity," is a key Russian Orthodox theological concept.)

The melding of the ethnic and the religious in the moral authority of the collective tradition was something that members of the parish seemed to feel in their bones. One typical but particularly eloquent example of this was a member's response to our interviewer's question: How do you describe the Protection Cathedral to other people?

> Well, that it is basically a typical phenomenon of Russian life. The Cathedral, if you see it, and especially when you enter it, you completely lose the feeling that you are in America. The paintings, the interior décor, and even the façade—you have a total impression of it being relocated from Russia, namely from nineteenth-century Russia, not that Moscow Soviet Russia of ours, but exactly the nineteenth-century Russia. The spirit, the singing, the service. . . . To those people . . . I [say], "If you want to see and feel Russia, you don't need to travel far away; you can feel it here." And to those people who need spiritual experience, I say, "Instead of trying to find something exotic and extravagant, it is best to touch upon the tradition; and in this sense, this Cathedral is simply an embodiment of that tradition."

## Moral Authority and Civic Engagement

Table 3.1 provides a summary of our findings regarding the locus of moral authority in each of our research sites. Here we show the actual counts of individualist versus collectivist references to moral authority in the interviews or in public events we observed. The observed findings are grouped according to our theoretically derived initial categorization of groups as individualist or collectivist. The "Documents" column indicates the number of transcripts or field note documents that included codes for the moral authority variable. Note that, on the whole, the expected patterns appear in the data. In the individualist category, just over 70 percent of the references to moral authority referred to it in individualist terms. In the collectivist category, the percentages were reversed, with just over 80 percent of the references being articulated in collectivist terms.

Examining the data from individual congregations, however, reveals some interesting nuances and anomalies. Not all particular groups matched the expected general pattern. In the individualist category, the BAPS Swaminarayan Hindu temple was an outlier. In the collectivist category, St. Lambert Roman Catholic Church and Victory Outreach both had a significant number of individualist references to moral authority. Looking at these cases a bit more closely will provide some insight into how the moral authority variable may interact with other religious variables, especially sectarianism, to produce unexpected

Table 3-1    References to Locus of Moral Authority by Site

|  | Documents | Individual | Collective |
|---|---|---|---|
| *Individualist* | | | |
| BAPS Swaminarayan | 16 | 2 | 7 |
| Gayatri Pariwar | 21 | 3 | 1 |
| ISKCON | 33 | 25 | 10 |
| HanMaUm | 20 | 2 | 1 |
| Ling Shen Ching Tze | 15 | 16 | 1 |
| Naperville COB | 28 | 5 | 2 |
| Truth Lutheran | 12 | 6 | 1 |
| Total | 145 | 59 | 23 |
| *Collectivist* | | | |
| Five Holy Martyrs | 13 | 0 | 2 |
| Maternity BVM | 9 | 0 | 3 |
| St. Lambert | 31 | 5 | 7 |
| Victory Outreach | 10 | 0 | 12 |
| Holy Virgin Protection | 26 | 0 | 15 |
| St. Demetrios | 15 | 0 | 1 |
| Synagogue FREE | 22 | 0 | 5 |
| Islamic Foundation | 22 | 2 | 1 |
| Islamic Cultural Center | 25 | 0 | 6 |
| Total | 173 | 7 | 52 |

patterns of behavior. The patterns we observed, both the expected and the unexpected, also raise some questions and suggest some predictions about how these religious variables might affect the civic engagement of new immigrant groups.

The BAPS Swaminarayan Hindu temple differs from many other Hindu temples in the extent to which it combines its religious mission with ethnic/cultural goals. Swaminarayan Hinduism began as a nineteenth-century sectarian Hindu reform movement in the Gujarat region of India and is deeply rooted in Gujarati culture (Williams 2001). In the group's brochures it refers to itself as a socio-religious movement. The temple in Bartlett, Illinois, where we did our research, built a large cultural center some years before it completed the central *mandir*. It is explicit in stating that one if its primary purposes is the preservation of Gujarati language and culture in the United States. It has extensive programmatic activities in pursuit of that mission—activities aimed at both Gujarati immigrants and at its non-Indian neighbors in suburban DuPage County. Unlike many other Hindu temples (the large temple in Lemont, a southwestern suburb of Chicago, is a good example), it does not offer shrines and services for a broad range of Hindu religious practitioners across the various Indian subethnicities. Instead, it focuses on one particular Hindu movement—one that is rooted in a particular ethnic community.

Thus, despite Hinduism's tendency to highlight the moral authority of individuals in approaching the divine, we found that, in public events and in our interviews with leaders and laypeople, topics of conversation continually returned to collective interests. We will discuss this further in the following chapter. Here, it is important to note that these sectarian interests are embodied in at least some of the movement's authority structures. Of particular importance is a religious hierarchy of sadhus headed by Pramukh Swami Maharaj, a popelike figure considered to be the fifth spiritual successor of Bhagwan Swaminarayan.

Lay practitioners also revealed abstract conceptions of moral authority in their interviews with us, and these frequently reflected the importance of the guru. Comments often revealed a kind of bimodal conception that partook of both the broader Hindu individualism and the more collectivist Swaminarayan approach. For example, one interviewee told us, "The key is to keep control of your mind and only attach it to a 'true person,' a guru." On one hand, the individual has the authority and the responsibility to exercise spiritual self-control, but on the other hand he or she chooses voluntarily to submit to a religious hierarchy.

It appears, then, that sectarian religion is well served by (may even require) at least an element of collectivism in its locus of moral authority. A sectarian movement depends on a collective identity that defines itself over against others in some way, and locating moral authority in the collective fosters and reproduces such an identity. Ethnically based or guru-based sectarian Hinduism operates in just this way. For the BAPS Swaminarayan community, both types of sectarianism are operative. The same is true of the Gayatri temple, although the ethnic identification and commitment to the guru are less intense than at BAPS. At ISKCON, there is openness to multiple ethnicities; but there is a much stronger focus on the founding guru and subsequent lineage. Thus, we also find an element of collectivism in their references to moral authority.

St. Lambert Roman Catholic Church also deviated from the pattern we predicted. As a Roman Catholic parish, we initially categorized it as having a collectivist conception of moral authority, in line with traditional Catholicism. In fact, the data for this parish were split about evenly between individualist and collectivist references to moral authority. In the case of St. Lambert's we can see how a congregation's primary moral projects may influence how they conceive of moral authority. St. Lambert has developed a particular sense of its mission that leads it to value individual moral authority more highly than it otherwise might have.

St. Lambert is located in Skokie, an ethnically diverse suburb just north of Chicago. In the past two decades, both parish and town have seen a dramatic increase in new immigrants from a variety of ethnic and religious traditions. In addition to the many "old" members from the still predominantly white surrounding neighborhood, the parish includes Filipino, Mexican, Sri Lankan, Haitian, and Cuban members as well as various other smaller immigrant groups. At a Taste of St. Lambert's dinner, the buffet table included food from Syria, Mexico, India, Hong Kong, Ireland, the Philippines, Sri Lanka, Poland, China, Italy, Cuba, and the United States. Under its current pastoral leadership, the congregation has embraced ethnic pluralism and has granted considerable autonomy to various ethnic groups to organize special celebrations of saints' days and other ethnically based religious practices.

The Filipino group is the largest and most visible of the new ethnicities in the parish. The Feast of San Lorenzo, an important festival for the Filipino community, has become a major annual event for the entire parish. The parish also supports home-based devotions in which statues of three saints important to Filipinos (San Lorenzo, Santo Niño, and Our Lady of Fatima) circulate among the homes of Filipino members of the parish. The three statues pass from family to family throughout the year, residing in each home for two weeks.

One informant mentioned that the archdiocese looks somewhat askance at this practice, and has a goal of moving ethnically based worship away from homes and into the church. But the fact that the practice continues with the blessing of the parish religious leaders points to how the commitment to supporting ethnic diversity has led to at least a modicum of democratization in the religious life of St. Lambert's. Clearly, parishioners there continue to recognize and submit to the authority of the parish and archdiocese religious hierarchy. On the other hand, the pastor, in a Maundy Thursday service during Holy Week, actually used the quintessentially Protestant phrase "priesthood of all believers" to describe the congregants' place in the church.

It is not surprising, then, that our data turned up a number of references to more individualistic conceptions of moral authority. Nearly all of them were references to the freedom given by parish leaders (particularly the current pastor) to individuals to pursue spiritual and ritual practices that were meaningful from their various backgrounds. As one Filipino interviewee told us, "We didn't do anything until eight years ago! It's different now. We wanted to do this devotion for so many years and we couldn't do it. And [when Father Luszak came] I asked him could we do it. And Father said, 'Oh, sure! What do you need to do it?' So I read all the books about it, and then he read all the books and all that. 'Sure!' he says, and the San Lorenzo is the beginning of the different ethnic celebrations in St. Lambert."

## Conclusion

Our interviews and observations show that religious groups vary significantly and systematically in how they articulate or instantiate conceptions of moral authority. But it is also clear that these conceptions interact with other religious factors to produce the particular ideas and practices embodied in the life and thought of local immigrant congregations. What impact might this have on civic engagement?

One important effect is how conceptions of moral authority will influence a group's ability to find compatriots (or, conversely, opponents) in the U.S. public square. The tendency of Eastern religions to emphasize individualist notions of moral authority gives them something in common with key dominant religious and cultural values in the U.S. context. We would expect them to have some affinity with American middle- and upper-class educated groups such as mainline Protestants or even Reform Judaism. It is perhaps no accident that so many of the U.S. converts to Buddhism are drawn from these groups, or that so many of the interfaith initiatives involve them as well (Numrich 1996; Wuthnow 2005). At the other end of the moral authority spectrum, we find that African American Protestants, like Muslims, have a collectivist conception of moral authority and thus provide a significant potential pool of converts for Islam. We can also observe emergent cooperative initiatives between African American Protestants and Muslims (Selod 2005).

These potential affinity groups raise some interesting questions for the civic engagement of recent immigrants. For example, will the Eastern religions' affinity with privileged groups in the U.S. context and Islam's affinity with disprivileged groups affect the content and efficacy of the public engagement of Hindus, Buddhists, or Muslims? Given the salience of race as an organizing principle in the U.S. public square, will Eastern religions come to be viewed as white, while Muslims are seen as black? If so, how will this affect their opportunities for effective civic engagement?

A second effect of the locus of moral authority is in how it may facilitate or inhibit civic engagement itself. Groups such as Muslims or Orthodox Christians, who place a strong emphasis on the moral authority of their collective tradition, may find engagement with others in the public arena difficult or threatening. The stronger a group's collective identity, and the more exclusivist their view of Truth, the more difficult it will be to find common ground on which to cooperate or engage with others. To the extent that they must engage, alternative worldviews may seem threatening. We can observe this effect in how Muslims have engaged the public school systems—especially in curricular or extracurricular activities that clash with the expectations that Muslims have about how they should practice their religion in everyday life. We also see it in the difficulty many Orthodox Christian congregations have in engaging in ecumenical initiatives. On the other hand, for groups such as Hindus and Buddhists, who give much greater latitude to individuals in the religious and moral choices they make, engagement with others may be easier. If truth can be discovered and experienced on multiple paths, there is less of a threat when paths cross.

Of course, other religious characteristics may complicate the effect of conceptions of moral authority. Some Hindu groups who hold strong ethnic identifications may be hindered in engaging others similarly to Muslims or Orthodox Christians. The fact that Islam is monotheistic in ways that Hinduism and Buddhism are not may give it some common ground with the dominant Christian and Jewish groups in the U.S. context. The increasing use of the category of Abrahamic Faiths rather than Judeo-Christian Tradition indicates that this shared identity is already emerging. But the long history of the monotheistic religions also tells us that such common ground will be the locale for conflict as often as it may provide soil for amity.

Finally, an immigrant religion's ideas on moral authority will influence its trajectory of religious and social change in its new American context. This will likely be particularly significant for groups such as Buddhists, Hindus, and Muslims who lie outside the American religious mainstream (that is, groups in the northwest and southeast quadrants in fig. 3.1). Groups that are individualist on both dimensions of the moral order map will be drawn to one or the other end of the mainstream culture. On one hand, they may move toward the right by developing a more collectivist notion of moral authority. Above, we noted that the BAPS Swaminarayan temple exemplifies such a shift. On the other hand, immigrant religious groups may be drawn toward the left by developing a more collectivist notion of the moral project. Certain expressions of "engaged Buddhism" (where Buddhists become more actively involved in social concerns), while not prevalent in either of our research sites, is an example of this trajectory (Queen 2002; Rothberg 1998).

For Muslims, who tend toward the collectivist end of both dimensions, religious or cultural change is likely to take other forms. A move toward the American religious or cultural left would require becoming more individualistic on the moral authority dimension. The increasing significance of Sufism in American Islam is an example of this trajectory, and one we observed in one of our research sites. Moving toward the right would involve individualizing how Muslims conceive of the primary moral project. While this can be observed in some settings with regard to economic and political behavior, most Muslim communities remain committed to building the *ummah* as their primary moral project in the religious field.

Thus, immigrant religions have a broad range of possibilities for the trajectory of their religious or cultural change. Assimilation, or Americanization, is not as unilinear or straightforward as popular ideas would have it. It is a complex and multidimensional process, what Portes and Zhou (1993) call segmented assimilation. Paying attention to how particular religious differences interact with the American context suggests that such processes will occur differently for different groups. In the next chapter we will focus in more detail on differences in how religious groups conceive of their primary moral projects. When we are able to understand multiple religious characteristics (such as sectarianism, moral authority, and moral project) and focus on how they interact, we will have a broader and richer perspective on how religion matters for new immigrants' civic engagement.

# 4    The Moral Projects of Immigrant Congregations

*From the Council of Trent in the sixteenth century onward, canon law stressed that the parish served all of the souls living within its boundaries. . . . The term had a geographical as well as religious meaning. . . . [I]n each instance a society no more than two or three generations away from a culture on the margins of industrial Europe used the parish to define community in a new environment.*

—John McGreevy (1996)

In his Sunday morning sermon, Ray Castro, the pastor of Victory Outreach Church, was discussing the problems his congregants faced as they navigated their everyday life in a blighted urban neighborhood. "The prisons can't deal with the streets," Pastor Castro declared. "The police can't deal with the streets. The courts can't deal with the streets. The government can't deal with the streets. Only Jesus can." Victory Outreach is a neo-Pentecostal Hispanic congregation affiliated with a larger international organization of the same name. It focuses on the rehabilitation of drug addicts, gang members, and prostitutes in its southwest Chicago neighborhood. Victory Outreach sees its primary moral project as the rescue, reform, and rehabilitation of individuals, accomplished by introducing each one to faith in Jesus and a personal encounter with the power of the Holy Spirit. As a consequence of how it defines its moral project, Victory Outreach has a deep distrust of collectivist solutions or action and develops citizens who are engaged in public life as individuals confronting other individuals in parks and on street corners.

A few miles to the north sits Maternity BVM, a Catholic parish in a similar Hispanic neighborhood, Humboldt Park. Maternity BVM's ministries also serve primarily poor or working-class Hispanics. Although their socioeconomic contexts and the class composition of their congregations are similar, there are significant religious differences between the two congregations—most importantly in how they define their primary moral project. Maternity BVM views its moral project in more collectivist terms, pursuing community development and structural change aimed at the improvement of its neighborhood as a whole. This

Maternity BVM Catholic Church involves itself in neighborhood social concerns. Photo by Jerry Berndt.

congregation is more optimistic than Victory Outreach about the role of government and the courts. Maternity BVM is particularly involved in promoting the economic and legal rights of day laborers and attempting to influence legislation on amnesty for undocumented immigrants. It offers its building as a safe space for immigrants to meet and mobilize around these issues without fear of Homeland Security. U.S. Congressman Luis Gutierrez regularly uses the church's facilities to meet with constituents, documented and undocumented alike. Thus, while both Victory Outreach and Maternity BVM offer their space as a safe haven for the development of individuals as empowered agents who act in the public sphere, the content of the consequent acts of citizenship is strikingly different.

### Defining the Moral Project

We draw the notion of moral project from the heuristic map of the religious or moral order in the United States introduced in the previous chapter (see also

Kniss 2003). Recall that the map consists of two dimensions representing two central issues in any moral order. One is the locus of moral authority and the other is the content of the moral project. The moral project dimension addresses the question of where moral action or influence should be targeted. At one end of the continuum, the moral project seeks the maximization of individual utility, while at the other, the maximization of the (collective) public good.

Figure 3.1 provides a graphic representation of this idea. Note that at one end of the moral project continuum religious groups focus primarily on the individual. Groups located near this pole of the dimension hold much in common with the libertarian notion in U.S. political culture that champions the maximization of individual utility as the primary moral project. Libertarianism applies individualism to questions of economic and political relationships, valuing a free market where free individuals act in their own rational self-interest in the competition for valued goods and resources. Networks formed by the individual pursuit of self-interest in a free market are the bases of the social bond. The religious counterpart to libertarianism holds that the primary moral project is the individual's salvation and moral improvement. The problems of the world can be solved "one soul at a time." Congregations are networks of individuals in pursuit of religious goods, whether those may be salvation, enlightenment, ecstatic experience, or personal well-being.

At the other, collectivist, end of the moral project dimension, we find communalist projects. Here, the primary moral project is the collective good rather than individual utility. In political economy, communalism favors a regulated market over an unregulated free market. Egalitarianism and cooperation are valued over self-interested striving and competition. In religion, communalism identifies the primary moral project as establishing a just and righteous social order rather than reforming individuals. Religious communalists such as Christian liberation theologians are more likely to talk about social justice than about individual salvation.

It is tempting to think of the libertarian end of the moral project continuum as identified with the religious right, and communalism as identified with the left. Certainly there are strong affinities or correlations in that direction, but there are also important anomalies. Communalism, for example, is not exclusively the province of leftist theologians. As Hart (1992) shows, communalist ideas can be operative among mainstream Protestants and Catholics in the United States. As we will see, most Muslims also view their primary moral project in collectivist terms.

Based on our conceptual distinction, we divided the congregations we studied into three theoretically derived categories—congregations we expected to focus on individualist moral projects, those we expected would emphasize collectivist projects, and congregations we expected would fall somewhere in the middle of this continuum. We assigned particular congregations to these categories based on what we knew of their broader religious traditions and their own particular expression of these traditions.

In the first category we placed the three Hindu congregations, the two Buddhist congregations, and the evangelical and Pentecostal congregations, because each of these religious traditions stresses moral projects oriented toward the individual. In the category for collectivist moral projects we placed the three Catholic congregations, the Lubavitch Hasidic congregation, and one of the Muslim mosques. Again, this placement was based on what we knew of characteristics of the broader religious traditions. In the middle category we included the mainline Protestant congregations, the Orthodox Christian congregations, and a Muslim mosque where there was a significant Sufi presence (where we expected a mixture of the collectivism of traditional Islam with the individualism of Sufi mysticism).

## Individualist Moral Projects

As figure 3.1 predicts, we find most evidence of individualist moral projects in congregations from Buddhist, Hindu, and conservative Protestant traditions. Hinduism, a complex and varying set of traditions and practices, is not easily characterized in a few sentences. But one core idea shared by all the religious varieties falling under the label of "Hindu" is the notion of *samsara*, the transmigration of souls. According to this idea, all living beings are caught up in a cycle of birth, death, and reincarnation. A primary religious goal (or moral project) is liberation (*moksha*) from this cycle through unity with the absolute or ultimate soul, *Brahman*. Unity is attained via mystical ascetic contemplation and proper religious practice. Although many Hindu groups have developed institutional forms that address secondary religious goals of lay people, such earthly institutional concerns are viewed by religious virtuosi as ultimately detracting from the primary goal of liberation from samsara. The ultimate liberation project, then, is a moral project oriented toward the individual.

Buddhism, like Hinduism, originated in India and shares the primary religious goal of liberation from samsara. Buddhism focuses on self-centered material desire as the tie that binds individuals to the cycle of birth, death, and rebirth. The goal then is detachment from material concerns, an enlightened consciousness achieved through religious practices such as chanting and meditation and adherence to the Buddha's teachings (*dharma*). Buddhism's diverse schools and orders represent a huge variation in religious ideas and practices; still, they share the primary moral project of individual enlightenment and release from samsara, even while they address the more earthly or mundane penultimate religious goals of lay practitioners.

Conservative evangelical and Pentecostal forms of Protestantism would claim little in common with Hinduism and Buddhism, but they do share a concern with individualist moral projects. The most important moral project for these Protestant groups is bringing individuals to a "born-again" (evangelical) or "spirit-filled" (Pentecostal) experience—that is, a spiritual rebirth. Other moral projects and the social and political agenda that follow from them are rooted in this fundamental notion that large problems can be solved one soul at a time. The focus is more on questions or problems of individual morality than on structural morality (i.e., "social justice," to use a term from the language of the collectivist Christian left). This shows up in large-scale sociological studies of conservative Protestants as a group or "subcultural identity," to use Smith's (1998) term. The identity is held together by shared commitments to collective forms of moral authority, but the moral projects—the specific content of morality—are oriented toward individual concerns. Hunter (1987), for example, shows that evangelical college students are much more likely to be concerned about individual morality issues such as the use of controlled substances, sexual behavior, or cheating than are students at large. Smith (1998) does not address many details about particular moral projects in his survey data, but his in-depth interviews demonstrate that evangelicals nearly always return to individual lifestyle concerns, and individually oriented actions (the "one soul at a time" strategy) whenever they discuss the specific whats and hows of moral action.

One of the best places to look at the question of conservative Protestant moral projects is with regard to race. Race, racism, and race relations have been core issues in U.S. politics and culture for the past two centuries. U.S. religious groups have offered a variety of responses to issues of race across the entire individual-collective moral project spectrum. Conservative Protestants have most frequently adopted projects at the individual end of the spectrum. They often speak against the "evils of racial hatred" (e.g., Henry 1947, 44), but less often address the structured economic and political racial inequalities that are more likely to be issues on the Christian left. Emerson and Smith (2000) show that evangelicals, when asked about the best ways to work against racism, are much more likely to suggest getting to know people of another race than to propose a more collectivist solution like working to racially integrate residential neighborhoods. They refer to this as the "let's be friends" strategy.

In the set of congregations we studied, the HanMaUm Zen Center exemplifies a group oriented toward individualist moral projects. Located in Skokie, a diverse suburb just north of the Chicago city limits, it primarily serves a Korean clientele. There are also a few Westerners who are attracted by the Zen meditation the temple offers. The temple is led by several Korean nuns and is affiliated with a sectarian movement headed by the Korean nun Dae Haeng Kun Sunim, within the Chogye Order of Korean Seon (Zen) Buddhism. The temple provides valued religious goods and services to individual participants, but it has few connections to its locale, provides few social services, and does very little cooperative work with other religious groups, even other Buddhist temples.

The focus on individual moral projects came through clearly in our interviews with leaders and participants at HanMaUm. We asked one of the nuns in charge of the temple, "What are your main responsibilities at the temple? Do you help with the services or the classes or the volunteers?" Her answer: "My first duty is my own practice to be a better nun, to reach the enlightened level." The nun's answer reflected the official teachings of the HanMaUm movement's head, Dae Haeng Kun Sunim. In an edited collection of her teachings she notes that teachers function primarily as role models—temporary crutches that individuals can use until they can see for themselves. "Without using words, mountains silently tell us, 'Live like a mountain.' Water silently tells us, 'Live like water.' Flowers silently tell us, 'Live like a flower.' The root of a weed in harsh soil tells us, 'Live wisely.' All things tell us to live like them. Therefore, there is nothing that is not a teacher" (Haeng 1999, 167–168).

Interviews with participants in the Skokie center also demonstrated the centrality of individual projects. Most told stories of finding HanMaUm in a time of personal crisis. One woman, a nurse, told how she and her family had been baptized in a Methodist church when they moved to the suburbs twenty-three years before. She returned to the Buddhist temple after the sudden death of her nineteen-year-old daughter in a car accident. "You know the difference between Buddhism and Christianity?" she said. "The Christians just keep talking and talking and talking. But the Buddhist way—the way the Sunim treated me: she just left me alone. I would come to the temple and cry and cry. I was here for months and the Sunim didn't bother me at all. Then when I talked she just listened and listened. I really found comfort—I couldn't find comfort any other place." She went on to describe how Buddhist teachings helped her to release her anger toward the driver of the car in which her daughter had died.

Other stories may have been less dramatic but provided similar accounts of disruption or personal crises related to job issues, geographic mobility, or child-rearing problems. But none of the interviewees looked to the temple for programmatic solutions to these social problems. They did not expect job training, child-care services, parenting support groups, or political advocacy by the Buddhist community to address structural causes of social problems. Rather, they looked for personal solutions that would help them as individuals to deal with difficulties. As one person told us, "I need my religion badly. I need somebody to tell me what I am doing is right; or I need, you know, spiritually I need someone." Another said, "Whenever I feel like 'Oh! I don't have any more strength!' then I come over here and I talk to nuns and I meditate. And that's how I 'build up'."

Out of all the interviews and observations at HanMaUm, we coded only four references to communalist or collectivist moral projects—and two of the four were pejorative references to such projects in other religions. Christians, for example, were criticized for using social services and job networking to evangelize immigrants. One of the nun/teachers in the temple noted that a focus on collectivist religious identities was divisive and worked against the unity of all humanity.

## Collectivist Moral Projects

The religious traditions we included in the collectivist category—Roman Catholicism, Islam, and Judaism—clearly contrasted with our individualist cases in how they talked about and carried out their primary moral projects. The differences in their talk and practice are in tune with differences in their basic religious assumptions and authoritative sources.

Catholic views on moral projects are collectively oriented, highlighting the role of the church in the world—a church that is coterminous with a human community and a geographic place, such as a parish, diocese, city, or nation. This leads Catholic congregations to feel an institutional responsibility for the quality of life in their neighborhood or region as a whole. McGreevy (1996) documents the important role played by immigrant Catholic parishes in American cities historically, especially with regard to race relations. In the first waves of Catholic immigration to the United States, parishes often served the needs of particular ethnic communities in ethnic neighborhoods. This, of course, complicated race relations, but it also led to cooperation with a growing labor movement and an affinity with the emerging social gospel in the early-twentieth-century United States (Dolan 1985).

More recently, with shifts in neighborhood residential patterns and the decline of original ethnic identities, parishes continue to maintain old collectivist projects and establish new ones that serve the needs of their geographic locales. These often target a more diverse ethnic population that includes Catholics and non-Catholics alike. Parish schools are a good example of this, as are local interfaith initiatives (Wedam 2000). Other kinds of collectivist projects are also prevalent among Catholics.

Islam, likewise, views its religion as coterminous with a particular community and/or geographic place. The important theological concept of *ummah* captures this core Muslim value. "Ummah" is a difficult word to translate accurately from Arabic to English, but as Cragg (1975, 73) notes, "It has elements of 'nation,' 'community,' 'people,' and 'religion'—all fused into [a] characteristic Islamic quality and ideal." Throughout the history of Islam, this core notion of ummah has produced a close connection between faith, politics and the state, particularly in the notion of *dar al-Islam*, territory governed by Islamic law (Shari'ah). These important religious ideas have spawned myriad collectivist moral projects in Islam.[1]

In the context of the contemporary urban United States, Muslim immigrants (like earlier Catholic immigrants) have established local religious communities that, while officially espousing universalism, tend to serve the needs of particular ethnic communities and geographic locales. They have also, like Catholics, been active in establishing parochial elementary and secondary schools and, more recently, student associations in universities. (Schmidt [2004a] documents this for Chicago.) The Chicago Bosnian immigrant community established the nation's first Muslim religious organization, a benevolent society, in 1906 (Numrich, forthcoming b; Schmidt 2004a). It was a precursor to the Islamic Cultural Center, one of the congregations in our study.

Finally, Judaism is also a religious tradition whose primary moral projects are collectively oriented, aimed at building and maintaining a community with a common identity and system of religious laws. Thanks to the many diasporic pressures in Jewish history, its communities are not as geographically instantiated as Catholic or Orthodox Christian communities. Rather, Jews primarily share a community of memory and tradition. Zionism, however, attempts to reclaim a geographic core for the Jewish community and is the most prominent example of a contemporary collectivist moral project within Judaism.

Some commentators suggest that Reform Judaism in the United States has adopted a "Protestantized" worldview and abandoned the collectivist moral orientation of traditional Judaism. For example, Friedland notes, "As Jews have been integrated into the larger, modern culture, dominated by consumerism and individualism, commitment to both ethnicity and religion has waned." But he goes on to suggest that even Reform Judaism is organized around synagogue life and that synagogue congregations can construct "communities of meaning" that engage the larger civic community in the moral project of *tikkun olam*, the "healing of the world" (Friedland 2001, 44–46).

One of the Catholic parishes we studied provides a good example of a religious community oriented toward collectivist moral projects. Maternity of the Blessed Virgin Mary is located in the Humboldt Park community of Chicago. Humboldt Park is the primary center for the Puerto Rican population in Chicago, but it is also home to a number of Mexican and Central American immigrants. Maternity BVM reflects that diversity in its congregational life. The neighborhood deals with the expected litany of social problems in U.S. urban Hispanic communities. Unemployment, underemployment, and unfair labor practices abound. Immigration status is a concern for many residents. The usual urban problems associated with poverty are part of the everyday life of Humboldt Park's residents. As a pillar congregation for the neighborhood, Maternity BVM finds ways to address the concerns of its parishioners and the neighborhood as a whole. But here you will find much less talk than at HanMaUm about helping individuals to cope spiritually with the problems in their lives. At Maternity BVM, in consonance with a theology that centers on the church as the collective body of Christ and includes social and political concerns as relevant theological topics, the moral project is viewed in much more collectivist structural terms.

This is apparent both in how leaders and participants speak abstractly about moral projects and in how the church structures itself programmatically. Like the leaders at HanMaUm, leaders of Maternity BVM recognize individual problems related to immigration, and they understand the importance of spiritual and religious support of individuals. But it was evident in most of our interviews there that references to spiritual problems and resources quickly move to collectivist solutions. As one of the priests told our interviewer, "We would hope that the reason why we exist is because we are a church, and so we hope that our principal activity would be worship. But then, you know, serving the welfare of our members asks that we don't be wholly inwardly focused. How can we be a service to the wider community?" A lay parish leader noted, "Church is not only Sunday, church is every day. What you hear on Sunday—that should give you nourishment to move on and act on, because of the needs that you have for your community. But it cannot be just one person. It has to be more people that show an interest in things that are affecting the community."

Similarly, a nun associated with the parish discussed the family and personal problems faced by immigrants; but even though she operated the parish counseling center, she didn't refer to individual or psychological solutions to immigrants' problems. Rather, she focused on collectivist institutional responses. "I think people who are involved in the church, people who are involved in their school, make sure their kids finish school, they are going to make it. I don't care what country they come from, if they stay involved in church and school, and try to get involved in the community, the block clubs—there is something to be said about the stability that the children get from those institutions that help them along."

Maternity BVM puts its collectivist talk into action. The parish provides resources and a supportive context for a variety of collectivist moral projects. Several religiously based collectivities call the parish home. These include a charismatic prayer group and at least two groups organized around saints that are important to particular ethnic groups in the parish. These groups, while they may focus on individual religious practice and piety, do so within the context of a collective identity. They use religious experience to strengthen and maintain the goals of the group. The congregation also organizes collectively to address the pressing social problems facing their parish and their neighborhood. The parish operates Providence Family Services of Chicago, a family counseling center that also offers after-school tutoring and computer training. They host immigration workshops organized by the United Neighborhoods Organization, a faith-based organization begun in Los Angeles that serves the needs of Hispanic immigrants. As noted earlier, U.S. Congressman Luis Gutierrez has used the parish as a safe place to meet with immigrant constituents regardless of their immigration status. Under the umbrella of community organizations like the Humboldt Park Empowerment Partnership, Maternity BVM cooperates with other collectively oriented religious and community groups (including liberal Protestant congregations) to address neighborhood problems such as gentrification or unfair and illegal practices involving day laborers.

## Mixed Approaches

We expected several of our research sites to fall somewhere in the middle of the spectrum between individualist and collectivist approaches to the moral project. Our placement of these congregations in the mixed category derived from what we know about the broader religious ideas and practices in which their particular communities were rooted.

Orthodox Christian churches, for example, combine an emphasis on the collective character of the church as a core societal institution usually coterminous with a nation or ethnic group and an equally strong emphasis on individual, even mystical, spirituality and religious experience. The central theological concept of *theosis* (or "divinization," the transformation of individuals into beings with divine qualities) makes individuals a primary moral project for Orthodoxy. Theosis occurs primarily through the act of worship, so there is significant emphasis on religious experience. Epiphanies (a communication or manifestation of the divine in this world, in which human individuals are direct participants) play an important role in Orthodox theology and practice—hence the central role of icons. In our study, we placed both of the Orthodox Christian congregations in the mixed category.[2]

Some Muslim groups also belong in the mixed category. While maintaining a commitment to the religious concept of ummah, many Muslim communities who have resided outside of dar al-Islam, some for centuries, have also participated in and made accommodations to modernity and modernism. A modernist or liberal Islamic perspective has emerged within global Islam in response to the challenges of modernity to traditional Islam (Esposito 1998; Khan 2003). In this, influences of classic Western liberalism may produce a greater affinity for individualism, as well as less interest in making Islam coterminous with the state in traditionalist fashion. A second significant individualizing factor within Islam is Sufism, a tradition that, like Orthodox Christianity, highlights mystical spirituality and individual religious experience (Waines 2003). One of the mosques we studied, the Islamic Cultural Center, rooted in the Bosnian immigrant community, fit the mixed category on both these counts.

With regard to the mainline or liberal Protestant denominations, we would normally have expected these to focus on collectivist moral projects—i.e., being more concerned about social justice and the church as a collective community than about individual salvation or piety, emphases more characteristic of conservative Evangelicals and Pentecostals. However, immigrant congregations, even those affiliated with mainline or liberal Protestant denominations, are often the product of missionary versions of their denominational traditions. These may be quite evangelical in their flavor and hence more focused on born-again religion than many of their mainstream denominational compatriots. This was certainly the case for the two mainline Protestant congregations we studied—an Indian Church of the Brethren congregation and a Chinese Lutheran church—and we placed both of them in the mixed category. The latter, Truth Lutheran Church, provides an excellent example of what we mean by a "mixed case."

Truth Lutheran Church is located in Naperville, a railroad town dating back to the nineteenth century and now an exurban center of high-tech industry in

Chicago's metropolitan region (Numrich 2000a). The church is located near the center of town in a historic building, the former town library. It values and prominently displays its affiliation with the mainline Evangelical Lutheran Church in America (ELCA). Its services follow ELCA liturgical forms, and leaders follow ELCA directives in how they organize their congregation's polity structure. In these respects, Truth Lutheran is like many of the pillar congregations located at downtown intersections of midsized towns across the United States. In other respects, however, it doesn't fit the stereotype. The congregation is almost entirely from Taiwan and mainland China. Services are in Mandarin and English. The music is led by a praise band typical of the contemporary worship style that has become so popular in evangelical Protestant circles. The texts of songs are projected on a screen and reflect an individually oriented and experiential piety that is foreign to traditional Lutheran modes of worship. Thus, the congregation, led by its Taiwanese pastor, negotiates a middle course between evangelical and mainline Protestantism.

The sermons we heard on Sunday mornings reflected the mix of individualist and collectivist moral projects. As one would expect in a Lutheran church, there were numerous references to "grace." But the pastor's teaching regarding how grace was to be accepted and reflected in parishioners' lives varied. In one sermon, for example, he noted that grace requires Christians to put God's word into practice. His examples ranged from the collectivist projects of addressing large-scale economic problems (he referred specifically to natural disasters and economic problems in Taiwan) to individualist projects like tithing (where he argued that individuals will be blessed by God if they tithe).

Interviews with members of the congregation also reflected the full range of individual and collective moral projects. One member echoed the individualist sentiments of the Korean Buddhist quoted above when she noted that, after moving to the United States from China, her life had "too much pressure, too hard work." The people at Truth Lutheran and the pastor's teaching helped her to "feel spiritual," to "become better and better" as a Christian. Otherwise, she said, "I feel I am so weak, I will die." Another member noted the important role the church played in teaching children "how to be a good person." More collectively oriented projects were also noted by interviewees. A typical example was the member who, when asked what was the most important thing she got from the congregation, said, "I think an extended family. I think there are a lot of people at church that watch out for us, in terms of our family. . . . I feel very comfortable in it, getting to know people from grandmas and grandpas to little kids. . . . Sometimes it is hard, because everyone is watching, but at the same time you know that there are always people who you can go to."

Truth Lutheran's organized programmatic activity is constrained by the congregation's size and limited resources, but what activities there are reflect a range of individually and collectively oriented projects. They engage in evangelizing efforts aimed at individuals—activities like "bring a friend" night or Bible studies for newcomers. But at the collectivist end of the spectrum, they also cooperate with other congregations to raise funds for world hunger. They collaborate with other Naperville churches in responding to community issues and have even hosted a town hall community forum with Naperville's mayor.

## Moral Projects and Civic Engagement

Table 4.1 provides a summary of the patterns we found in the congregations we observed with respect to how people spoke about their moral projects. The "Documents" column indicates the number of transcripts or field note documents that included codes for the moral project variable. Included in the individualist cells are positive references to individualist projects and negative references to collectivist projects. The inverse is true for the collectivist cells in the table. The data demonstrate what we hypothesized based on the theory and empirical examples discussed earlier. Individualist congregations were more likely to speak of their moral projects in individualistic terms, while congregations from collectivist traditions were more likely to talk about collectivist projects. References were more evenly distributed in the mixed category. In each group, however, there are congregations that do not fit the pattern we expected in our a priori coding. As is often the case, an examination of atypical groups can yield some interesting insights.

### Sectarianism and Moral Projects

Three congregations that we had coded as individualist based on our theory actually split about evenly between individualist and collectivist orientations in their references to moral projects: the BAPS Swaminarayan Hindu temple, the Ling Shen Ching Tze Buddhist temple, and the Victory Outreach Protestant congregation. In fact, at BAPS, a little more than half of the references to moral projects were collectivist in their orientation. All three of these atypical congregations were coded as high on the sectarianism variable vis-à-vis their larger religious traditions. A closer look at the BAPS data offers some insight into how sectarianism may interact with a congregation's commitment to moral projects.

Half (eleven of twenty-two) of the references to collectivist moral projects in the BAPS data referred to one of their primary goals as ethnic preservation. Respondents referred to their temple as a cultural center and explicitly stated that, intertwined with their religious commitments is an interest in preserving Indian (especially Gujarati) cultural heritage. The temple offers instructional classes in Gujarati language, dance, and drama, as well as an array of other cultural events and services. Social service is also a major focus of activity, including international disaster relief and economic development. Much of this has also had an Indian and Gujarati focus, especially after the earthquake in Gujarat in 2001.

Table 4-1    References to Locus of Moral Project by Site

|  | Documents | Individual | Collective |
|---|---|---|---|
| *Individualist* | | | |
| BAPS Swaminarayan | 16 | 18 | 22 |
| Gayatri Pariwar | 21 | 10 | 6 |
| ISKCON | 33 | 27 | 18 |
| HanMaUm | 20 | 10 | 2 |
| Ling Shen Ching Tze | 15 | 14 | 13 |
| Victory Outreach | 11 | 18 | 14 |
| Total | 116 | 97 | 75 |
| *Mixed* | | | |
| St. Demetrios | 15 | 19 | 20 |
| Holy Virgin Protection | 26 | 3 | 18 |
| Naperville COB | 28 | 8 | 8 |
| Truth Lutheran | 12 | 8 | 7 |
| Islamic Cultural Center | 25 | 8 | 9 |
| Total | 106 | 46 | 62 |
| *Collectivist* | | | |
| Maternity BVM | 10 | 2 | 24 |
| Five Holy Martyrs | 13 | 11 | 7 |
| St. Lambert | 31 | 3 | 15 |
| Synagogue FREE | 22 | 2 | 3 |
| Islamic Foundation | 22 | 2 | 5 |
| Total | 98 | 20 | 54 |

Even when speaking of such activity in collectivist terms, however, the ultimate goals and values have an internal and even individualistic flavor. For example, one leader of the temple told us,

> As I mentioned, one reason for BAPS's tremendous success in terms of volunteers and volunteer hours locally, nationally, and internationally is because we genuinely believe that by volunteering we're doing good for ourselves, meaning we have a personal stake in the act of volunteering. It's not . . . just

to do good for others, but, in fact, to do good for us. And the way that happens is [that] when you volunteer, when you come into contact with people of various backgrounds and various temperaments and various skills, and polished and unpolished people as you do in normal everyday life over and over again, you tend to conquer your own temperament. You tend to be a little bit more patient. You attempt to be a little more understanding and tactful and diplomatic. . . . The main purpose is to learn self-control, and if you can do that, you're more disciplined and you're more likely to move further on the pathway to salvation, toward a higher body.

A similar internal focus to collectivist projects can be seen at Victory Outreach and Ling Shen Ching Tze, as well. Victory Outreach speaks of its rehabilitation center and its congregation as a "family." Ling Shen Ching Tze speaks of its corporate projects (for example, classes in Tai Chi, Feng Shui, karate, and computer skills) as ways to improve the lives of their own members and to attract others into the temple. It appears that sectarian groups with individualist moral projects need to pay more attention than other individualist groups to collectivist concerns. Maintaining a sectarian stance over against co-religionists or "the world" requires strong internal cohesion and identity, and collectivist moral projects pursue that goal. This, in turn, is likely to reduce or hamper a congregation's civic engagement. Thus, many of the Ling Shen Ching Tze references to collectivist (sometimes even externally focused) moral projects expressed frustration at their lack of success in attracting or engaging others from outside their temple.

### Moral Authority and Moral Projects

There are two other atypical cases that require closer examination. Holy Virgin Protection, a Russian Orthodox congregation in the mixed category, shows an imbalance toward the collectivist side of the spectrum (eighteen of twenty-one references). Five Holy Martyrs, a Roman Catholic parish in the collectivist category, had more than half of its moral project references coded as individually oriented. These cases reinforce what we said earlier regarding how congregations may serve ethnic collective interests, but they also highlight how the moral authority variable may interact with people's notions of the moral project.

Like the cases cited earlier, Holy Virgin Protection (HVP) is also fairly sectarian in its religious and cultural outlook. The Russian immigrant community is a smaller and less integrated group than many other immigrant groups in Chicago. Further, HVP is part of the Russian Orthodox Church Outside of Russia (ROCOR), an older and more conservative group within the Russian Orthodox family that has maintained an antagonistic relationship to the church (and state) in postrevolutionary Russia. So, not surprisingly, many of the references to collectivist moral projects in the interviews are focused internally on how the church serves as a community for Russian immigrants.

Other references reflect the central role of the church and its leadership hierarchy (the Russian Orthodox moral authority) in determining how Orthodox Christian believers carry out their moral projects. For example, consider the following from an interviewee recounting a conversation with a priest regarding his decision to be baptized into the church as an adult.

And he wanted to know what I was going to do when I was baptized, to see what my next steps would likely be: "Will you go to church? Do you know that Jesus Christ commanded his apostles to be in the church? The church is the mother. It must govern everything. Everything must come from it." And, basically, I agree with that. The church is what the priest manages to make of it. Everything depends on the priest. The entire church life depends on the priest, on what kind of person he is, how people relate to him.

This interviewee spoke extensively of the congregation as a community (a collectivist moral project) to which all members contributed, an organism of which each was a part. But he also noted that the shape of that community was determined by the church hierarchy, especially the priest.

Five Holy Martyrs (FHM), the other outlier, also demonstrates a congregation's interactions with ethnic experience and religious hierarchy. As a Roman Catholic congregation, we expected it to reflect Catholic collectivist views on the moral project. And while typical Catholic collectivist moral projects were part of the life of the parish and were reflected in the interviews, just over half of the references were to individualist moral projects. FHM is one of the large historic parishes in the very large Polish community in Chicago. As such, it serves many of the individual needs of new Polish immigrants, such as Polish-language services, job-seeking networks, and assistance with immigration paperwork. The interviews reflected these individually oriented projects. The parish did not need to be *the* community for new Polish immigrants. The Polish community is old and well-established, with a broad range of social organizations. The parish was one of many such organizations providing a particular set of services.

As for the interaction with moral authority, FHM (at least during the period that we observed and interviewed) had a somewhat tenuous relationship with the larger Catholic hierarchy. There were pastoral transitions, not all priests spoke Polish, and the geographic parish itself was in transition from a predominantly Polish neighborhood to one populated primarily by Mexicans. This made for weakened and somewhat problematic relationships with its broader Catholic context, a situation likely to affect how the congregation viewed its moral projects.

### Impact on Civic Engagement

To sum up, we expect that religious communities' conceptions of their primary moral projects will have an important impact on how they engage with others outside their particular local congregation—both with co-religionists and with society more broadly. Groups that define their moral projects individualistically will no doubt engage other individuals around questions that affect individual interests and well-being. Groups that define their moral projects collectively will be more likely to engage other collectivists around questions that affect larger social structures and processes. To bring this closer to the ground: If substance abuse is a problem to be engaged, we would expect conservative Protestants to feel an affinity with "just say no" policies and to engage in individual rehabilitation efforts. And we would expect Catholics, on the other hand, to address economic or social problems that make drug abuse more likely and to engage others around, say, drug-related legal issues that may punish some groups more than others.

## Putting It All Together

Figure 4.1 combines the coding for each of our sixteen research sites on each of the three religious variables. For the moral project and moral authority variables, we calculated scores for the ratio of collectivist to individualist references in the data. Research sites whose scores fell into the middle third of the range on each variable were coded as mixed. In the figure, we use font type to indicate whether the congregation was sectarian, mainstream, or practiced a mixture of sectarian and mainstream religious expressions.

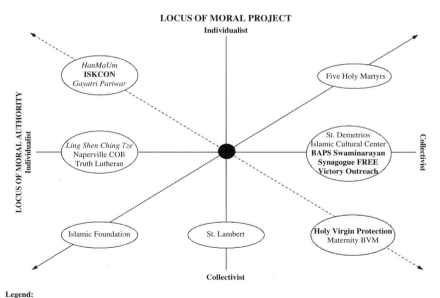

**LOCUS OF MORAL PROJECT**
Individualist

HanMaUm
**ISKCON**
*Gayatri Pariwar*

Five Holy Martyrs

*Ling Shen Ching Tze*
Naperville COB
Truth Lutheran

St. Demetrios
Islamic Cultural Center
**BAPS Swaminarayan
Synagogue FREE
Victory Outreach**

Islamic Foundation

St. Lambert

**Holy Virgin Protection**
Maternity BVM

LOCUS OF MORAL AUTHORITY
Individualist

Collectivist

Collectivist

**Legend:**
**Bold** = Sectarian Religious Expression
*Italics* = Mixed Sectarian/Mainstream Religious Expression
Regular = Mainstream Religious Expression

Figure 4.1   Research Site Mapping Based on Coding of Religious Variables (Figure by Laurie Cooper Stoll)

There are several things to note when looking at all three variables together. First, the majority of our research sites lie off the mainstream diagonal shown in figure 3.1. For the moral authority and moral project dimensions, most congregations are mixed or high collectivists on both or mixed or high individualists on both. Although this is atypical in the American religious system, perhaps we should not be surprised that immigrant religions are atypical. It does suggest that civic engagement for immigrant religious groups is likely to express itself in ways that may seem unfamiliar to older players in the public square. (It also means that, in the chapters to come, we can refer to individualists and collectivists without always specifying the particular religious dimension, given that groups' positions on the dimensions are often similar.)

Second, it is interesting to note that scores are much more polarized on the moral authority dimension than on the moral project dimension. (Only one congregation, St. Lambert, fell into the mixed category on the moral authority dimension.) This suggests that conceptions of authority are well-articulated and defended by religious groups, but that social practices deriving from religious conceptions of the moral project may be more vulnerable to conflict and change, especially when transplanted into a new social or cultural context. If so, then civic engagement around particular moral projects will be more likely to involve give-and-take interactions than will issues that seem to strike at core assumptions on moral authority.

Finally, if we think of individualists and collectivists as representing two different clusters of immigrant congregations, figure 4.1 indicates that sectarian expressions are found on both sides. Sectarianism is a third dimension that will provide nuance to any general claims about individualists and collectivists. Clearly, it will have a significant impact on civic engagement, but that impact will occur all over the map.

Thus, we expect sectarianism to interact with conceptions of moral authority and moral projects to shape how immigrant religious groups engage public life. We noted some of these expectations above, but there are many questions left to be explored. For example, what kinds of coalitions (or oppositions) might we expect based on groups' shared or opposed definitions of moral authority, moral project, and/or sectarian distinctions? To continue the earlier example of responses to substance abuse, might we expect individualists and collectivists among non-Christian groups to ally themselves with their Christian counterparts? What kinds of social and cultural changes might immigrant groups experience as their fundamental conceptions are modified or challenged in the American context and in engagement with other religious or civic groups? We will explore these and other questions as we examine the involvement of immigrant religious groups in issues related to occupation, education, marriage and family, and language.

# PART TWO

## SACRED ASSEMBLIES IN SOCIAL CONTEXTS

# 5

## "Making It in America"

OCCUPATIONAL AND ECONOMIC
ADAPTATION IN IMMIGRANT
CONGREGATIONS

*The first step in obtaining an American foothold
was to find employment. . . . In their religious faith
immigrants recognized almost the only pillar of the
old life that had not crumbled in the course of the
Atlantic crossing. To it, therefore, they clung both as
a means of preserving their identity and as a source
of security and solace in a bewildering world.*

—Maldwyn Allen Jones (1960)

"A lot of Koreans who immigrated to the United States, even though they were
Buddhists in Korea, they became Christians [here]. . . . People think, 'If I go to a
big Korean church, there is more opportunity for me to get a different job or
meet different people.' " This statement, made by a forty-three-year-old Korean
Buddhist travel agent who attends HanMaUm Zen Center in suburban Chicago,
echoes the literature regarding the high ethnic in-group commitment and strong
social networks found in immigrant Korean churches (Kim and Kim 2001). When
acquaintances ask why she does not avail herself of the many material opportunities afforded by Korean churches, she replies, "Well, I am Buddhist and I am
happy that I'm Buddhist. It fits into my personality. That's what I practice, and it
makes me a better person."

The direness of their economic situation and the trauma of their transnational sojourn may not be as stark for all recent immigrants as British historian
Maldwyn Allen Jones described for an earlier American immigrant generation.
Even so, congregational activities and perspectives retain their relevance to religious immigrants at work in America today. In this chapter we ask not only how
congregations alleviate palpable material needs, but also how they bring religious meaning and vocational clarity to their members' work life. This is, after
all, central to what it means to be a sacred assembly. Our Korean Buddhist travel
agent attends HanMaUm Zen Center for religious reasons (among other reasons, to be sure), and she chooses not to change her religious affiliation despite

the nonreligious reasons her fellow Korean immigrants find alluring. Here again we will see how religion matters in such people's lives.

## Occupational Issues in Recent Immigration

In Alejandro Portes and Ruben Rumbaut's *Immigrant America: A Portrait* (2006), the chapter "Making It in America: Occupational and Economic Adaptation" surveys key aspects of the complex process of making it in America, including the socioeconomic circumstances of different immigrant groups, each group's position in the hierarchy of key indicators (such as income and education), and the kinds of reception immigrants receive from the host society. Religion is mentioned only once in that chapter and is discounted as an explanatory factor in their analysis.

Portes and Rumbaut's book typifies the larger immigration literature.[1] We learn much about occupational and economic issues facing recent immigrants but little about how religious immigrants and their congregations address those issues. This lacuna is being filled by scholarship in congregational studies (e.g., Ammerman 2001, 2005; Chaves 2004; Cnaan 2002; Ecklund 2005; Farnsley 2000; Schwadel 2005; Slessarev-Jamir 2003b), to which we add our voice. This chapter begins where the larger immigration literature tends to end.

### Occupational Distribution

All sectors of the American economy now thrive on immigrant workers (Suarez-Orozco, Suarez-Orozco, and Qin-Hilliard 2001, xii). The wide occupational distribution of recent urban immigrants differs from the classical period of American immigration when most entered the socioeconomic pyramid at the lower strata (Bodnar 1985). Today's bimodal clustering includes highly educated professionals at one end and unskilled labor at the other (Numrich 1997; Suarez-Orozco, Suarez-Orozco, and Qin-Hilliard 2001, 380).

The immigrant interviewees in our study (N = 104) clustered noticeably in the higher strata of the socioeconomic pyramid. By far the largest occupational group (29 percent) fell under the professional and technical category according to current Office of Immigration Statistics nomenclature ("Yearbook of Immigration Statistics: 2004"). Students (14 percent) were also strongly represented who, though not currently high earners, nevertheless hold high status and portend future socioeconomic success. We also interviewed several religious workers (13.5 percent), not a separate category in the government nomenclature. Educationally, our interviewees as a group held a remarkable thirty-nine bachelor's degrees, fifteen master's degrees, and five doctoral degrees (three of them MDs). Thus, we heard from many relatively well-off and well-positioned immigrants, making the occupational obstacles discussed later all the more poignant.

We do not have the necessary hard data to determine the overall socioeconomic status of each of the congregations with any precision. However, we can identify some significant occupational patterns across congregations, based on interviewee comments and our own assessments, using Census Bureau categories.

The prominence of the professional/technical category stands out. This group has a high representation in ten of the sixteen sites. At the other end of the occupational status hierarchy, four of the sites feature large numbers in the operators/fabricators/laborers and unemployed categories. Somewhere in the middle, several sites have a significant number of members in service, sales, and administrative support. Most of the sites have a noticeable mixture of occupations in their memberships; in other words, socioeconomic diversity is typical.

Immigration scholars study ethnic occupational niches and economic enclaves (e.g., Portes 1995). We found evidence of these among our congregations, such as Indian nurses and computer technologists, Chinese laboratory technicians, and Hispanic day laborers. However, we were surprised at how few of our interviewees indicated that they work alongside fellow members of their congregations. As we shall see later in this chapter, immigrant congregations provide both formal and informal networks for job placement, but these do not necessarily funnel members to the same employer.

Some large congregations become relatively important employers in their immigrant communities. A few of our research sites employ first-, 1.5-, and second-generation members, such as Five Holy Martyrs (a Polish Catholic church) and Synagogue FREE. Both Islamic parochial schools hire significant numbers of teachers, administrators, and staff. The principal of one school was raised in the school's parent mosque, the assistant principal of the other rose to that position after volunteering in the school for some years. One staff member started her daughter in the preschool program at the same time she entered her graduate degree program. "They were always looking for people in the community who were interested to work here," she told us. "They were always open to me working here, so when I finished graduate school, they had the job opening for me and I took it. I thought it would be nice to work in the Muslim community for a while and be with my daughter, have the same hours." It was her first job following graduate school.

Typically, few second-generation youth pursue a professional religious worker track, such as pastor, priest, or monastic. Personal, parental, and social incentives tend to push American-born children into secular occupations, leaving immigrant congregations little choice but to import clerical leadership from the homelands (e.g., Mann, Numrich, and Williams 2001; Numrich 1996). We found nothing to dispute this trend in our congregational pool.

Immigration scholars also study the informal or unregulated economy (Portes 1995), where the risk of worker exploitation is high, as we shall see with regard to day laborers. A separate but related area has to do with legality. Although we excluded direct questions about immigration status from our interview protocol, we nevertheless heard of illegal situations, such as work visa violations and undocumented immigrants. This brings us to our second broad occupational topic, the obstacles immigrants face in trying to make it in America.

### Occupational Obstacles

"Proficiency in English is probably one of the most crucial factors in facilitating immigrants' socioeconomic success and related adaptation" (Lee and Edmonston 1994, 123). English proficiency includes more than grammatical skills, which even native speakers may lack, but also foreign accents that may affect relationships with employers, fellow employees, and customers or clients. English deficiencies of any kind can make or break an immigrant's job application and contribute to his or her occupational successes and setbacks.

Asked about his work history, a retired Russian Jewish man explained to us, "I tried to get a job, but it didn't work out. I didn't speak the language and my age caused suspicious attitudes. As years went by, the employment situation was getting worse and worse." English deficiency and age both might have conspired against this man, but language alone can present a sufficient occupational impediment for younger immigrants. Another Russian Jewish man, an accountant in his forties with a bachelor's degree, speaks both Russian and English with some proficiency. When asked how his knowledge of these languages affected his current job situation, he responded, "In a very big way, in a crucial way. Of course, a lot depends on me. I need to make efforts. But that pulls me back and prevents me from getting promoted to a job I could aspire to. Objectively, I see that I simply can't rise one step up on the professional ladder." He also admitted that he had difficulties communicating at work.

A twenty-year-old Russian Christian man who works in contracting also experiences difficulties communicating at work. "It's specific words I sometimes don't know and it's—the job that I have is very hard, because you have to speak with customers a lot and discuss a lot of things. So there are a lot of specific terms. That's why it's hard."

We encountered a surprising case that points up the insidiousness of the language issue in immigrant occupational choices and opportunities. A woman of mixed European parentage who grew up in North Africa was offered a teaching position at a local college, with this cautionary word from the school's hiring official (as described by an interviewee): "Let me give you an advice. What if one of the students comes and says, 'Why do you bring us a teacher with an accent? We want an American.'?" You have the credentials for the position, he admitted to our interviewee, "You can take [the contract] and sign it, but this is a personal advice: I am sure I will hear from the students around [here]."

The interviewee went home and thought it over. "I said, 'Well, here are my two youngest kids. I wouldn't want a Spanish person to teach them English. I'd want an American.' So I immediately called him and told him, 'No, I refuse the job.' He was very understanding." We are not sure how to assess the hiring official's "very understanding" attitude. Could it have been relief that the school would not have to field complaints from students about an instructor's accented English?

We heard numerous complaints about discriminatory practices and systemic impediments in the work world. One religious leader at HanMaUm Zen Center explained (through an interpreter) that many Korean immigrants sense something wrong at their workplaces but cannot put their fingers on exactly what: "They felt something where they cannot tell exactly, you know, discrimination, or something. But you know, they don't feel comfortable working, as in their own country—you know, different culture, different manner." According to this interviewee, some Korean students have difficulty changing their residency status in order to get jobs: "When they don't have permanent—the resident card, or something like that—then they cannot get a job with a certain amount of money, you know. It's not—they have to compromise in that kind of situation."

Job instability and exploitation cut across immigrant groups. Many of the light industries that have sustained Hispanic blue-collar workers in Chicago are closing, explained a 1.5-generation Mexican woman from Maternity BVM Catholic Church on Chicago's west side. "Curtiss [a candy manufacturer], that is closing down too," she complained. "Within the next two years they are going to be out of here 'cause they are going to another state. So that again leaves our community without jobs." Out-of-work people in this community often turn to day labor companies, an alternative that draws the ire of this woman and many others: "Day labor, I know you have heard of day labor jobs. Really, that is the minimum wage job, but they are making money from you. You can get a job from there, a temporary job, daily pay, but they are making money from you. I know that because I know friends that work in factories and they tell me, 'M., they might get five dollars but we are paying them nine dollars an hour for these people. We are paying the company the daily pay and the man that is working, he is only getting minimum wage.'"

A white religious leader at Maternity BVM likewise had little good to say about day labor operations, placing them in the larger context of immigrant vulnerability. When asked, "What do you think are the major problems facing the immigrant community here in Chicago?" this leader described the snowball effect of being an undocumented worker in a neighborhood with no jobs: No documents, no legal driver's license or automobile insurance; therefore, you take risks in driving to places of employment. "They can't get a decent job. These guys over here who run [names two day labor companies] and all these little joints around here take advantage of them. And they know they are working with false cards and they give them a job anyway. . . . So without those blessed documents they are confined to being poor."

We posed the same question to a key religious leader at Islamic Cultural Center of Greater Chicago: "In your experience, what would you say is the biggest challenge that a new immigrant who comes to Islamic Cultural Center faces?"

> They complain about instability in terms of jobs. When they find a job, they are not used to being told by the boss, "Go home. Don't need you. Maybe we'll call you if we need you." That kind of thing. They are not used to that. So they complain it's very unstable in terms of jobs. . . . They compare that with what they had in Bosnia, or some of them in Germany because many of these refugees came from Germany. They left Bosnia for Germany. They stayed in Germany for a few years. Then they came here. And now they compare America with Germany and with Bosnia. And that's what they find. It's tough, tough to find a good job and to stay.

We asked what types of jobs are especially difficult for Bosnian immigrants to find and keep. "Truck drivers, some simple jobs for simple people who don't have too much education or who have education but it's not useful here. So they take anything. You have doctors, medical doctors, who do jobs like janitorial work or doorman."

This kind of downward job mobility seems common among recent immigrants. One immigrant woman who had taught English in a Russian university, a seemingly marketable skill, has nevertheless had difficulty finding a job here. "She's sort of been doing other things," said her American husband, including a temporary job as a translator that did not bring in enough income for the family. Now she does data processing at the company where her husband is employed.

Multiple job trajectories are also common as immigrants search out a livable wage in an unstable American economy. Two of our interviewees, one Greek, the other Indian, contrasted the numerous job opportunities in the United States to the dearth in their respective homelands. Another interviewee, a fifty-five-year-old member of Gayatri Pariwar Mandir, did fieldwork as an electrical engineer for a power company in India. Over a span of more than two decades in Chicago he shifted from consulting, to communications technology at a bank, to a position with AT&T. Thus the occupational trajectory does not always move downward, or stay in that direction for long. Another Gayatri member with a bachelor's degree in accounting from India was hired at a company here to do data entry. Disappointed, she nevertheless convinced herself, "It doesn't bother me. Job is job, no matter what." But within a few months she received a promotion to claims processor, and in two years became an assistant accountant at the company.

Most of our interviewees did not complain about specific workplace tensions, such as conflicts with peers or superiors. (Of course, this does not mean that workplace tensions are rare in their experience.) One exception, a Chinese

Christian woman, described how her fellow factory workers, all of a different immigrant ethnicity, "picked on" her daily in the first six months of her employment. She said, "When I came home, I cry, I pray to God, 'How come you give me this situation?'" A Chinese Buddhist woman implied difficulties at her workplace in explaining her religious identity to others. "If you are working in a Chinese firm, that's easy. When you work in, you know, an American firm, okay, it's just very, it's hard to make them understand that we are Buddhist."

We were not surprised about the responses to the interview question, "Is your workplace unionized?" Only about one-fourth of those interviewees for whom this question was relevant (N = 19) answered "Yes," consistent with what we know of immigrant occupational patterns and the generally weak position of American unions today. We were a bit surprised by the overwhelmingly negative response to our follow-up question to those not currently members of a union, "Would you join one?" Only three interviewees said "Yes," two of the three being nurses (one Buddhist, the other Catholic). The Buddhist nurse, who attends HanMaUm Zen Center and is nearing retirement age, was adamant about joining a union if the chance afforded itself: "Yes! I think it would be more powerful. You see a lot of teachers have unions. So once in a while, every two, three years, if they don't get a raise, then they go on a strike. So their pay scale is always advanced. But nursing just stay pretty much [the same]. Also, our healthcare system is very bad. Everybody knows about it. So then the healthcare system is hurting themselves. Money is very tight, that's another major fact."

## Congregational Activities and Perspectives

The preceding section indicates the multiplicity of occupational issues facing immigrants today, in terms of both distribution patterns and employment obstacles. As Portes (1995, 24) reminds us, sociologists of immigration view immigrants "not simply as individuals who come clutching a bundle of personal skills, but rather as members of groups and participants in broader social structures that affect in multiple ways their economic mobility." Since congregations play an important role in these broader immigrant social structures, we must ask how they help their members address pressing occupational and economic issues.

### Social Service Provision

Recent scholarship confirms that social service provision is not the primary purpose of American congregations generally. After analyzing the extensive data of the National Congregations Study, Mark Chaves (2004, 46) concluded that "congregations typically engage in social services in only a minor and peripheral way." Nancy Ammerman's research in the equally extensive Organizing Religious Work Project, although more generous in assessing the extent of social service provision by congregations and their partner organizations, confirms that congregations' "primary task is not the delivery of social services . . . [but rather] the spiritual wellbeing of their members" (Ammerman 2001, 4, cf. 2005). This nonmaterial succor should not be minimized, for it can be "empowering" and can provide great "spiritual strength and moral guidance" (2001, 5, 31).

Formal and long-term social service programs are uncommon in American congregations generally, including in the areas of occupation and economic needs (Ammerman 2001; 2005; Chaves 2004; Cnaan 2002). Immigrant congregations tend to reflect this larger reality—only four of the congregations we studied have established their own formal occupational programs or services. Congregational leaders and members do sometimes refer employment inquiries to outside agencies. Among immigrants, these connections often feature co-ethnic and/or co-religious organizations—for instance, in the Chicago area, the Hellenic Foundation (Greek Orthodox) and Jewish Vocational Service.

In contrast to the dearth of formal initiatives, immigrant congregations deliver a good deal of informal and ad hoc social services, like short-term help for the needy and other individual assistance (Ebaugh and Chafetz 2000b). There were numerous reports of occupational networking in the immigrant congregations we studied. Individuals often get tips and referrals about job possibilities from fellow members and clergy. Describing the informal network at the BAPS Swaminarayan temple as "guerrilla tactics of how to find a job," one interviewee mimicked a typical interchange between members: "I'm looking for a job." "Hey, I'm a supervisor at this company and we're hiring. I'll give you a good recommendation."

Some formal congregational initiatives, like English as a Second Language (ESL) and computer literacy programs, have a direct bearing on members' occupational readiness, but they also bear on other aspects of citizenship. Sometimes congregational programs have serendipitous occupational effects. Maternity BVM Catholic Church, for instance, organizes summer youth work teams that participate in Habitat for Humanity house building projects, the most prevalent form of American congregational partnership in the area of economic development (Ammerman 2005). "All those things are very good for our young people to start learning [about various occupational tracks]," one interviewee explained. "You know, you don't have to wait until you are an adult. Who knows, when you are young, you find out maybe this is something I want to get into, maybe be a carpenter, maybe be an electrician, an architect, you know, all those gifts that they all have. They can start learning that from when they are teenagers, they don't have to wait until they are in their twenties."

### Religious Perspectives on Work

Far more pervasively than formal or even informal provision of occupational services, immigrant congregations address the pressing occupational issues of their members' lives by applying religious perspectives, including the kind of spiritual succor mentioned above. One of the core tasks of any congregation is "providing theological [for non-Christians, read: "religious"] interpretations of events in daily life" (McKinney 2005, 361), such as giving religious meaning and vocational clarity to the workplace. Work consumes a large portion of daily life for most adult members of any congregation, and it often occupies the thinking of both young people anticipating a working adulthood and retired people reflecting back on the work of a lifetime. The field of management and leadership training has begun to recognize the fact "that people do not, alas cannot, leave their beliefs and commitments at the workplace door," any more than they can leave other aspects of their "whole person" (Hicks 2003, 40). Congregations attempt to transform work into a vocation—that is, a religious calling. In drawing attention to this factor in the analysis to follow, we contribute to a neglected topic in economic sociology, the values and moral considerations underlying economic action (Portes 1995).

We heard numerous testimonials from our interviewees about how their religious beliefs and understandings give meaning to their work lives and influence their workplace behavior. We offer a selected few here and include more in our next section.

"How are your services different from, say, secular employment agencies that find jobs?" we asked a staff person in Synagogue FREE's job referral program. "You see," came the reply, "their [secular agencies'] work is built around maximizing their profit. . . . Their goal is to rip [off] more money. Since I am a face of the synagogue, primarily, as a social worker I must have somewhat different goals. And they are achieved, little by little." This social worker clearly derived satisfaction from the imputed higher moral status of a faith-based service agency.

Another staff member of Synagogue FREE attributed both his membership and his job at the congregation, at least partially, to completing his personal *tshuva* (return) to Judaism: "In this case it is a return to carrying out what every Jew must carry out, to certain rituals of Judaism. I did this in Jerusalem, . . . and because of that, when I came to America, I was looking for a synagogue where I would be a member, and it so luckily happened that I was able to find a job here according to my [occupational] specialty."

A Swaminarayan Hindu shared his emotional testimony about landing a new job as an information technologist at a Fortune 500 company in Chicago. He had been laid off from another company a few weeks earlier, when prospects in the IT sector were grim. After filling out his application at the new company, he went to the temple and prayed before the divine images for help. After his first job interview, the interviewer told him that, since she liked him personally, she would be honest with him—he had no chance of getting the job. But he knew that God would help him because of his prayers, so he told her that if she moved him forward in the interview process, he would certainly get the job. She laughed, saying she'd let him know.

On the following Friday, the woman called to inform him that he would be interviewed by her supervisor on Monday. He went back to the temple on Sunday and prayed again. On Wednesday he was offered the job, and he went again to the temple, this time asking for a high salary, which he received the next day. He told us that God had given him the job plus a high salary because he had prayed for them and they were "good" for him. For this reason, God could not refuse his wishes.

As Raymond Williams (2001, 164) explains about Swaminarayan Hinduism, "the acquisition of wealth and the prudent use of capital are justified and viewed as directly willed by god. Success is viewed as the result of his grace."

A 1.5-generation Chinese woman from Truth Lutheran Church used religious terms in talking about her proclivities in graphic and commercial arts. "I do have the talent from God," she testified. She admitted to being a bit frustrated, however, since her current employment situation does not challenge her to maximize her gifts. Even so, having such gifts puts a vocational perspective on workplace frustrations—she can fulfill her divine calling in spite of the situation.

## Analyzing Congregational Activities and Perspectives

Religious differences in moral authority, moral project, and sectarian tendencies shed light on how and why immigrant congregations respond to occupational and economic issues differently.

### Individualist Orientations

Three of the congregations have individualist orientations in both moral authority and moral project: Gayatri Pariwar Mandir (Hindu), ISKCON (Hindu), and HanMaUm Zen Center (Buddhist) (see fig. 4.1).

Gayatri Pariwar Mandir, one of only four congregations in our research pool with formal programming around occupation, instituted a major initiative a few years ago. The temple and a local firm coordinated the regular placement of about fifty women in house-cleaning jobs, storing their equipment and supplies at the temple. Although discontinued at the time of our interview, the coordinator at the temple expressed interest in reviving the program and had made inquiries with the city about possible joint efforts.

This program exemplifies the individualist focus of Gayatri's moral project, which addresses the quality of life of individual workers rather than the economic structures in which those individuals work. As an interviewee explained about another temple program, the purpose of yoga instruction is to help members who complain of being "totally distressed and demoralized, I mean tired and working, like that."

The Gayatri movement places work in a larger spiritual context of how individuals should live a good and true life characterized by "high thought" or "high thinking." Such a life is incompatible with luxurious excess. The moral ideal should be "plain living and high thinking," in the words of the group's founder, Pragyavtar Gurudev ("The Demand of the Times," 11). As one of Gurudev's disciples writes of his early travels in India with Gurudev:

> From this tour I learned that a man living luxuriously cannot be at [sic] spiritually minded person. One must always lead a simple life and have high thinking. The second thing that I learnt was that one must do one's own work. . . . Gurudev also told me, "Son, there are no coolies in foreign countries. One has to personally carry one's own luggage." From that day I started doing my work myself. When I see a person leading a luxurious life and becoming big, I feel that he does not have knowledge. (Sharma 1999, 66)

No matter how high one advances in one's career track, it all counts for naught without a transformation of one's inner character. *Learning Torch*, the Chicago Gayatri temple's quarterly newsletter, printed a piece written by Swami Jyotirmayananda (2001) of the Ramakrishna lineage, titled "How to Change Your Life." "An ordinary clerk may become a government official," writes the author. "A lawyer may become a judge. An ordinary student of philosophy may become a professor. But the deeper part of their personalities continues to be the same." Such individuals will continue to manifest their underlying personality deficiencies.

> When deprived of their favorite objects, they still grieve and lament just as they have done in their earlier years. When encountering objects of their liking, they lose their balance of mind through elation. Veiled by the mask of external prestige and public recognition, they continue to be what they have been all along. The external mask has further hindered them from receiving the healthful atmosphere of nature. Men who mask their old uncultured self with glittering degrees and titles received from the world become more uncontrolled with reference to their defects and negative habits. (8–9)

Significantly, Gayatri, like many Hindu groups, believes that the world will change as individuals change. "The call of the times is for change and reform," said Pragyavtar Gurudev (*Learning Torch* 2001), "the people's mind[s] must be prepared accordingly. . . . The creation of the new era will be achieved—not by bricks and mortar but—by changing the direction of thinking of the people. High thinking is dependent only on simple living."

"Creation of a new era" is a recurrent theme in the Gayatri literature. The Chicago temple's mission statement locates itself within "a universal constructive movement for resurgence of a new era by educating people to think righteous ways. To revolutionize the way of thinking in every walk of life by developing divinity in man to establish heavenly environment on the earth." Righteous thinking will produce righteous workers in every sector of society. Social workers, for instance, "should not only be independent and be without pride or ego, they must also be free from greed" ("The Demand of the Times" n.d., 29).

The ISKCON movement within Hinduism similarly invests work with spiritual meaning. An Indian religious leader at the Chicago ISKCON temple reflected stoically on his numerous jobs since joining the movement in the 1970s. Whether he worked mattered not at all—if he had money, it was because God wanted him to have money, if not, God did not want him to have it. His stoicism derives from what Travis Vande Berg (2005) calls ISKCON's "master frame" or interpretive schema—that is, its understanding of "Krishna Consciousness [which] emphasizes anti-materialism, spirit-based language and identification, and universalism and addresses the need to develop a Krishna Conscious society and self as an alternative to those provided by Western materialism" (118). Vande Berg, who studied ISKCON temples in Chicago and Toronto, describes how this movement's antimaterialist perspective influences the serious devotee's self-perception and valuation of everyday activities like work. ISKCON devotees see themselves as "spirit-souls" who use their temporary bodies and circumstances to worship Krishna. This is living "properly," a term they often invoke—that is, seeking spiritual rather than material ends in life.

The HanMaUm movement within Korean Chogye Zen Buddhism also provides a spiritual—and individualist—perspective on work for its members. Recall the Korean Buddhist nurse from HanMaUm Zen Center who adamantly advocates unionizing her profession. Her collectivist sentiment in this area appears

ISKCON devotees live a monastic lifestyle, deemphasizing material concerns and everyday activities associated with work and occupations. Photo by Jerry Berndt.

anomalous and did not surface elsewhere in our interview with her. She characterized the HanMaUm expression of Buddhism as everyday practice that guides her in being a good nurse. When we asked her to list the most important temple activities or programs for new immigrants, she replied that the temple offers opportunities for people to learn everyday thought and practice as taught in Zen Buddhism. Ironically, the temple discontinued a special program devoted to this because working members could not fit it into their busy schedules.

An analysis of the teachings of HanMaUm's charismatic founder and leader, the Korean Buddhist nun Dae Haeng Kun Sunim, reveals the doctrinal and ethical underpinnings of this group's individualist orientation toward work. "The essential part of spiritual practice in Daehaeng Sunim's teachings," writes a scholar-nun of the HanMaUm movement (Hyeseon Sunim 2004), "is to believe in Juingong (主人空) that is the true self, the foundation, within us, to let go of and entrust everything to it." This has applications in every area of life, including occupation, and does not require a cloistered monastic lifestyle to carry out meditative practices:

> We don't need to give up our job or to leave our home to cultivate our minds; we are able to do spiritual practice as much as we want while living our life, as it is. Whatever we do in our daily life, if our minds are not away from the place of fundamental mind that takes care of everything, the twenty-four hours of a day can be the hours of polishing our minds. . . . Wherever you are, you are doing spiritual practice. You can cultivate mind while you are eating, working, driving, loving, sleeping, making a home, and managing your household. It is because spiritual practice is done with your mind, not with your body.

The emphasis here on meditative living, the spiritualization of every activity in one's life, can be seen as part of the larger engaged Buddhism movement of recent decades (Queen 2002), which has two main thrusts. One, the less prevalent, qualifies as collectivist in our sense of that term, in that Buddhists challenge institutional and structural injustices and violence. In Korea this kind of engaged Buddhism is quite recent and limited in scope (Tedesco 2003). The second and more prevalent kind of engaged Buddhism takes an individualist approach, as Donald Rothberg (1998, 272) explains: "Buddhism is to be brought into life 'in the world' in *all* its aspects, including the everyday contexts of families, interpersonal relationships, communities, and work. From this perspective, everything we do is potentially an act of engaged Buddhism." According to Rothberg, this predominant approach of "inner responses" has resulted in "little collective transformation at the levels of institutions" and only preliminary social or collectivist analyses by engaged Buddhist writers (283). HanMaUm Buddhists fall into this individualist category of engaged Buddhism.

## Collectivist Orientations

Maternity BVM Catholic Church's occupational programming reflects collectivist orientations in both moral authority and moral project. In addressing the exploitation of day laborers, the church not only offers spiritual perspective and succor, it also mobilizes the church's membership and the larger community to effect structural economic change.

We attended a community meeting on day labor issues held in Maternity BVM's auditorium in the spring of 2001. The meeting was cosponsored by several religious and community groups, the latter including Chicago Coalition for the Homeless, Near Northwest Neighborhood Network, Logan Square Neighborhood Association, Chicago Workers Center, and West Town Leadership Project. Five day-labor companies had been invited to send representatives to the meeting, but only two showed up. Nearly three hundred people attended, approximately two-thirds of them Hispanics, one-third whites, and a small number of African Americans. Many wore English/Spanish T-shirts saying, "Here we are all equal/Aqui todos somos iguales." An Illinois state senator and a U.S. congressman participated, and a local Spanish-language TV station covered the event.

The atmosphere was decidedly adversarial, bearing the earmarks of a political rally. One banner portrayed two buildings, a day labor agency and a company office, and two workers, a man and a woman, breaking the chain connecting the two operations. Each of the empty chairs for the day labor agencies that did not send representatives was filled with a sign showing the company's name inside a bull's-eye target. Several people gave testimonies of workplace abuses before the meeting formally began. After each, the crowd booed and hissed their disapproval. One man pleaded, "Who in the audience can survive on $35 a day? And then have to pay 3 percent for transportation [to a job site]?"

The formal meeting began with a prayer of invocation given by a white priest (not from Maternity BVM) who is a major organizer in the local day laborer rights movement. Alternating between Spanish and English, he thanked God for the gathering and asked for divine help in the workers' claims for justice and dignity, stressing God's preferential option for the oppressed and the workers' right to economic security.

During the meeting, the two representatives of day labor agencies responded to the earlier testimonies. One agreed that all the complaints were legitimate except the one about the 3 percent transportation fee taken out of the paycheck. The other representative did not accept the validity of certain other complaints. People in the audience protested both speakers.

Congressman Luis Gutierrez ended the meeting by proclaiming his support of the day laborers' right to organize and to work and live with justice. After this, the organizers asked the TV crew to leave the premises, presumably so that they would not cover the next activity—a protest rally at one of the day labor agencies. Several buses and cars awaited outside the church to take people to that site.

The moral authority for collectivist advocacy of immigrant workers' rights and larger economic justice comes from the highest offices of the Catholic Church. In his 1981 encyclical, *Laborem Exercens (On Human Work),* Pope John Paul II addressed the issues surrounding immigrant labor in the section titled "Work and the Emigration Question."[2] "Every possible effort should be made," wrote the Pontiff, "to ensure that it [emigration] may bring benefit to the emigrant's personal, family and social life, both for the country to which he goes and the country which he leaves." He continued with a collectivist moral project to meet this expectation: "In this area much depends on just legislation, in particular with regard to the rights of workers." Further:

> The most important thing is that the person working away from his native land, whether as a permanent emigrant or as a seasonal worker, should not be *placed at a disadvantage* in comparison with the other workers in that society in the matter of working rights. Emigration in search of work must in no way become an opportunity for financial or social exploitation. As regards the work relationship, the same criteria should be applied to immigrant workers as to all other workers in the society concerned. The value of work should be measured by the same standard and not according to the difference in nationality, religion or race. For even greater reason the *situation of constraint* in which the emigrant may find himself *should not be exploited.*

In his Labor Day message the same year as the meeting described above, the Archbishop of Los Angeles, Roger Cardinal Mahony, chose to reflect on *Laborem Exercens* on its twentieth anniversary. In "The Dignity of Work and Workers: The Message of *Laborem Exercens,*"[3] the cardinal said, "Some low-wage workers who labor in many important industries come from abroad and are vulnerable to exploitation because they do not enjoy permanent legal status. A legalization program for these workers would help protect their basic labor rights and ensure that all workers in the United States are afforded a living wage and decent working conditions." Here again a collectivist moral project is promoted—namely, economic change through legislation. It explains the motto AMNESTY NOW on the fliers at the rally at Maternity BVM Church, pointing to the connection between illegal immigration and worker exploitation.

### Mixed Individualist and Collectivist Orientations

Congregations may combine individualist and collectivist orientations in various ways. For instance, St. Lambert Catholic Church draws from a mix of individualist and collectivist sources of moral authority while pursuing a collectivist moral project. That combination places St. Lambert in a category of collectivist tendencies. Naperville Church of the Brethren combines an individualist moral authority with a mix of individualist and collectivist moral projects, thus falling into a category of individualist tendencies (fig. 4.1). We elaborate here on some of our other congregations to illustrate how their mixed approaches address occupational and economic issues.

We consider Truth Lutheran Church a theologically evangelical congregation within a mainline denomination (Evangelical Lutheran Church in America). Two members told us of the frustrations they have experienced in their jobs. One, the Chinese woman we met earlier whose fellow factory workers hassled her daily when she started the job, explained how she eventually overcame their hostility with kindness by bringing homemade Chinese fried rice, egg rolls, and candies to work. This led to some promotions, but she eventually left that job to start her own Chinese restaurant. This was clearly an individualist approach to rectifying an unsatisfactory situation in the workplace.

A Chinese Buddhist woman from Ling Shen Ching Tze Temple, a congregation in the same mixed category on our conceptual grid, takes an equally individualist approach to her work situation. She explained that her fellow workers wonder why she is so adept at handling the pressures of their occupation. In her mind, this ability stems from "getting her soul at peace" at the temple each week. She also told us of the time her savings account at the bank increased markedly during a period when she did not make significantly more income. When her husband inquired, she attributed the windfall to a new ritual she began doing before a particular Buddha statue in their home.

These views stem from the teachings of the True Buddha School with which Ling Shen Ching Tze Temple is affiliated. The True Buddha School recognizes people's need for economic sufficiency, even prosperity, but within a spiritual context. Quoting from the booklet "Questions and Answers on the True Buddha School," "Although spiritual cultivation is considered by the True Buddha School to be the most important goal in human existence, it also acknowledges the necessity of financial sufficiency for its cultivators in the modern world. In order to bring prosperity to sentient beings, the True Buddha School has included among its Eight Principal Deities Practices the Yellow Jambhala Practice (the Yellow Jambhala is the wealthiest god in the spirit realm)" (4).

The booklet continues, "Within our True Buddha Tantric Dharma are many practices that one can do, to pray for children, health, blessings, wealth, status, purification, subjugation and magnetization" (33). After death, individuals are tried in a series of courts, one of which, called King Wu Guan, arbitrates business-related misdeeds, such as evading taxes, using faulty scales to gain an advantage in transactions, and selling imitation medicine that causes a patient more suffering. Such offenses result in one's soul being dispatched to "the Combined Major Hell situated at the due east of the Fertile Reef beneath the ocean," with its sixteen minor hells that mete out the appropriate punishments (*Yuli—The Holy Book*, 14). All of this indicates an individualist moral project regarding work—individuals, not collective entities, are the moral agents that can effect positive change in the workplace. The negative incentive of afterlife punishment is directed at individual souls.

Three of our congregations fall into the same mixed category cell on our conceptual grid, Synagogue FREE, Victory Outreach Church, and the BAPS Swaminarayan Hindu temple. Although each congregation has overall collectivist tendencies, individualist notions surface as well.

Synagogue FREE is one of four congregations in the research pool to establish formal programming around occupation, a job referral service as part of its extensive provision of immigrant assistance. Synagogue FREE's perspective on work is summed up in an essay by the popular Lubavitch author Tzvi Freeman, titled "Our Daily Bread: Meditations on Earning a Living."[4] "The reason you have a business is to reconnect all these fragments [of work] back to their Creator. And the gauge of your success is your attitude. . . . The common conception of how the system works is faulty. They see a career as 'making a living.' A career doesn't make anything. What you receive is generated above, in a spiritual realm. Your business is to set up a channel to allow all that to flow into the material world." Here we see no challenge to the structure of the system, no collectivist moral project, in other words, but rather advice to individuals on how to redeem the value of their work by placing the system within a larger, divine context.

In a sense, another congregation in the research pool that offers formal programming around occupation places this at the heart of its mission. Victory Outreach/Alcance Victoria, the parent group of the Chicago church, began in the Boyle Heights district of East Los Angeles in the late 1960s and "has become a vast and highly organized movement spanning the globe and touching and improving the lives of many" (Leon 1998, 166). Although many members today are working class, the core of the movement's initial ministry, as well as the emphasis of its continuing self-narrative, is the rehabilitation and redirection of social and economic misfits, the rescue of drug addicts, prostitutes, gang members, criminals, and other negative elements in the Hispanic community.

Although the Victory Outreach movement draws from a collectivist moral authority grounded in conservative Protestant Pentecostalism, its moral project is decidedly individualist in addressing social problems. As Luis Leon (1998, 184) explains, the movement's founding pastor, Sonny Arguinzoni, teaches that "ministry . . . must always come before spending energies on social justice 'causes.'" "It is not our job to propose legislation resolving immigration conflicts," says Arguinzoni regarding an issue very much a part of many of his members' lives. Another pastor considers illegal immigration "a matter of personal conscience" (188). Leon (192) sums up what Victory Outreach offers its constituents, who have few economic options and limited occupational prospects: "By stressing individual [divine] election and achievement, the discursive and ritual community of Alcance Victoria confers self-worth, ultimate meaning, purpose, and a way to make sense of a harsh world. . . . Alcance Victoria enables people to work happily and productively within their social limitations."

The BAPS Swaminarayan movement offers an informative example of a group that manifests some collectivist tendencies within a typically individualist religious tradition (Hinduism). As we suggested in chapter 4, the sectarian identity of BAPS helps to explain its collectivist tendencies, since strong over-againstness vis-à-vis co-religionists or "the world" requires high internal cohesion and identity, a goal well served by collectivist moral projects.

Much of Swaminarayan teaching emphasizes an individualist understanding of work and the fruits of one's labor. The sacred text, the *Shikshapatri,* exhorts business owners to be prudent, honest, and just in their dealings, a Hindu version of the classic Protestant ethic according to Raymond Williams (2001, 162–164), although Swaminarayans dislike the analogy. "The pursuit of material gain and pleasure are appropriate to the life of the householder," Williams explains, "but the pursuit must be controlled by a moral discipline. Otherwise it would lead man to disaster and cause failure to attain salvation." Wealth per se is not evil, rather attachment to wealth and all else ephemeral. "In this way [of detachment] the devotee is able to leave the world from within. Thus, a rich man can be saved."

What takes this individualist orientation in collectivist directions is the Swaminarayan emphasis on social welfare. Williams notes a favorite saying of Swaminarayan himself, "Accumulation of wealth is a great danger; distribution of wealth is a blessing" (164). In a paper on philanthropic trends in the Hindu community of the United States, Priya Anand (2004) describes the signature BAPS merger of spiritual and social agendas, quoting a statement from their own literature:

Many ask, "How can you mix spirituality and social service"
We ask, "How can you separate the two?"
    Those who wish to sincerely serve society must be spiritually pure and only those who are spiritually pure can sincerely serve society! (22)

The BAPS service delivery infrastructure is enormous, providing aid in five general areas according to Anand: disaster relief, health care, rehabilitation, environmental care, and education. In Anand's assessment, BAPS and similar Hindu groups "provide need-based solutions . . . for the poorer sections of society, [the] aged and the people with disabilities" (49). Of course, need-based approaches tend to translate into individualist moral projects, but the BAPS movement also mounts significant collectivist moral projects in India and elsewhere around the world.

We saw an indication of the tensions that sometimes develop between individualist and collective tendencies during our first formal visit to the BAPS temple in suburban Chicago. We viewed a video presentation, "The Millennium Vision," about an initiative of the group's current spiritual leader, Pramukh

Swami, designed to keep Indian culture from being lost through assimilation in North America. Our host for the visit admitted that some people question the great outlay of money on BAPS centers in the United States and Canada (in Chicago, an anticipated $15 million at that time). Why not spend the money on hospitals, schools, and other social projects? He replied that the cultural value of the centers justifies the expense.

The motto for their efforts in Chicago was "Save Our Heritage." We saw a slide presentation usually shown to Indian audiences at fund-raising events or in financial institutions, law offices, and the corporate world. It explained how an unsupported Indian cultural heritage will be diluted by the time it reaches the second generation. Immigrant parents, like our host's own, he noted, come to the United States for the opportunity to succeed on their own merits and to gain access to a world-class education. They attain great economic and educational success, but the preservation of their cultural heritage suffers. One slide in particular, "Economic and Educational Success without Cultural Preservation: Is It Worth It?" drew stunned silence from Indian audiences. The host asked, "Don't you want your children to benefit from the same cultural upbringing that you had in India?"

The host felt that such efforts at culture preservation would slow the decline process far more effectively than individual efforts made by immigrant families. The Millennium Vision initiative combines both individualist and collectivist tendencies in a moral project to rescue cultural identity from the competing values of success and wealth. The appeal is to individuals, but the goal is collective survival as a people.

## Implications

Our findings both confirm and supplement recent scholarship on American congregations in important ways. First, like all congregations, the immigrant congregations in this study provide far more informal and indirect social services than formal and direct ones, including economic and occupational services. This is consistent with the Houston study of immigrant congregations conducted by Helen Rose Ebaugh and colleagues. As they report, immigrant needs are "met substantially within their congregations, but their primary mechanism is through informal social networks" (Ebaugh and Chafetz 2000b, 374).

Second, our findings shed light on the dynamics involved when congregations do establish formal social service programs. Religious identities and doctrinal perspectives inform congregational choices about such programs, as they do in the areas of political advocacy, community improvement, and civic involvement—in other words, in areas beyond the spiritual succor that forms the heart of a congregation's raison d'être. Certainly, many factors enter into decisions about such activities, such as congregational resources and programming priorities, but religion matters as well, perhaps even more fundamentally than these other factors, and therefore warrants the increased scholarly attention of recent years (e.g., Ammerman 2001, 2005; Chaves 2004; Cnaan 2002; Ecklund 2005; Farnsley 2000; Schwadel 2005; Slessarev-Jamir 2003b).

The typical dichotomy found in Christian circles between liberal collectivist and conservative individualist moral projects (Ammerman 2005; cf. Bosch 1980, chap. 4; Chaves 2004) also surfaces among immigrant congregations of other religious traditions. But this simple dichotomy can be complicated by a congregation's moral authority and sectarianism. A group's strong sectarian identity, for instance, might move its moral projects in collectivist directions even though the group is mostly in the individualist camp, as in the BAPS Swaminarayan case. Moreover, either an individualist or a collectivist orientation can motivate a congregation to establish a formal program to address the occupational and economic needs of its constituents, but the targets of their efforts will differ depending on their particular orientation. Individualist-oriented programs aid individual workers without attempting to change economic structures. Collectivist-oriented programs aid individual workers as a by-product of their primary goal of changing economic structures. Combined approaches keep these poles in some balance, although they may favor one orientation more than the other.

We can thus make some informed, though cautious, predictions about the congregations in our study (and other immigrant congregations) that have not established formal programming, should they do so in the future. Hindu and Buddhist congregations would likely establish individualist-oriented programs consistent with the doctrines and ethical teachings of their parent traditions. Their primary target would be individuals at work, their strategy to transform mere jobs into vocations with larger spiritual meaning. Catholic congregations would likely establish collectivist-oriented programs consistent with Catholic social teachings. Their primary target would be the economic systems in which individuals work, their strategy to redeem the value of work by creating just systems. The mixed cases are less predictable, though our insight about strong sectarianism predicts a collectivist tendency in the moral projects of such groups. But we must add one further point here with regard to the role of ethnic identity in this last scenario. Those groups with a strong ethnic component to their sectarianism, such as Swaminarayans and Hasidic Jews, tend to favor collectivist moral projects more than those groups that emphasize the universalism of their teachings, such as evangelical Protestants. This would explain why both Korean evangelical Protestant congregations in Elaine Ecklund's (2005) study manifest collectivist expressions of civic engagement—both downplay their Korean-ness, one in its emphasis on multiethnic diversity, the other (a second-generation church) in distancing itself from the immigrant generation's conflation of ethnic and religious identity. We can predict that those Muslim congregations who emphasize the multiethnic unity of the Islamic *ummah* will likewise tend toward collectivist moral projects around occupational and economic issues.

In a third area, we found no evidence to challenge the impression that Christians exceed other religious groups in establishing formal social service programs, whether in congregations or through other types of organizations, coalitions, and initiatives (e.g., Slessarev-Jamir 2003a). Of the sixteen immigrant congregations in our study, only four have provided any kind of formal services around occupational issues, and half of these are Christian. But we must be careful in interpreting our data on this account. Most of our eight Christian congregations do not provide any kind of formal occupational services. Some of our congregations, both Christian and non-Christian, serve fairly well-off constituencies that do not need such services, while others that do serve needy constituencies lack the human or financial resources to establish formal programs to serve them.

A fourth finding of this study goes back to the issue of a congregation's raison d'être. The tendency of our interviewees and congregations to separate the spiritual from the material, or the sacred from the secular, is so pervasive as to merit close consideration, for the implications are as subtle and subject to misinterpretation as they are significant. What Vande Berg (2005) concludes about ISKCON applies to most members of our congregations, namely that they are attracted more for religious or religio-cultural reasons than for the social services they might receive. The same sentiment was expressed by Buddhist monks in a study of Asian faith-based organizations and social service provision in the Chicago area (Slessarev-Jamir 2003a, 20): "Many of the monks continue to emphasize that Buddhist temples are places of spiritual guidance, meditation and teaching, rather than social service agencies."

This is significant because it runs counter to the emphasis on the cultural, ethnic, and social functions of immigrant congregations in the recent literature. In contrast, we consider this sentiment—that their primary raison d'être is spiritual rather than mundane—to be the default position of congregations. Chaves (2004, 126) is correct to place the admittedly meager record of congregations in the areas of social services and political activism in perspective: "Relative to other organizations whose primary purpose is neither social service delivery nor politics, congregations engage in a fair amount of at least some types of this activity—enough to warrant exploring its nature and varieties." In other words, the amount of social service work that is carried out by congregations is remarkable given that such work requires special justification in congregational decision making.

Finally, with regard to the civic impact of individualist versus collectivist orientations, we sense a refrain in the literature favoring collectivist over individualist approaches to accomplishing significant structural change in society. For instance, in his epilogue to the Religion in Urban America Program report, R. Stephen Warner expresses his initial disappointment at the minimal collectivism of Chicago congregations—their efforts "leave much to be desired" in addressing the deep structural problems of urban America, he writes. Yet Warner quickly challenges his own collectivist bias, admonishing his readers that current congregational efforts "should not be slighted." Moreover, he continues, dichotomous approaches to public policy that pit collectivism versus individualism (our terms) should be abandoned (Warner 2000a, 305, 306).

Ram Cnaan writes about American congregations generally: "Congregations are, as a rule, highly involved in service delivery that helps people solve personal problems and meet material needs. They are less involved in efforts to bring about social and political change. . . . Despite our probing, few congregations reported any involvement in social justice issues" (2002, 69, 242). In other words, American congregations, including immigrant ones, tend to take individualist rather than collectivist approaches to social problems like economic inequity and occupational obstacles. Still, we should not ignore the pervasive social influence of individual decisions and actions, like those of religious people guided by their moral traditions. Other observers who note the dearth of collectivist action taken by congregations nevertheless judge congregational influences to be considerable. Mark Chaves (2004) finds this is true in the area of cultural activities, particularly in transmitting religious meanings through worship, education, and the arts. Nancy Ammerman (2001, 31) makes a case that "even when congregations have no overt ministries or other connections in the [larger] community," they serve those communities well by providing "places where people gather for spiritual strength and moral guidance, where they find a caring community in which to express themselves and find a home." Research on the role of religious identity and spirituality in the workplace notes a growing dissatisfaction with material success, "the realization that obtaining material goods only goes so far in meeting one's needs. The quest for spirituality in the workplace, on this view, is part of the search beyond income for human fulfillment, meaning, and purpose" (Hicks 2003, 38). We have certainly seen this in individualist cases like Gayatri Pariwar Mandir and HanMaUm Zen Center, but even in the collectivist case of Maternity BVM Church, immigrants seeking a just and livable income also have nonmaterial needs for human dignity.

Lowell Livezey (2000, 20) and colleagues, in their study of Chicago congregations in the Religion in Urban America Program, concluded that "programs of social service and social action account for but a fraction of the religious contribution to the quality of urban life." But this kind of "social ministry," to borrow language from Christian circles, is not the whole story of what congregations do for the city. "To understand that contribution fully," Livezey continues, "it is necessary to examine the cultural life of religious organizations and to recognize that cultural production and community formation are not necessarily inward-looking and private but are often effective forms of public action." The cultural production so central to congregations is "one kind of religious public action," with "a prominent moral dimension" (22). Translating this into our theoretical framework, even individualist moral projects can have significant social and civic consequences.

# 6

## Religion, Education, and Civic Tensions in Immigrant Congregations

*Religion and education have been related throughout American history in a most intimate way, yet also in a way often laden with tension and ambiguity. . . . How to achieve creative cooperation within this tension, without sacrificing the one kind of school to the other [parochial versus public], is one of the problems for the future.*

—Will Herberg (1961)

Islamic Foundation is one of the largest and most successful mosques in metropolitan Chicago. Located in affluent west suburban DuPage County, the tenth highest-ranked county in the nation in median household income, according to the 2000 census, Islamic Foundation operates a parochial school accredited and recognized for its excellence by the State of Illinois.[1] Interviews with school staff and parents revealed the civic tensions inherent in faith-based education that Will Herberg identified four decades earlier, when American Islam barely registered on the country's demographic radar screen.

"What would you say is the biggest challenge these students face, being raised as American Muslims in a non-Muslim environment?" we asked a school administrator. "For the students," we were told, "the biggest challenge is the struggle and temptation that they see around them in mainstream society. I mean, they are Muslims, and our aim is to produce Muslim identities. We want to produce clear Muslim identities, but American citizens as well who would be totally comfortable in mainstream society but not lose their identity. This is easier said than done."

Note the use of the phrase "mainstream society," twice, by this interviewee. Islamic Foundation's parochial school represents no radically separatist religious enterprise completely at odds with American society. Rather, its moral project, reflecting that of its parent mosque, is to produce Muslim American citizens who will maintain their distinctive religious identity without succumbing to perceived temptations of the larger culture. The inherent tension of being a religious citizen is not easy to negotiate, as Herberg noted and as religious groups throughout American history have discovered, and it manifests itself along a continuum of over-againstness vis-à-vis the larger American society. Educational efforts in immigrant congregations carry inherent tensions with the larger society as congregations promote what it means to live a distinctively religious and moral life. Establishing a parochial school marks a significant step in institutionalizing this tension, yet this does not necessarily mark a retreat from positive civic engagement.

An Islamic Foundation School parent talked about the relationship between public and parochial education in America, expressing some of the tension she herself feels in negotiating her child's religious and academic needs. "There is so much more out there," she said, referring to the public school system.

> As a parent I feel responsible, competing with public education which has been in existence in this country for at least one hundred years. When you look at private education versus public education, there are a lot of things that are lacking in the private. I think in the academic sphere, you don't have all those bells and whistles that you'll find in public schools. But at the same time, the environment here is so healthy, I feel, and so nurturing. I think that the psychology of little ones especially is so important, to foster this healthy mind, this happy mind. They should feel secure and be able to charge the world [i.e., face it confidently]. So I am very comfortable with my choice of Islamic Foundation for my child for K through five. But maybe after she reaches middle school, I might choose a different environment just because academics might play a bigger role at a different stage in life. But right now I think that it serves our needs wonderfully.

Here we see a Muslim parent, like many religious parents in America (immigrant and nonimmigrant alike), making educational choices for her children out of a calculus of mixed motivations. How do such parents and their religious leaders promote the benefits of a faith-based education in a society that is both religiously diverse and influenced by secular ideologies? How do they negotiate the inherent tensions between faith-based education and the larger society which is often criticized in that very education? What are the civic implications of the educational programming offered by immigrant congregations?

## Education in Immigrant Congregations

Many immigrant congregations offer educational programs in nonreligious topics and skills such as English as a Second Language (ESL), citizenship, or vocational training. Scholarship on post-1965 immigrant religions has emphasized the ethnic reproduction and immigrant adaptation facilitated by educational programming in congregations, typically underanalyzing the religious component

Muslim parents may use the mosque and Islamic parochial schools for religious and worldly education. Photo by Jerry Berndt.

of many ethnic identities. Here we focus on the religious aspects of educational programming in immigrant congregations, especially the religiously informed moral components of such education, examining what is taught, why, and how.

In a sense, much of what a congregation does can be considered faith-based education—that is, instruction in how to remain faithful to the worldview, practices, and expectations of an inherited religious tradition. Rituals, sermons, social activities, informal conversations—these and other components of congregational life carry important didactic content. Additionally, congregations typically establish formal programs with a more intentional and pointed educational function, like the religious education or catechetical instruction found in Christian contexts. These include children's programs of various types, such as Sunday or weekend schools, weekday classes (often after school or in the evening), short-term retreats or camps, preschool and other child care programs for young children, focus groups for youth, and parochial schools. Adult education is usually provided as well, to a greater or lesser extent, such as lectures, seminars, topical series, workshops, and small groups for scriptural study or practical application of religious principles to life and work. The purpose of all such faith-based education, in immigrant congregations even more so than in nonimmigrant ones, is "inescapably particularistic," to borrow the insight of sociologist R. Stephen Warner (1994, 65). That is, it applies the wisdom and insights of the inherited religious tradition to the contemporary context of the local congregation.

The content of the overall educational programming found in immigrant congregations falls under two main categories: religious identity and morality. The first inculcates the particular identity of the congregation and the religious tradition or lineage in which it stands, ranging from sectarian to mainstream expressions. The second category includes the religiously informed moral authority and moral project of the congregation and its larger tradition or lineage. Of course, in practice, religious identity and morality are intertwined in congregational education, with morality flowing from religious sources, as in the following excerpts from an English *khutbah* (sermon) preached at Islamic Foundation:

> Most respected Brothers and Sisters, I just recited from the Book of Guidance [the Qur'an]. This book is a complete guide, whether it relates to individual behavior, community affairs, or international problems. It contains the basic rules and regulations for certain situations. Allah [God] tells us that these are the things He likes, and these are the things He doesn't like. . . . We must spend time to educate our children, teach them in their beginning stages. Within a few days, a bird can start flying, functioning, but the human child Allah has given sixteen or seventeen years to learn how to live in this world, to learn what Allah likes and dislikes. It is the responsibility of the parents and leaders of the *ummah* [the whole Islamic community] to tell them and to establish educational institutions.

One interviewee from Islamic Foundation listed the priorities of the mosque's educational programming in this order: "spiritual, then moral, and then social, and lastly material aspects of human life." This description points to the all-encompassing purview of religion, with morality and moral education as high priorities. Immigrant congregations embody this moral sensitivity, often through critical judgments of the mores of the larger culture. "Across the gamut of recent immigrant religions, concern is raised about the secular and material enticements of modern American society," writes Numrich (2007, 27) in a survey of immigrant religious views on the family.

> To summarize the conservative critique coming from many new immigrant religious groups, America has abandoned its original moral compass, and dissolute Americans today give in to passions and proclivities fueled by modern ideologies such as individualism, feminism, secularism, and materialism. . . . The fears of the immigrant generation find intense focus in efforts to protect their American-born offspring from these social ills by inculcating traditional Old World values through educational, cultural, and religious programs.

Such moral conservatism is partly fueled by a growing religious conservatism in the immigrants' sending countries, yet, as Numrich points out, "moral conservatism is a common byproduct of the immigration experience" that also characterized the classical period of American immigration history. As historian Timothy Smith (1978, 1175, 1176) noted in a seminal essay, "migration was often a theologizing experience" that produced an "immigrant Puritanism"—a phrase Smith borrowed from another historian of American immigration—"a predictable reaction to the ethical or behavioral disorientation that affected most immigrants, whatever the place or the century of their arrival." Immigrant groups may vary in the specific objects of their moral concern due to socioeconomic, doctrinal, or other variables, but moral concern is pervasive, particularly among parents (Ebaugh and Chafetz 2000b, 433).

### Immigrant Parochial Schools

Establishing a parochial school marks a major step for an immigrant congregation. Not all immigrant congregations desire to do so, while some with the desire lack the institutional resources to make it so, at least in the short term. Those that do establish parochial schools combine both means and motivation, the latter including some degree of sectarian tension with the larger society. If it were not so, parents would be satisfied to send their children to public schools.

Parochial schools have been around since colonial times and have played a significant role in American immigrant history. Of the three largest non-Christian religious groups in post-1965 American immigration (Muslims, Buddhists, and Hindus, in order of size), only Muslims have established a notable parochial school presence. Both of the mosques in our Chicago study operate parochial schools, but none of the other non-Christian congregations do so. Four of our eight Christian sites operated parochial schools during our study period—all three Catholic parishes (one of which has now closed) and one of the two Orthodox churches.

### *Islamic Parochial Education in Chicago and the Nation*

Islamic Foundation (established in 1974) opened its elementary school in 1988, adding higher grades in subsequent years to fill out a K–12 program.[2] Islamic Cultural Center of Greater Chicago (whose first mosque was established in 1954) in north suburban Northbrook houses the Averroes Academy, which opened in 1999, for grades K–5 and is named after the noted medieval Islamic intellectual Ibn Rushd (known in the West as Averroes).[3] Note that in both cases a number of years elapsed between the establishment of the mosque and the opening of a parochial school. Although both mosques provided other educational programming for children early in their histories, full-time day schools came later and in stages (Averroes Academy currently has plans to expand beyond grade five).

Local and national data indicate that the majority of immigrant mosques do not operate parochial schools. In metropolitan Chicago, only four immigrant mosques out of a total of approximately fifty either operate or house parochial schools: Islamic Foundation (Islamic Foundation School); Islamic Cultural Center of Greater Chicago (Averroes Academy); Mosque Foundation (Aqsa School for girls, Universal School for boys); and Muslim Community Center (Muslim Education Center). In addition, two independent Islamic schools exist locally, Chicago Preparatory School of America and Institute of Islamic Education. Extrapolating from data in the Mosque Study Project report (Bagby, Perl, and Froehle 2001), slightly more than 20 percent of immigrant mosques nationally operate parochial schools, which would put the total number of such schools at around 185.[4] A substantial majority of these schools do not extend through grade twelve. The report explains that a mosque is more likely to have a parochial school if it is large rather than small, located in city neighborhoods and suburbs rather than city downtowns and rural areas, and situated in the South rather than other regions of the United States. The report does not offer any information about the religious identities or motivations of those mosques that operate parochial schools, although such information about mosques generally appears elsewhere in the report. In contrast to the relatively small number of immigrant mosques with parochial schools, a substantial majority operate weekend schools, according to the report.

The relationship between parochial and other private schools to government regulatory bodies varies from state to state. Illinois curricular requirements for nonpublic schools are rather minimal, stipulating only that "the children are taught the branches of education taught to children of corresponding age and grade in the public schools." Nonpublic schools need not be registered, licensed, or accredited by the Illinois State Board of Education.[5] In 2003–2004, three Chicago-area Islamic schools (Islamic Foundation School, Aqsa School, and Universal School) were accredited by the North Central Association's Commission on Accreditation and School Improvement,[6] and two (Islamic Foundation School and Universal School) received nonpublic school "Recognition" status by the Illinois State Board of Education.[7] Both statuses indicate quality of program above and beyond minimum state requirements.

### Philosophies, Curricula, and Extracurricular
### Programs of Islamic Parochial Schools

The following statement appeared under the heading "Our Philosophy" in the Islamic Foundation School's 2000–2001 handbook for parents and students:

> To stop our young generation's assimilation into a materialistic, secular and non-Islamic society.
>
> The Islamic Foundation School not only takes Muslim children out of the non-Islamic environment of public schools, but also provides the much-needed Islamic education and Islamic environment favorable for the development of an Islamic personality. Our school's mission is to daily instill and

inculcate Islamic teachings and values in the minds of our young children. It will help them grow in Islamic faith as practicing Muslims—without sacrificing individual excellence in the mastery of skills necessary to survive, flourish, compete and succeed in this modern age of technology.

This statement maintains a relatively strong sectarian "over-againstness" vis-à-vis the larger American society, especially in the sentence "To stop our young generation's assimilation into a materialistic, secular and non-Islamic society." The phrase about mastering modern technological skills is generic, never specifying that those skills need be employed in the United States. Taken as a whole, the statement implies an isolationist mentality in a hostile culture.

This over-againstness and implicit isolationism were noticeably toned down under the same heading, "Our Philosophy," on the school's Web site one year later (2002). The sentence about stopping the young generation's assimilation to a morally corrupt, non-Islamic society was missing from this version, while the following sentences were added: "The mission of the Islamic Foundation School, in cooperation with the Muslim community, is to provide excellent education in an atmosphere of faith and to prepare students to be life-long learners and contributing members of society." "It [the school] will also help our young children to get necessary training to become future Da'ees [Propagators, a variant of *da'wah*] of Islam."[8] We do not know how much the events of September 11, 2001, might have contributed to this change in sentiment, but the shift toward positive civic engagement in American society is clear, even as the importance of maintaining—and propagating—Islam continues to be emphasized. Thus, a degree of tension between Islamic and American identities remains despite the recent tempering of the language of the school's philosophy statement. As we shall see, this typifies the tension found in all mainstream parochial education vis-à-vis a larger society from which it shelters its students even while training them to be faith-informed citizens.

Averroes Academy, the parochial school operated by Islamic Cultural Center of Greater Chicago, was established by a group of Muslim leaders called the North Shore Education Foundation (NSEF). The school describes its philosophy in a Web site statement titled "Our Mission." "Because NSEF believes that being American is clearly compatible with being Muslim, this school will provide a balanced approach to education both academically and socially," the statement explains. Additionally,

NSEF believes that this institution can make a positive contribution in this society by promoting justice and truth. Accordingly, the goals of such a program are three-fold:

• to provide an excellent academic curriculum, comparable to any public or private school in the area, with a heavy emphasis on reading, writing, and public speaking;

- to provide an Islamic education that nurtures the development of Islamic scholars and promotes the learning of traditional Islamic sciences, with a heavy emphasis on Arabic and Islamic jurisprudence;
- to provide an environment for American Muslim children which promotes Islamic spirituality and God-consciousness.

With these goals in mind, NSEF believes that this school, God willing, will produce exceptionally educated children with positive moral and ethical values who will go on to succeed in higher education and will make positive contributions to American society, including the Muslim community.[9]

Here the tension between parochial education and the larger society is tempered even further than at Islamic Foundation School, though it still persists. Averroes Academy clearly provides a Muslim alternative to the public schools—its Web site includes a feature titled "Why should I enroll my child at Averroes when they can go to the public schools?" But this is not an extreme isolationist alternative. The academy's founders made a conscious decision to resist a trend they perceived in Islamic school circles, as noted in an article about their 2001 fund-raising event posted on the Averroes Web site.[10] The article argues that the "gravest" challenge to the growing number of Islamic parochial schools in the United States has nothing to do with minimal resources, as many might think, but rather stems from a "lack of intellectual vision on the role and the function that Islamic education should play in a non-Muslim society. This lack of vision is manifested in an isolationist Islamic education where Muslim children are being taught in a closed environment, hardly exposed to the American culture, which is portrayed as a threat to the Islamic values and beliefs." The article blames much of this isolationism on the immigrant generation that confuses ethnic culture with Islam. "Averroes Academy has been trying . . . not to fall into this traditional pattern," the article notes. Quoting the fund-raiser's organizer, the president of the Council of Islamic Organizations of Greater Chicago, "Averroes Academy achieved a great goal for a small school only two years old, that is to provide Islamic education while being in touch [with] the American society."[11]

Averroes Academy's fund-raising event the following year, in 2002, was the first to be held post-9/11. The announcement included a statement from the president of the North Shore Education Foundation that applied a progressive or modernist Islamic perspective to the difficult realities faced by Muslims in contemporary American society: "At Averroes Academy, we have always believed that a sound education which combines traditional secular subjects with Islamic tradition and virtue is the only viable alternative to the status quo. As such, it has become increasingly clear that today more than ever, American Muslims need to hear the voices and ideas of those thinkers whose vision supplies deep rooted commitment to Islamic spirituality, without the political rhetoric that threatens the sanctity and credibility of the American and European Muslim community."

The keynote speaker for this fund-raiser was a British convert to Islam. The announcement made the reason for the choice clear: "It has been a tradition for years that American Muslims seek the knowledge and erudition of scholars from Muslim countries, [but] now more American Muslims are finding guidance in the spiritual and intellectual leadership of Muslim Western scholars. . . . More American Muslims are finding the ideas and views of Western scholars better suited to express their cultural particularity within the mosaic of the Muslim world without hindering the established set of values of the Islamic paradigm." Clearly, Averroes Academy finds a progressive or modernist Islamic perspective most suitable to educating Muslim children in a Western society.

Curricular offerings at both Averroes Academy and Islamic Foundation School combine Islamic and secular studies; the Islamic component provides the religious value added of a parochial school education, the secular component complies with state education requirements. "The Islamic Foundation School is committed to the education of each child as a *whole*," stated the school's Web site in 2005, the final word italicized in critique of the putatively incomplete education offered by the public school system.[12] Parochial courses include "Qur'anic studies, Hadith [traditions about the Prophet Muhammad], Prophet's *seerat* [biographies], Prophet's companions, Islamic teachings, Islamic morals, Islamic history, Arabic reading and language, and the rights and obligations of each individual Muslim to himself/herself, to the parents, to our community in this country and all over the world, and to all humanity." At Averroes Academy, "the Islamic Education curriculum is aimed at nurturing the development of Islamic scholars and promotes the learning of traditional Islamic sciences such as Arabic, *Fiqh* [Islamic jurisprudence] and Qur'an recitation and memorization."[13] This religious grounding intends to promote academic, civic, and social success: "Averroes Academy will give a high priority to the Islamic education of our children as we prepare them to achieve high academic standards thereby preparing them to excel for future successful and prosperous avocations and careers (*InshaAllah*) [God willing]."

Required secular topics often receive religious treatment and interpretation in parochial schools. For instance, Islamic prescriptions about socializing between the sexes makes coeducation per se problematic, while mixed physical education classes pose an added affront to Islamic views on modesty. The largest Arab mosque in Chicago, Mosque Foundation, has established separate schools for boys and girls, but smaller Islamic schools may not be able to afford dual instruction and increased costs. Even the relatively well-off Islamic Foundation School must compromise. "For now," a published story explains (Franklin 2001, 16), "boys and girls learn in the same classrooms, something that wouldn't happen if space allowed separate facilities. The children are told that it is proper to mix during classes, but not outside of class and especially not socially." To such idealistic expectations, one alumna of several Islamic parochial schools in Chicago replies (Abd'l-Haleem 2001, 5), "Yeah right. Let me tell you, a lot can happen in three minutes of chaotic herding [between classes], not to mention unlimited after-school time." This student felt liberated scholastically when she transferred to an all-girls' school, where she could study "unhindered by the subconscious awareness that they [boys] are in the room, aware of your every move." She does not fall into the opposite kind of idealism, however, thinking that such segregation can ever be complete for this age group, yet she was thankful to be relatively free of the "dynamics of intermingling" during school hours.

To some degree, all secular topics are suffused with religious meaning in the context of parochial education. Language used throughout Averroes Academy's Curriculum Guide illustrates this, from Qur'anic quotes like "God will raise in rank those of you who believe and those who are given knowledge," to simple expressions of pious hope like "InshaAllah [God willing] the students at Averroes Academy will develop critical and inquiry skills that will foster value and appreciation for science."[14]

Like curricular offerings, extracurricular programming at parochial schools also provides a religious context and perspective for all activities. Islamic Foundation School offers basketball, student council, clubs, a literary magazine, and fund-raising events. "We make a big thing out of both Eids," one school official told us, referring to the two annual Islamic holidays, "because we feel that it is equivalent to Christmas for the Christians. So we always set aside the whole day for parties and for special treats." All the high school students went to a ski resort on one Eid. "They skied all day. They had a great time, the girls went with their *hijab* [traditional head covering] and everything, the girls with the female teachers and the boys with the male teachers. We had a wonderful time."

Islamic Foundation School also participates in the cooperative Muslim Scouts of Greater Chicago program. Upon accessing this program's Web site,[15] one is greeted by a child's lilting rendition of the traditional Muslim greeting, *Asalaamu Alaikum* (peace be with you). The home page notes that the program is open to students from Islamic Foundation School, a nearby independent Islamic school, and "all Private, Public, and Homeschooled Muslim Youth." The Web site and its links reveal a close interweaving of Islamic and Scouting philosophies. Clearly, the goal here is to nurture upstanding Muslim-American citizens. As we read in one place, "Girl Scouts is the pre-eminent organization *Where Girls Grow Strong!* You can help today's Muslim girls become tomorrow's leaders inshaAllah." The same intersection—with its inherent tensions—between civic and religious identities that we have noted with regard to Islamic parochial schools can be heard in a statement by one of the local Muslim Scout organizers (Yates 2003): "There's a big cry [from the Muslim community] not to be isolated but to keep our Muslim identity. . . . We're trying to do it without offending anyone. We're trying to do it to bridge our communities."[16]

Muslim home schooling presents another case in point of an educational initiative with potential for civic disengagement that instead forges constructive links to the larger American society. Muslim home schools in the Chicago area may number around two dozen (Horan 2002). Muslim parental motivations for home schooling are the same as for full-time Islamic schools. "Many Muslims choose to school their children at home as a means of preserving religious values and of minimizing the negative influences of society," writes Nimer (2002, 61), although the word "many" probably overstates the extent of the trend. It appears that Muslim parents readily traffic their children between home school and other educational options, including public schools (Horan 2002). A perusal of the Web site of the Muslim Home School Network and Resource reveals many links to non-Muslim resources, including Christian home schooling initiatives and materials, such as a review of the animated Christian video series called "Veggie Tales," which is recommended for use by Muslim families.[17]

The two research sites in Chicago reflect the mainstream Islamic parochial school movement in the United States. Although the literature is still scant (see Haddad 1997, 237n134; Leonard 2003b, 112, 114), we know enough to make three generalizations about this movement.

First, many immigrant Muslim parents have ambivalent feelings about American society and American public schools which affect their educational choices for their children. In the benchmark study by Haddad and Lummis (1987), Muslims as a group expressed mixed feelings about the need for Islamic parochial education. Fully 40 percent of respondents answered "Not important" to a question about the importance of providing a mosque-based Islamic school as an alternative to public schools. The authors listed the following reasons for parental resistance to Islamic parochial schools: satisfaction with the public school experience and quality of instruction; skepticism about the quality of instruction offered by Islamic schools; concern that Islamic schools might be too strict or conservative religiously; high costs; and fear it would isolate them from American society (51). Haddad and Lummis summarized the parental dilemma over choosing a non-Islamic school: "The tension comes in reconciling the desire for an academically excellent education, which is possible in some American institutions both public and private, with the fear that such exposure to different value systems may lead their children away from the principles of Islam" (168).

Second, we can safely generalize that religious and/or religiously motivated moral concerns usually tip parental decisions in the direction of an Islamic education, outweighing other considerations like those identified by Haddad and Lummis. In a survey of research, Karen Leonard (2003b) discusses the motivations of immigrant Muslims for establishing Islamic schools. These include, negatively, "a major concern about sex and violence in American schools" and objections to sex education curricula and coeducational activities. Positive motivations include teaching Islamic subjects and fulfilling the ideal of panethnic

Islamic identity: "Many Muslims see the establishment of Islamic schools in multi-ethnic America as a step in bringing the international umma into being" (113).

Many Muslim observers emphasize the negative motivations for Islamic education in a non-Islamic and secular-influenced society. Freda Shamma (1999) proposes a curriculum founded on the Islamic doctrine of *tawhid* (divine unity), a God-centered curriculum in contrast to the secular curricula of public schools. Louay Safi (1999, 37) writes,

> While Muslims have been impressed by the vibrant American culture, and hence willing to learn from its strengths, they have been equally alarmed by its downside. Particularly of concern to Muslims is the increasing moral laxity of the American society, reflected in sexual promiscuity, violence, pornography, drug abuse, and other social ills that have been on the increase. The perceived moral laxity has prompted many Muslim parents to search for alternative schooling and social activities for their children, and hence brought them closer to Islamic centers, and highlighted the importance of community.

Safi contends that a secular educational philosophy created the current moral crisis in America and lays out a philosophy of an integrated Islamic education to address this crisis: "The mission of Islamic education is to reintegrate the fragmented consciousness of modern man by once again repositioning divine revelation at the core of human consciousness, the binding and nurturing core which the secular project has managed to destroy" (43). According to Safi, Islamic education will work hand-in-hand with the political maturation of the American Muslim community, which stands ready to transform America: "American Muslims, I contend, could contribute profoundly to the restoration of the spiritual and moral core of modern civilization which has been fading away with the advancement of hardcore secularism. Indeed, American Muslims are in a position to restore the spiritual and moral dimensions of modern life while continuing to be faithful to the true spirit of liberalism" (33). The last sentiment expressed in this quotation locates the Islamic parochial school movement as a largely mainstream initiative, rather than an isolationist enterprise, consistent with our findings in Chicago.

One mosque leader in Chicago bemoaned the fact that more Muslim parents do not choose an Islamic education for their children. Many parents are "too busy, too greedy," he opined, "and then the parenting is left to the [public] schools on their behalf. And [public] schools cannot do this." He went on to talk of the "tremendous peer pressure in public schools. Public school [Muslim] children tend to forget whatever they learn in the mosque. Once they stop coming to Sunday school, they don't care too much about learning about religion. . . . They simply become more involved in worldly affairs." At one public event at his mosque, this leader told the audience that Muslim parents often ask him whether four or five years in Islamic school can make a difference in their children's lives. He always tells them, "Yes. Even one day can make a difference."

A third generalization about the mainstream Islamic parochial school movement in the United States concerns its inherent tensions with the larger society. Like mainstream parochial schools of any religious tradition, Islamic schools attempt to shelter their students from society's negative influences while training those students for faith-informed citizenship and socioeconomic success in that very society. As Asma Gull Hasan (2002, 145) puts it, Islamic schools "focus on helping students strike a balance between Islam and American culture." This balance is insured both by state accrediting requirements and by the schools' own sense of citizenship. Islamic educators often bemoan the weakness of the religious value-added component of Islamic parochial education given the reliance on public school standards and curricula, an irony not lost on proponents of a parochial alternative to the public schools (e.g., Schmidt 1998, 95–96; Shamma 1999). As the principal of Islamic Foundation School explained in a published article, Islamic schools "constantly walk a fine line" between parental factions—on one side those whose disdain for the negative elements of American culture overshadows any concern about the quality of education offered by Islamic schools, on the other side those who place quality of education over Islamic content (Franklin 2001, 16).

Some in the Muslim community wonder just how successful Islamic schools can be in producing good Muslims. As an administrator at one of the Islamic schools in our study explained, the very discipline problems and immoral behaviors that Muslim parents feared in the public schools are increasing in this school: "I foresee these will become bigger problems in the future because this is reality. I mean these children are living in this society, we will see these types of things coming up. We don't expect that all children who attend our school are perfect angels and that they will be doing everything which is Islamic and appropriate and they do not make any mistakes. That's not gonna happen." Another interviewee who attended both this Islamic school and public school pointed out that a parochial school education is only one factor in the lives of its students. Regarding one classmate who attended Islamic school through twelfth grade: "If you saw her, you wouldn't think she would have come from Islamic school. She did not change at all, even though she went to school and everything. So I mean it depends if the person wants to change, too. Environment can only do so much."

Garbi Schmidt (1998) discusses the tension between immigrant Islamic schools in Chicago and the dominant culture. Schmidt explains that the Islamic schools were established over against the feared Other of "American society and norms" and "vocalized segregation from it, or, at least, an interaction with Otherness on *their* terms" (91). Yet Schmidt ends her discussion with a classroom exchange about the potential for a positive reformulation of Islam in interaction with its American environment. In contrast to the initial motivation for establishing separate Islamic schools, "the fulfillment of an Islamic utopia was here [in this classroom discussion] presented as inherently connected to American society" (103). Elsewhere Schmidt summarizes the relationship between ideology and practicality in this regard: "Ideologically, Muslim full-time schools legitimized their existence through the rejection of the Other. Practically, they were forced to include it" (107).

This evolution from relative social isolationism toward increasing positive civic engagement is illustrated by the full-time parochial school founded in 1989 by Muslim Community Center, the oldest post-1965 mosque in metropolitan Chicago (Livezey et al., forthcoming). This evolution also characterizes our two research sites in Chicago, although the respective parochial schools of both Islamic Cultural Center of Greater Chicago and Islamic Foundation began with less isolationist sentiments than Muslim Community Center's school. In contrast, nonmainstream Islamic schools, like the Qur'an recitation school described by Schmidt (1998, 104–107), virtually opt out of relationship with the American social Other altogether.

The report by Nimat Hafez Barazangi (1991) captures the philosophy and practices of what we have labeled the mainstream Islamic parochial school movement in the United States. Barazangi takes great pains to establish "the contrast between the Islamic and Western worldviews" and how these fundamentally different worldviews "impinge strongly on the ways in which their respective philosophies of education are set forth" (157, 158). Given the fact that American-born and/or -raised Muslim youth identify more with Western American values than with Islamic ones, Islamic parochial schools must provide an "educational intervention" that makes explicit and critical comparisons between the two value systems (171). Significantly, Barazangi sees the intention of this approach as "to preserve the Islamic identity in an integrative manner within the pluralistic Western society" (172). Explaining the word "integrative," Barazangi (174n20) states: "The term *integrative* is used here to indicate the ability to maintain the Islamic belief system at its central concept level, *tawhid* [divine unity], and to objectify this belief system in the Western secular environment without (1) compromising the Islamic principles, (2) sacrificing national/ethnic group attachment, (3) living dual, but separate lives (Islamic and Western), or (4) withdrawing from the outside society." Here we see continuing tensions between Islamic parochial education and the larger society, but not to the extent of isolationism.

### Islamic Parochial Education in Comparative Perspective: Lutheran and Catholic Parallels

How does the emerging mainstream Islamic parochial school movement compare to parochial education among other immigrant religious groups in the United States? We can begin to answer this question by identifying which groups have established parochial schools (and which have not) and by examining parochial school philosophies and practices across religions. This will help us to understand the common religious motivation for parochial education as well as the reasons why only certain groups act on this religious motivation by making parochial education a priority moral project.

In the classical period of American immigration, Lutherans and Catholics stood out as the torch bearers of parochial education. (The majority of Jewish children during the classical period of American immigration attended public schools, due largely to their parents' desire to assimilate them into American society. Jewish "day schools" [parochial schools] were found mostly among the Orthodox.)[18] Before the institution of the American public school system, Lutherans had established approximately four hundred elementary schools. In the century between 1840 and 1940, driven by the huge waves of German and Scandinavian immigrants, nearly three thousand more Lutheran schools arose in what one Lutheran historian calls "the major Protestant educational undertaking during two centuries." By the early 1960s, Lutheran elementary schools in the United States numbered a still impressive 1,684, more than 80 percent of them affiliated with the conservative Missouri Synod denomination (Beck 1965, vii, 433).

Even more impressive was the Catholic initiative. Approximately 70 Catholic elementary schools existed in the British colonies and the French and Spanish territories by the beginning of the Revolutionary War, with perhaps another 75 established in the early years of the republic (Burns, Kohlbrenner, and Peterson 1937). In 1924, when federal restrictions put an end to the classical immigration period, Catholic elementary school enrollment passed the 2 million mark, with more than 7,000 schools. By the mid-twentieth century, Catholic elementary schools had 2.5 million students, whereas enrollment in all Protestant schools combined had dropped to less than 150,000, the majority of whom attended Missouri Synod Lutheran schools (Curran 1954). One Catholic historian (Fisher 2002, 79) calls the Catholic elementary school system "one of the greatest achievements in U.S. religious history." The massive University of Notre Dame study in the 1960s, summarized in the report *Catholic Schools in Action*, described the American Catholic educational system as having "no parallel anywhere in the world" (Neuwien 1966, 9).

Chicago's part in this achievement is remarkable as well. Writes local Catholic historian Edward Kantowicz (2000), "ethnic Catholics generally began with a school rather than a church. In parish after parish, priests and people built the school building first, as a unifying force for parishioners to rally around, with church services held in the basement until a more suitable house of worship could be built." We read in the *Five Holy Martyrs Diamond Jubilee* commemorative book (1985, 64) the words of Archbishop Mundelein at the dedication of new parish facilities in 1920: "The fine churches can wait; the schools must come first." According to Kantowicz, "by the end of the nineteenth century, three-quarters of the 114 Catholic parishes in the city of Chicago included a school. Eventually these schools formed the largest private school system in North America. At their peak in 1965, the Chicago Catholic schools enrolled over 300,000 children in city and suburbs. Only two public school systems in the country—those in Chicago and New York—were larger."

The philosophies driving Lutheran, Catholic, and Islamic parochial education are remarkably similar in basic respects. In all three cases the religious and religiously informed moral content of parochial education offers a preferable alternative to public education. The view here is that parochial education is holistic, integrated, and morally superior, supplying the religious component that the public school system not only lacks but also has replaced with inferior secular norms and values. This has important civic implications for the nation, according to parochial school proponents across religions. Parochial education at once withdraws students from a morally flawed society in order to educate them as positive change agents of that society.

> The *primary objective* of Lutheran parochial schools has at all times and in all synods been the inculcation of Christian doctrines and principles of life and their coordination with the entire curriculum of the school. It is the long-established conviction of the Lutheran Church that education and religion must go hand in hand; that a nation cannot make the right kind of citizens by a godless education and bringing in religion afterward. Most Lutheran bodies have held that this can be achieved only by means of the full-time parochial school, and they accordingly at some time in their history fostered schools and promoted the movement. (Beck 1965, 408)

Beck specifies the religious value added of a Lutheran education beyond that offered by public education and its underlying secular ideologies: "The philosophy and the teachings of Christianity thus become just as much a part of the total curriculum as do the basic tenets of democracy as a political or economic or social system, or those of Pragmatism, or Utilitarianism, or Existentialism, or any other philosophy that is made inherent in the objectives, materials, and methodology of the secular or general schools" (473). Thus, "the history of the Lutheran school reveals that there is a distinctive place for parochial schools in a democracy" (416). We note here the tension of being a moral voice both apart from and a part of the larger society.

The Catholic school movement began in earnest in the nineteenth century largely out of concern that the public school system would erode the faith of the growing numbers of immigrant Catholics because it was dominated by non-Catholic ideologies—Protestantism early in the century, then increasing secularity (Burns, Kohlbrenner, and Peterson 1937; Lannie 1970). In the waning years of the nineteenth century, liberal Catholic leaders, led by Archbishop John Ireland,

and conservatives, led by Archbishop Michael Augustine Corrigan, clashed over the relationship between the two school systems. The liberals sought common ground and cooperation with the public schools; the conservatives brooked no relationship with the public schools as "hotbeds of materialism, hedonism, and immorality" (Walch 1996, 84). The controversy officially ended in 1893 when the Vatican sided with the liberals: "It was an important day when the pope confirmed that the church had no fundamental disagreements with the principles of public education" (98; cf. Burns, Kohlbrenner, and Peterson 1937, 160–167).

This rapprochement should not be overstated, however. Catholic education has always maintained important philosophical differences with public education, as witness its continued existence as an alternative school system. Given the larger context of anti-Catholic (and related anti-immigrant) sentiment in the nineteenth and twentieth centuries, Catholic educators needed to stress the assimilationist or "Americanization" function of their parochial schools. The church's twofold purpose in parochial education was "to preserve the faith in the immigrant and to prepare him for American citizenship" (Burns, Kohlbrenner, and Peterson 1937, 176). This dual religious and civic focus continued beyond the classical period of Catholic immigration, as the Notre Dame study explained in the 1960s: "The central consideration, therefore, is . . . how does the Catholic school carry out the mandate to provide religious training, while at the same time serving the purposes which are those of education for life in the United States at this period in its history?" (Neuwien 1966, 2). Here, again, religion offers the value added that is missing from public school education and that is needed in the public square: "Thus one can discern a marked continuity of thought in the declarations made by the teaching authority of the Church on the subject of education. Because man is endowed by his Creator with rights that in turn impose duties, moral training in the rational use of those rights and in the performance of the duties that accompany them is inseparable from education; and religion provides the only light in which the significance of moral action can be adequately understood" (19).

In Chicago, St. Lambert's parish school (now closed) advertised itself in a brochure as "A progressive alternative to public education," providing students with "The St. Lambert Advantage: St. Lambert School is dedicated to fostering the spiritual, moral, intellectual, physical, emotional and social development of our children to face the challenges of modern life by preparing them to be Catholic adults who bear witness to the good news of Christ, for in our children lies the hope of the future." The brochure expressed the dual religious and civic focus of Catholic education in general: "We believe in Catholic education because it emphasizes high academic standards and spiritual formation. We strive to provide the moral leadership needed to mold tomorrow's citizens."

The sentiments in this local Catholic parochial school statement match those in the two local mosques described earlier. In an article titled "Islamic Schools as

Change Agents" (Moes n.d.), posted on the Web site of the Islamic Society of North America, the author draws out the "parallels between Catholic and Islamic schools."

> Muslims have objected to public schools on both the grounds that motivated Catholics to establish a separate school system. Firstly, on philosophical grounds, it can be argued that Islamic education is not compatible with secularism since the "revealed knowledge" found in the Qur'an and Hadeeth literature supersedes scientific knowledge. Secondly, anti-Muslim rhetoric and bigotry has also been identified in the public schools and their texts. It must be noted that the lines drawn between Muslims and secular Americans have not been as pronounced as those between nineteenth-century Catholics and Protestants, though recent events affecting our nation have made anti-Muslim rhetoric more of an issue since 9–11–2001. . . . In fact, the goals for establishing Islamic schools are not much different [from Catholic schools]: Firstly, to promulgate the teachings of the religion and secondly to safeguard the students from such evils of society as drugs, racism, and premarital sex.

Hasan (2002) also draws out the parallels between Islamic and Christian (especially Catholic) parochial education, including the inherent tensions in being a religious citizen: "Islamic schools are similar to Catholic schools or other parochial schools in emphasizing the importance of one's own religion. An Islamic school has the same goals as does a Catholic school—to create an environment that is still very American but is sheltered from influences that work against Islam and Catholicism or that make kids feel 'weird' and different being a Muslim or Catholic" (146–147).

Regardless of religious identity, parochial education movements tend to move from initial sectarian impulses toward relative rapprochement with the larger society. In other words, they "mainstream," and in the process they compromise some of their religious and moral distinctiveness. This has certainly occurred in the Lutheran and Catholic cases. In the 1950s Curran (1954) pointed out that the principal cause of the decline in number of Lutheran parochial schools was theological rather than linguistic—not the loss of German as much as the loss of a compelling sense of the importance of religious education. Only the Missouri Synod, one of the most sectarian Lutheran denominations, held forth as other Lutheran bodies abandoned the field of parochial education. Said Curran, "Apart from the Missouri Synod, the Protestant parochial school systems failed" (128).

Catholic education had mainstreamed by the twentieth century, as we have seen. Jesuit sociologist Joseph Fichter's (1958) study of one urban (nonimmigrant) Catholic school in the 1950s suggested that parochial and public schools were more alike than the independent private school was to either of them, private schools being socially privileged and elitist. The Catholic school Fichter studied reflected the demographics of its community, and its students were remarkably similar culturally to their public school peers. Moreover, this Catholic school was thickly interrelated with the public schools and contributed financially, civically, and morally to the larger community.

In a 1960s study facilitated by the National Opinion Research Center, Greeley and Rossi (1966) found that Catholic schools per se had not fostered the broader societal divisiveness of the time and argued that Catholic education tended to inculcate tolerant and liberal social attitudes, especially at the high school level and beyond. In a striking conclusion that went to the heart of the "protection of the faith" rationale for parochial education, Greeley and Rossi found "no evidence that Catholic schools have been necessary for the survival of American Catholicism" (227). A steady decline in the number of Catholic schools nationwide in recent decades certainly stems largely from social and economic factors (D'Agostino 2000), but also from a diminishing sense of the importance of full-time Catholic education. Analysis of parish data in Illinois by Michael Cieslak (2004) led to the conclusion that "it may be difficult to establish new Catholic schools, even in areas where existing Catholic schools have waiting lists" (106). The high cost of building and operating such schools was a key factor here, but ambivalence about the importance of parochial education was even more important. Both the purpose and the clientele of Catholic education have changed, particularly in no longer serving primarily immigrant populations (Cieslak 2005). The Catholic school movement will look different in the twenty-first century, predicts Cieslak, "if for no other reason than because Catholics have been well integrated into society and no longer need the social isolation that Catholic schools offered" (185).

## Islamic Parochial Education in Comparative Perspective: Buddhist and Hindu Cases

Immigrant Buddhists and their descendants have experienced social marginalization comparable to that of their Catholic and Muslim counterparts, yet Buddhists have established a minuscule number of parochial schools. In the classical period of American immigration, the majority of Buddhist immigrants to Hawaii and the mainland United States were Japanese, most of them affiliated with the Jodo Shinshu Hongwanji-Ha or Nishi Hongwanji branch of Japanese Buddhism,[19] either the Honpa Hongwanji Mission of Hawaii[20] or the mainland Buddhist Mission of North America, the latter renamed Buddhist Churches of America (BCA) in 1944.[21] An examination of twenty-four temple links on the BCA Web site revealed no parochial schools among them,[22] although several temples operate Japanese "language schools."

In Hawaii today, there are only three Buddhist schools out of a total of 132 private schools on the state roster,[23] two of the three being affiliated with Honpa Hongwanji Mission: Hongwanji Mission School[24] and Pacific Buddhist Academy,[25] the latter having the distinction of being the first Buddhist high school in the United States (Essoyan 2003). (The third school is affiliated with a Japanese Zen Buddhist group.) The philosophy of the two Honpa Hongwanji schools in Hawaii expresses the dual focus of religious and civic training that characterizes mainstream parochial education generally, with only a minimal sense of tension between the two: "The Pacific Buddhist Academy offers families a college-preparatory high school with a standards-based, academically challenging curriculum that is rooted in Buddhist values. As Hongwanji Mission School does for preschool through Grade 8, the Academy develops individuals who can effectively contribute to Hawaii's multi-cultural society and the world beyond it."[26]

But why so few Buddhist parochial schools over the long history of Japanese immigration to the United States? Education has always been a central moral project in Buddhism. "Historically one of the most important functions performed by the Sangha [the Buddhist monastic community] was education, for until the advent of European colonial powers and Christian missionaries nearly all education took place within the precincts of the temple grounds" (Swearer 1970, 71). In precolonial Ceylon (modern Sri Lanka), for instance, "Monks taught reading and writing (mainly but not only to boys), and at the same time taught moral values and literature: virtually all literature was Buddhist and inculcated Buddhist ethics" (Gombrich 1988, 147).

During the classical period of American immigration, Japanese Buddhist temples in Hawaii and on the mainland established so-called language schools that taught Japanese culture, values, and Buddhist tenets in addition to the Japanese language (Hunter 1971; Kashima 1977). These schools usually convened outside of public school hours and became a focal point of the contentious Americanization debates of the time. Critics, who typically did not distinguish between Americanization and Christianization, saw the language schools as cells of foreign influence in American society: "Every day, wrote Bishop Henry Restarick of the Episcopal Mission [in 1907], children were sent to a Buddhist priest and taught the Japanese language and patriotic principles. Thus the Buddhist schools, the [Christian] clergy alleged, were a menace to the Americanization of the Territory" (Hunter 1971, 90). Japanese Buddhist educators and officials responded with assurances that the schools served important moral and civic functions for the immigrant community. In 1910 the Honpa Hongwanji Mission declared that its schools promoted "the encouragement of American thought and system." The head of the mission, Bishop Yemyo Imamura, "consistently and vehemently admonished Hawaii's young Americans of Japanese ancestry to abide wholeheartedly by the principles of Americanism and instructed his priests to do likewise." Imamura saw the two school systems, public and Buddhist, as complementary, together stressing citizenship, family values, and morality, familiar concerns of parochial educators generally, as we have seen (Hunter 1971).

If immigrant Buddhist temples have promoted educating their children in this way, then why not through full-time parochial schools that would provide an alternative to the public school system, particularly when the latter was so hostile to Japanese culture in general and to Buddhism in particular? Three factors are salient. First, immigrant Japanese Buddhists lacked the social and financial resources to establish full-time parochial schools. But this was not a sufficient impediment, for, if it were, more parochial schools would have been established as the community prospered in later generations. A second, and more significant, reason for the lack of parochial schools was the strong desire to assimilate as much as possible into American society rather than to exacerbate tensions with the majority population by opting out of the public school system. Assimilation accelerated with the growth of the Nisei (second generation) after 1920, as "Buddhists borrowed Christian terminology and approaches, while some traditional Buddhist practices underwent a process that became known as Protestantization, in which they came to resemble America's dominant religion, Protestant Christianity" (Mann, Numrich, and Williams 2001, 33). In the throes of the decades-long Americanization controversy in Hawaii, many Nisei parted ways with their elders and opposed even the part-time language schools at temples (Hunter 1971). A third reason for the lack of parochial schools has to do with the individualist orientation of the Buddhist educational moral project, which emphasizes personal morality rather than a collective religious identity.

If we are correct in our analysis, then we would expect parochial schools to emerge along the sectarian edges of the immigrant Buddhist community, in groups where the importance of maintaining a distinctive religious identity is more pronounced. We know of one possible example in California, at a Buddhist temple called City of Ten Thousand Buddhas, founded by the Chinese master Venerable Hsuan Hua.[27] This temple runs two schools, Instilling Goodness Elementary School and Developing Virtue Secondary School. As a brochure explains, "The curriculum reflects a commitment to educate the whole person. Accordingly, the elementary school emphasizes respect for parents, teachers, and elders, while the secondary school guides students to fulfill their personal and civic responsibilities, to cherish their families, their nation, and all living beings." The brochure features a quotation from Venerable Hsuan Hua: "A nation's true wealth is in its students and schools." Even in this sectarian Buddhist case, there are familiar civic sentiments of mainstream parochial education found in other religious circles.

We know of no immigrant Hindu parochial schools in the United States. Raymond Williams (2004, personal communication) reports that BAPS Swaminarayans operate schools in India, plus one affiliated with their London temple. However, Williams knows of only one BAPS group in the United States that has discussed establishing a parochial school. One Hindu group in Hawaii reported the sentiment among Hindu youth that parochial education could address the issues they face in their lives ("Dharma Suffers in U.S. Schools" 1987): "Most students thought that Hindu parochial schools could solve the problems, harmonizing education and religion, giving a sound knowledge of Hinduism. Then, as adults, they felt they could stand strong on the foundation of understanding and talk intelligently with their Christian and Jewish peers in a pluralistic society." This echoes the rationale for parochial education we have seen across religious groups. But, as with Buddhists, mitigating factors have been more powerful among immigrant Hindus, including remarkable success (at least in some strata) in assimilating into American society. If immigrant Hindu parochial schools do arise in the United States at some point in the future, we can predict that they will be established by sectarian groups such as the Swaminarayans. Not surprisingly, the only Hindu parochial education movement of any significance to date has been that of the sectarian group ISKCON, which was not an immigrant initiative and which virtually folded as a result of the abuse scandal of the 1990s (Vande Berg 2005; Vande Berg and Kniss, forthcoming). A small movement is also afoot in nonimmigrant circles to apply principles of yoga, a Hindu-inspired meditative practice, to public education through privately operated charter schools (Gallanis 2004).[28]

### Religion, Education, and Civic Tensions: The Recent Immigrant Case

Will Herberg understood the civic tensions inherent in faith-based education throughout American history, but he also envisioned a future agenda of achieving a kind of creative cooperation that would sacrifice neither parochial nor public school education. We framed our discussion in this chapter through an examination of the educational moral project of immigrant congregations, focusing particularly on mainstream (rather than sectarian) parochial school initiatives to produce American citizens who maintain their distinctive religious identities without succumbing to perceived temptations of the larger culture.

What have we learned about how recent immigrant congregations arbitrate the tension between religious and civic identities through their educational programming? And what have we learned about the effects of such efforts on American society; in other words, how does all of this matter beyond the four walls of an immigrant congregation or parochial school?

First, we see that civic tensions are inherent in faith-based immigrant education due to its moral critique of the larger society. The moral conservatism found across the board in immigrant religious groups fuels a tremendous amount of educational programming that falls along a continuum of over-againstness vis-à-vis larger society, with parochial schools indicating a relatively high degree of social separation.

Second, we have gained insight into which immigrant religious groups establish parochial schools and why, as well as why some parochial education initiatives wane. In the Lutheran and Catholic cases, early marginalization as immigrants resulted in substantial parochial school movements. As marginalization diminished, both movements waned, continuing to hold significant importance to the highly sectarian Missouri Synod Lutherans.

Of the three largest non-Christian immigrant groups today (Muslims, Buddhists, and Hindus), only Muslims have mounted anything close to a substantial parochial school movement. We agree with those who view Muslims as the contemporary counterpart to classical Catholic immigrants. As beleaguered multiethnic, minority religious groups, both established parochial schools as a bulwark against marginalization. The smaller scale of the Muslim movement today speaks to a hopeful attitude among Muslims about the prospects for integration into a more multicultural and accepting contemporary America. Times have changed, American society has changed, recent immigration differs from classical immigration.

But the immigrant Buddhist and Hindu cases complicate the picture. Neither group has produced a substantial parochial school movement in the United States, even though we might expect such a movement among Buddhists given their history of social marginalization comparable to the Catholic and Muslim cases. If we assume that, in principle, parochial education is attractive to immigrant religious groups given their inherent tensions with the larger society, we suggest the following hypothesis to explain the appearance of parochial education among some groups but not others: a substantial parochial school movement will emerge only within those immigrant religious groups for whom tensions with the larger society reach a critical level; for whom the moral project has a primarily collectivist goal; and for those who can muster the requisite material resources. Lutherans and Catholics in the classical immigration period and Muslims today combine all three of these factors. The waning of the Lutheran and Catholic parochial school movements occurred primarily because the tensions with the larger society dropped below the critical level, and secondarily because of the lack of material resources, again with the exception of the sectarian Missouri Synod Lutherans. The absence of a substantial parochial school movement among Buddhists and Hindus can be explained by the lack of sufficient tension with the larger society—for Buddhists, their own largely defensive efforts to assimilate in the early twentieth century account for most of this—and by an individualist moral project. In an immigrant context, the educational moral project in Islam has a collectivist goal of creating a multiethnic *ummah* in a non-Islamic society, whereas the educational moral project in both Buddhism and Hinduism has an individualist goal of creating good Buddhists and good Hindus. Islamic teachings about collectivist identity are much stronger than analogous teachings in Buddhism and Hinduism. We predict that parochial schools will emerge only along the sectarian margins of immigrant Buddhism and Hinduism where collectivist teachings maintain group identity.[29]

A third lesson from this chapter has to do with the mainstreaming tendencies of parochial schools—that is, their typical shift over time from relative isolationism toward positive civic engagement. Although more systematic and wide-ranging research needs to be conducted to determine the representativeness of our findings, we suggest that recent immigrant parochial education tends toward mainstream interaction with the larger society rather than sectarian withdrawal from it, and immigrant congregations are thereby entering into a creative and positive relationship with American society. Tensions remain between religious and civic identities, but immigrant parochial schools generally seek to inculcate religious identities and concomitant moral guidelines for life as a contributing member of American society, not in order to opt out of it. Thus, we suggest that immigrant parochial schools today function more as bridging institutions to the larger society than as bonding enclaves unto themselves (see Chaves 2004).

Parochial schools must make certain compromises that contribute to this mainstreaming process. Besides the obvious compromises with government accreditation stipulations, they must also accommodate the wishes of a clientele that tends to expand beyond a congregation's immediate membership into pools of potential new clients from the larger immigrant community, and perhaps even beyond. A spokesperson for one of the Islamic schools of our study estimated that 80 percent of the parents whose children attend that school are not closely affiliated in some way with the school's host mosque. Of course, these parents are overwhelmingly Muslims, but this remarkable figure still speaks to a wide client base beyond the core constituency of the mosque, bringing with it a certain amount of compromise with the wishes of large numbers of supporters. If the Muslim case follows the typical Christian pattern (e.g., Cieslak 2005, 176), today's immigrant Islamic schools will someday appeal to a clientele outside of their own religious communities, bringing even more compromise.

Thus, educational dynamics that could potentially disengage recent immigrants from American society have largely had the opposite effect. Parochial school initiatives have been minimal among recent immigrant religions, indicating, if not always satisfaction with, at least grudging tolerance of the American public school system. We have heard the ambivalence of immigrant parents and have seen the complex calculus they employ in making decisions for or against public schooling for their children. We assume that the relative dearth of parochial schools, even among Muslims, results at least partly from a sense that religious and moral educational needs can be adequately served by other congregational programming.

Although our interviewees from the Islamic schools in Chicago told us of minimal interaction with local public schools to date, they also expressed willingness to expand such interaction in the future. One interviewee from Islamic Foundation School described a new program of the Council of Islamic Organizations of Greater Chicago (CIOGC) that bodes well for such future interaction: "Currently the CIOGC is trying to work with the various full time Islamic schools to create some form of network so that these various schools can better themselves and one another. The CIOGC has met with previous Chicago Public Schools CEO Paul Vallas and the current CEO Arnie Duncan to attempt to leverage the CPS experiences and resources to assist our Islamic schools." According to its Web site,[30] the CIOGC has formed a Full-Time Islamic Schools Coordination Committee that represents and facilitates the efforts of member Islamic parochial schools, but also commits to using "its access and goodwill to seek and provide consultative services from the Public and Parochial school systems of metropolitan Chicago." This represents important links to civic peers in education. We also note the traffic that occurs between Islamic schools and public schools, mostly in students transferring back and forth, but also among teachers and administrators. The principal of one of the Islamic schools we studied in Chicago came out of the teaching ranks of the Chicago Public Schools and had not been affiliated with Islamic schools before taking up the current position.

We find in all of this evidence of a creative cooperation between parochial and public school education, though perhaps not exactly with the players Will Herberg had in mind in the 1960s. We recall the research question posed to the Gateway Cities projects by the Pew Charitable Trusts: How does religion either contribute to or impede the civic incorporation of new immigrants? In the case of Islamic parochial education, the answer tends toward positive civic engagement.

# 7
## Marriage Patterns in Immigrant Congregations

IMPLICATIONS FOR SOCIAL DISTANCE
AND GROUP IDENTITY

*The concept of "distance" as applied to human, as
distinguished from spacial relations, has come into
use among sociologists, in an attempt to reduce to
something like measurable terms the grades and
degrees of understanding and intimacy which characterize personal and social relations generally.*

—Robert Ezra Park (1924)

The renowned Chicago School of sociology, born out of the nation's first sociology department at the University of Chicago, established its reputation during
the classical period of American immigration history. Robert Park published the
article excerpted above in the year classical immigration came to a close with
the passage of restrictive federal legislation. Among many research interests,
Chicago School sociologists attempted to measure social distances between
groups, including that between immigrant groups and mainstream American
society. Beginning in the 1920s, Emory S. Bogardus, a graduate of the University
of Chicago's sociology department, quantified Park's notion into a social distance scale that continues to exercise sociologists and others today, even when
regarded circumspectly (Bogardus 1925a, 1925b, 1968; Lee et al. 1998; Lieberson
and Waters 1988; Pagnini and Morgan 1990; Spickard 1989; Yu 2001).[1]

Intermarriage is often regarded as indicative of minimal or no social distance
between groups. In the Bogardus scale, willingness to interact socially with
members of another population group is arranged along a continuum from
greatest distance (as fellow citizen) to least (as kin by marriage), the assumption
being that there is no social intimacy closer than marriage. Scholars today study
intermarriage rates as a barometer of immigrant assimilation into mainstream
American society and a harbinger of shifting ethnic and racial group identities
(Bean and Stevens 2003; Fu 2003; Jacoby 2004; Kibria 2002; Lee and Bean 2004;
Lee et al. 1998; Pagnini and Morgan 1990; Saenz et al. 1995; Sanjek 1994; Spickard
1989; Waters 2000).

Scholarly investigation of religious factors underlying intermarriage patterns typically focuses on macro-level religious identities like Protestants, Catholics, and Jews (Herberg 1955; Kennedy 1944, 1952; Lieberson and Waters 1988). But more microlevel subreligious identities also matter when it comes to marriage. Not surprisingly, given that our data came from religious associations (i.e., congregations), we encountered widespread disapproval of marrying outside of one's religious group. Only rarely did we encounter significant sentiment that the religious identity of a prospective spouse matters little in marriage considerations. For the most part our interviewees recognized religious identity as vitally important and worthy of preserving through marriage and childrearing practices.

But immigrant group identity is never one dimensional. Religious identity is always intertwined with ethnic or racial identity in complex ways. In this chapter we examine the evolving complexity of identities in immigrant congregations as seen in marriage preferences and patterns. We are aware of other important topics surrounding immigrant family life, such as generational dynamics, extended family relations, spousal gender roles, and divorce, yet we consider (inter-)marriage patterns crucial to both the long-term group identities of recent immigrants and the emerging demographic landscape of American society. We recognize the speculative aspects of our analysis in this chapter, especially given the fact that the second generation in most of our research sites is just now reaching marriageable age. We necessarily draw extensively upon respondents' personal opinions and attitudes here since the number of actual intermarriages in our sites remains small. Still, opinions reflect powerful motivations and norms and suggest large implications about future behavior.

## Evolving Immigrant Group Identity

We begin with several assertions about immigrant group identity. First, immigrant groups tend to prefer maintaining their specific complex of Old World religious and ethnic/racial identities in the new American context. Hence, the usual emphasis on a narrowly endogamous marriage—marrying outside the group is like abandoning the immigrant's transnational village.[2] Discussing Italian immigrants in the classical period of American immigration, Robert Park (1955, 162) noted that an immigrant man was considered lost if he never returned to his homeland village or if he married "an American girl" or "an Italian of another town" living in America. Contemporary Chicago interviewees also expressed concern about the potential for confused identities among the offspring of exogamous unions.

Second, immigrant groups experience social pressures against maintaining their specific complex of Old World religious and ethnic/racial identities in the new American context. "First generation—they usually marry within their group," explained a white congregational leader at Maternity BVM Catholic

Church. "Those who are born in Mexico marry Mexicans. [The others], they go to school, they speak English, they begin talking to each other and find out, 'Hey this guy is not Mexican, but he is beautiful' " (this said with a smile and a laugh).

Propinquity has long been recognized as a factor in intermarriage rates, the assumption being that face-to-face interaction with members of other groups increases the likelihood of dating and marriage across group boundaries. As the interviewee just cited indicated, American schools provide propinquity between immigrant and nonimmigrant students, whether at the elementary school, high school, or college levels. "It is so common," said a female Chinese immigrant from St. Lambert Catholic Church, one of the most diverse research sites, in response to a question about the frequency of exogamy in that congregation. "If my friend went and married an American, you know, we just say 'Oh, okay.' They live in a kind of different world, you know, because they have to go to an American college now."

Answering our question about how the congregation views exogamy, a Polish immigrant from Five Holy Martyrs, the historically Polish Catholic parish that now includes a significant number of Mexican members, replied with a chuckle, "It depends. You know, people say, 'Oh, what's she doing or what's he doing, it shouldn't be like that.' But you know, the young people, they look differently at this problem. They are more open. America is like that, you know, a different nation."

One Filipino couple from St. Lambert prays that their sons marry Catholics, preferably Filipino Catholics, yet they have adopted a practical resignation about the situation. "I mean, we have accepted the thing," explained the father. "That is the price we have to pay for living in this kind of a society and culture. There's no sense fighting it, I mean. We told the boys, wherever you're going to be happy, and that's it." Many of our interviewees expressed such resignation, to one degree or another, about the pervasive breakdown of immigrant identity boundaries in America.

Third, we invoke an assertion that has been around since the classical "triple melting pot" thesis (Herberg 1955; Kennedy 1944, 1952)—namely, that religion becomes increasingly more salient than ethnicity/race as immigrant group identity evolves in the American context. In other words, the breakdown of an immigrant group's identity boundaries tends in a certain direction, from a narrow initial complex of Old World religious and ethnic/racial identity to one in which ethnic/racial differences elide to some extent within a more widely construed religious identity. In the classical period of American immigration, Protestant, Catholic, and Jewish immigrant groups established ethnically defined enclaves but eventually sorted out into their respective larger religious categories that included multiethnic/racial groupings and significant interethnic/racial marriage. Muslims, Hindus, Buddhists, and other new immigrant religious groups are sorting out in similar fashion. In this view immigrant groups, especially in the American-born generations, tend to expand the boundaries of their religious identities beyond their initial mono-ethnic/racial confines.

This has great significance for future group identities in that previous ethnic/racial boundaries are breaking down while religious identities are being maintained, though redefined. After reviewing the complexities of immigrant group identity configurations, Ebaugh and Chafetz (2000b) suggest that the Greek Orthodox trajectory may become normative for other immigrant groups over the long run:

> [The Greek Orthodox] case suggests that, in the absence of significant numbers of immigrants, over the generations the distinctive ethnic flavor of what were once immigrant congregations wanes, as their American-born members' identities become more focused on religion than ethnicity, despite their common ethnic background. . . . [The future holds] the distinct possibility that, as in the Greek Orthodox case, second and subsequent generation-dominated religious institutions will likely be more pan-religious and/or more pan-ethnic in their practices, identities, and memberships. (402, 406)

The specific boundaries of the emerging more panreligious and/or more panethnic identity, to use Ebaugh and Chafetz's phrasing, will depend on the immigrant group. In the Greek Orthodox case, this includes a significant amount of intermarriage with other Orthodox Christians, thus creating a more panethnic Orthodox Christianity, as well as intermarriage with non–Orthodox Christians, a more panreligious Christian grouping. One leader at St. Demetrios Greek Orthodox Church in Chicago estimated that more than three-quarters of all marriages performed there include non–Orthodox Christian spouses, particularly Roman Catholics (mostly of Mexican or European ancestries).

"I think it's very difficult today to not have interethnic and interracial and interreligious marriage," said a fifty-five-year-old second-generation member whose Italian Irish wife converted to Greek Orthodoxy. "I think it's very difficult today because we're such a diverse society. I would love my daughter to marry a young Greek guy who is in the church, but I know that it's not really my decision. So, while I would like to influence her to do that, I really don't think that it's a horribly crucial factor in having a happy marriage today." He continued, explaining the dichotomy of views within the congregation: "St. Demetrios is such a diverse parish, having those with very strong traditional opinions and those who understand what the situation is today. They might not want it to be that way but understand that's how it is going to be."

We found evidence across the sixteen immigrant congregations of our research pool, spanning seven religious traditions, that religion is becoming more salient than ethnicity/race in marriage preferences and patterns. The real question is not whether ethnic/racial identity boundaries are expanding in these immigrant groups, but how far they will expand in each group and what religious factors are involved in each case. A further question then arises as to what this means for evolving ethnic/racial group identities in American society as a whole.

## South Asian Americans

The designation "South Asian" carries a large measure of artificiality for the immigrant generation since South Asians exist only in diasporic contexts like the United States. In South Asia we find Indians, Pakistanis, Sri Lankans, and others at a national level, and, often more significantly to the groups themselves, sub-national populations like those of India's cultural regions. Religious diversity complicates the picture even further since many South Asian nations and regions are multireligious as well as multiethnic.

South Asians' place in America's ethnic/racial hierarchy has always been ambiguous. Not fitting clearly into either white or black categories by the usual American criteria, South Asians have been labeled "Dark Caucasians" because of a dark complexion combined with physical traits considered white by the larger society (Takaki 1998). A national survey in 1978 garnered a variety of racial labels for Asian Indians, including white (11 percent), black (15 percent), brown (23 percent), and other (38 percent) (Xenos, Barringer, and Levin 1989). South Asians promise to contribute to the evolving ethnic/racial configuration of America in significant ways, and religious identities will certainly factor into their contribution.

Five of our research sites serve predominantly South Asian constituencies: Naperville Church of the Brethren (Gujarati Indians), Islamic Foundation (Indians and Pakistanis), BAPS Shree Swaminarayan Mandir (Gujarati Indians), Gayatri Pariwar Mandir (Gujarati and other Indians), and International Society for Krishna Consciousness (Gujarati and other Indians). Notable numbers of South Asians attend two other sites as well: St. Lambert Roman Catholic Church (Sri Lankans) and Islamic Cultural Center of Greater Chicago (Indians and Pakistanis). Our research pool thus affords us an opportunity to compare and contrast marriage patterns across several religious and ethnic/racial subgroupings within the South Asian American population. We find it helpful to organize our analysis according to the sectarian/mainstream distinction. We will also note where our distinction between individualist and collectivist factors pertain.

### Sectarian Groups

BAPS Swaminarayan Hinduism has a decidedly Gujarati Indian provenance and content. As Raymond Williams (1992, 240) explains, "Swaminarayan Hinduism has grown among Gujarati immigrants because of the effectiveness of an ethnic strategy," including use of Gujarati language and cultural symbols. Nevertheless, the cultural rhetoric invoked by this group emphasizes a larger "Hindu" or "Vedic" identity that will also appeal to Hindu immigrants from other regions of India.

BAPS Swaminarayan Hinduism is equated with true or essential Hinduism. For instance, a biographical sketch of the group's founder included in promotional literature claims that Lord Swaminarayan (b. 1781) "revealed the Vedic Philosophy of Akshar Purushottam [BAPS] worship" and established "one of the most progressive and purest forms of Hinduism." A section titled "Indian Culture" in the Chicago temple's inaugural booklet touts the lasting contributions and values of ancient "Vedic civilization," from science to the family. A book on Indian *mandirs* or temples makes the case that the Swaminarayans of Gujarat are simply "Carrying Forward an Ancient Spiritual Art" of India (Sadhu Shantipriyadas 2000, 116).

One Gujarati woman suggested to us that the Swaminarayan way is naturally attractive to other Indian Hindus since Swaminarayans follow "the right saint" and offer a meaningful and satisfying religious experience. Spouses who are not Swaminarayans initially, she said, will "get interested later on." Indeed, we heard of at least two local cases in which the non-Swaminarayan Hindu spouse eventually converted—in one case the wife; in the other, the husband.

In her research that began as part of our project, Farha Ternikar (2004) found that Swaminarayans stood out from her other Hindu interviewees in unanimously opposing intermarriage with either non-Indians or non-Hindus. Marrying a Hindu from another spiritual lineage is acceptable if that person converts to Swaminarayan Hinduism, but conversion of a Swaminarayan to another Hindu lineage is not. "This religion really makes me who I am today," explained a second-generation Swaminarayan woman (103). "I am not ready to convert. . . . It doesn't matter, as long as I don't have to change religions. And he's willing to convert."

A key lay leader of the Chicago BAPS temple explained why exogamy is far less common among Swaminarayans than in the Indian immigrant community at large. "I think it just comes down to, you know, the BAPS Swaminarayan religion is not a weekend-to-weekend belief. We believe that it should pervade our entire life. If that part is important to you, it just makes sense objectively to find somebody with that in common, because you will save yourself a lot of headache. I mean, it's as simple as that. And if you choose not to do that for whatever reason, it's going to be that much more difficult. That's the way I look at it."

That the strength of the sectarian BAPS identity favors conversion of the non-BAPS spouse recalls Darren Sherkat's (2003) commonsensical insight that the stronger religious spouse usually influences the weaker in matters of religion. The acceptance of converted spouses from other Indian Hindu groups indicates that BAPS Swaminarayans are willing to extend their ethnic boundaries beyond a regional Gujarati identity, but not beyond a panethnic Indian identity.

The ISKCON Hindu case differs in that its core sectarian doctrines undermine ethnic/racial distinctions of all kinds, thereby encouraging marriage beyond

Indian ethnic boundaries. But ISKCON is a complex case, not least given its origins as a new religious movement in the United States. In recent years ISKCON has been increasingly supported and led by Indian immigrants. In his dissertation that grew out of the RICSC Project (extending research to Toronto), Travis Vande Berg (2005) distinguishes several groups within ISKCON temples, including different types of Indian immigrants who affiliate to varying degrees of investment and hold varying understandings of the ISKCON expression of Hinduism. The majority of Indians who attend ISKCON temples are peripheral attendees who practice what inner circle members, or devotees, call a "generic Hinduism." The devotees expressed the distinctly ISKCON doctrines that speak directly to the issue of intermarriage. The following examples demonstrate the loyalty to ISKCON doctrine that we found to be typical in our conversations with devotees.

"Would you ever date or marry someone from another ethnic group?" we asked one Indian devotee in Chicago who was raised in the ISKCON movement and now lives the disciplined religious life of an unmarried householder (*brahmachari*) outside of the temple. "I personally look for qualities of, like if they were actually God-conscious, you know," he responded. "I think that would be more important than what they looked like or who they are, like race or anything like that, you know. How they are as a person really, truly. So I guess, yeah, I would."

"How do you think your parents would feel if you chose to date or marry someone not of your ethnic background?" we followed up.

> I think it might upset them a little bit. Not, you know, not nothing they would really hang onto, I think, 'cause they're pretty open-minded and they'd understand that, you know, that you don't have to be, like especially after being in this movement for a while, you see people from all different creeds, all different races, you know, everything is like, we all come together on one common point which is the Lord Krishna. So I don't think they would really have a problem with it, a longstanding problem with it. I mean like, initially they'd have to work over some of the bumps in the road, but you know.

"How are interethnic/racial couples treated at the ISKCON temple?" we asked an Indian married householder (*grhasta*) devotee in Chicago whose wife comes from a different region of India.

> That works because basically the god is the same thing. They don't see the different castes or different country or different color because they don't identify themselves with body. They see the soul as the same. So whichever country or whichever caste, it's the same soul. And soul is the part and parcel of Krishna. . . . So we don't differentiate based on these criteria. So there is no problem when Krishna is involved because the goal of the life is same for both the partners.

"See, the whole philosophy is to understand that you are not this body," explained another Indian brahmachari devotee. "So I may have an Indian body and you have an American body or, you know, I may have a dog's body or a cat's body. That's not what we look at. We look at . . . that we are a spirit-soul. And then when we marry each other, again, I mentioned that the contact point is keeping Krishna in your center. So if I marry an American body, if I marry some-one in a European body, or somebody in an Indian body, . . . that's not the goal. The goal is that, you know, we come together as a spiritual relationship."

Vande Berg (2005) explains the significance of the body-spirit dichotomy in ISKCON doctrine. One's true essence is spiritual, the "spirit-soul," not one's physical body, which is merely part of the ephemeral material world. This leads most ISKCON devotees, both Westerners and Indians, to use "-bodied language" when referring to different groups of people, such as "white-bodied" for white people and "brown-bodied" for Indian people, ironically downplaying the impor-tance of such superficial categories. By identifying themselves as "brown-bodies," Indian ISKCON devotees have "accepted Krishna Consciousness over [main-stream] Hinduism, [and] they have also accepted the spiritual identities provided by Krishna Consciousness over ethnically or racially based identities" (107).

Doctrinal approbation of interethnic/racial marriage is thus clear in ISKCON Hinduism, as long as the mates are both Krishna Conscious. There is one group of ISKCON devotees, however, who hold a different perspective on their identity that may lead them in another direction. Vande Berg explains that they call themselves "Indians," but not in the usual ethnic sense conveyed by that term. For these ISKCON devotees, who do not employ the "-bodied language" of other devotees, their particular kind of "Indian-ness" reflects the idealized religious culture propounded by ISKCON and purportedly native to ancient India. Vande Berg interviewed several of these "Indians" who "frequently explained that attending ISKCON [temples] was an important strategy in their efforts to ensure that their children remained Indian" (101–102). Obviously, these parents do not want their children to marry non-Indians, and thus favor an Indian endogamy similar to BAPS Swaminarayan Hindus.

Like ISKCON, our third sectarian Hindu group, Gayatri Pariwar Mandir, also holds the potential for exogamy beyond Indian ethnic boundaries. Although endogamous cultural preferences were clearly expressed at this site, so also was the notion that a mixed-ethnic/racial couple could overcome the obstacles through religious compatibility. A woman from the Punjab region of India clearly hoped that her children and grandchildren would continue to value Indian cul-ture, but "That's their life. After awhile, we have to let them go. . . . We brought them up, we give them what we can give them. The rest is up to them, and they have to bring up their family, not me." She wants them to attend temple and keep in touch with the Indian culture it expresses, but in the end, "That's just up to God and them."

A Gayatri Pariwar couple worships together. Photo by Jerry Berndt.

One immigrant man from the Maharashtra region of India, whose sister married a Roman Catholic, admires how their marriage honors both religions and how they encourage their children to choose for themselves. He believes that avoiding excessive religious conservatism and allowing each other to practice their respective religious traditions will help to ensure a healthy and viable intermarriage.

In all three of the sectarian Hindu cases we see ethnic/racial group boundaries expanding to one extent or another. The expansion moves furthest from the initial mono-ethnic/racial parameters of the immigrant group where religious identity is not integrally tied to ethnicity and where individualist notions of identity (e.g., ISKCON and Gayatri) weigh heavier than collectivist notions (e.g., the Swaminarayan emphasis on Vedic Indian-ness).

### Mainstream Groups

Our mainstream sites with significant South Asian constituencies all show potential for exogamy well beyond their current ethnic/racial parameters. Our Roman Catholic interviewees from St. Lambert tended to accept interethnic/racial marriages as long as they involve Catholics. The liberal, post–Vatican II Catholic perspective at this parish differs from the strict ethnocentric endogamy of Indian Knanaya Catholics, for example, who reject all exogamous pairings, including with other Catholics (Ternikar 2004, 97, 107; cf. Williams 1996, 147).

One Sri Lankan man from St. Lambert ticked off the many ethnic groups in that parish—Sri Lankan, Filipino, Indian, Pakistani, Afghani, American—explaining that it doesn't matter to him as long both spouses are Catholic, especially for the sake of the children: "It's more important to family life to have children trying to get the same religion. The religion [is more important] than the other stuff. I mean, we will be trying to tell them, 'Try to keep that,' because we know some families where the father is Buddhist and the mother is Catholic, so the child does not know which way to go. That is a big [problem] for them."

"The hardest thing to do is to marry out of your religion," said a Filipino father from St. Lambert. "Marrying out of your race or culture will not be as bad as marrying into another religion." This person mentioned Baptists and Jews as potentially problematic spousal choices, saying, "That is really hard—not for us, but for the person marrying outside their religion. Because most of our celebrations, when we get together, center around Catholic festivities." St. Lambert has worked assiduously to accommodate the various ethnic-specific Catholic expressions within its diverse membership.

Another St. Lambert member, a Cuba-born man raised in America, pointed to potential problems for practicing Catholics in interreligious marriages: "I cannot tell my children 'No.' It has to be their choice. [But] I would just make them aware, make them very much aware of the difficulties that that would pose because we are practicing Catholics." This person opened the possibility of marrying a non-Catholic Christian, again noting that ethnicity/race is not the issue: "We are a Catholic family and that plays a role in our lives. I think it's okay, for example, if they would marry someone who is not Catholic but still Christian. That would be easier. . . . [T]he one thing that I have to say to my kids is, 'I don't care if you marry white, black, Chinese, Japanese, whatever it is, okay. So long as they make you happy. I would like for you to marry somebody who is a Catholic because that would play a part in your lives.' But, again, it's not my choice to make. It's their choice to make."

Immigrant members of Naperville Church of the Brethren show signs of accepting marriages outside of their Gujarati ethnic boundaries as long as both spouses are Christian. As one youth explained, in agreement with the others in our focus group interview, "If you don't want to have any problems [with your parents], they should be at least Indian and definitely Christian, that's the number one thing. Our parents have all stressed that the number one thing is [being] Christian, but like it's hard for us to find that just because there are not a lot of Indian Christians, and even [more] there's not a lot of Gujarati Christians."

This statement implies the hierarchy of marital preferences in the immigrant generation at Naperville Church: first Gujarati Christian, then Indian Christian, then non-Indian Christian, but in any case "definitely Christian." This last caveat certainly has Indian Hindus and Muslims primarily in mind, but it would hold for non-Christians of any ethnicity/race. The pool of potential Gujarati or Indian Christians includes members of several Christian denominations. The small size of this pool, however, makes choosing a non-Indian Christian spouse much more likely, and this has caused intergenerational tensions at Naperville Church and other Indian Christian churches in the United States (see Kurien 2004, 179).

The Naperville congregation's acceptance of interracial marriage was tested during our research period when the daughter of a prominent church family married a white Christian man she met at an American college. Although everyone wondered what this marriage might mean for future trends among the second generation, the marriage seemed well received by all.

Both mosques we studied have multiethnic congregations today, although they differ as to which ethnic group has been preeminent in number and/or influence for most of their respective histories. At Islamic Foundation (established 1974), South Asians have predominated from the start; at Islamic Cultural Center of Greater Chicago, Bosnians have had preeminent influence as far back as the parent organization (established 1906). Bosnians continue to dominate even though their numbers have somewhat diminished recently relative to other ethnic groups attending the mosque, including Arabs and South Asians.

Two significant and related views of intermarriage emerged from interviews at both mosques. First, Islam accepts, even encourages, interethnic/racial marriages among Muslims. "The way Islam is structured," explained a young second-generation woman from Islamic Foundation, "it's not a culture, it's a religion. And you can structure a culture around Islam. . . . Islam is the skeleton and your culture is the flesh. So, I don't feel it's so necessary to marry into your own race." Muslims from a variety of ethnic backgrounds growing up in the United States are forging a new cultural identity through their shared religious identity as American Muslims: "Especially in America, 'cause yeah, I'm Pakistani, but I think I'd be able to relate to an Arab girl who grew up here more than I could a Pakistani who's from Pakistan. You know what I mean? Like growing up in America is its own culture, I think, so I would rather marry an Arab guy who grew up in America than a Pakistani FOB [a "Fresh Off the Boat" immigrant]. I couldn't handle it."

"Yeah, it's great," another young Indian woman opined regarding immigrant Muslims marrying across ethnic lines. "The main basis would be religion. If the religion is the same, I don't think it will cause a problem, especially when everyone is in America, it's a whole different ballgame. So, yeah, we have the best of both worlds. If you have like a Middle Eastern mom and an Indian/Pakistani dad, you get the best of both worlds. You have access to another language, you have access to another culture, different types of food, you know."

Despite such multicultural advantages to interethnic marriages, this interviewee prefers a fellow Indian/Pakistani mate. The complications of arranging a marriage—"and that's the only kind of marriage I would go for"—across too wide of a culture gap seem daunting: "I think that would be just another factor that would complicate matters." This person is not alone in this view—Islamic doctrine may permit it, but Muslim parents are not always prepared to accept interethnic/racial spouses for their children. "When I look at that," summarized one youth, "what I see is that our generation might be ready for it, but our parents' generation isn't."

Farha Ternikar (2004) confirms that generational tensions exist in Chicago's South Asian American Muslim community regarding interethnic/racial marriages among Muslims, including marriage across ethnic lines within the South Asian population (whether across nationalities, e.g., Indian-Pakistani, or across regions, e.g., Hyderabadi-Bihari). The American-born second generation appears generally open to interethnic/racial marriage among Muslims—Ternikar points to a popular Muslim matrimonial Internet site, Naseeb.com, that touts its multi-ethnic/racial clientele. Ternikar's findings in Chicago are consistent with a Houston study that found a clear trend toward ethnic exogamy in young Muslim marriages (Leonard 2003b). Garbi Schmidt's (2004b) research among Muslim youth in Denmark, Sweden, and the United States likewise uncovered an increasingly panethnic Muslim identity that rejects the immigrant generation's cultural expressions of Islam. The influence of mainstream, modernist Islam (see Esposito 1998, chap. 4; Khan 2003) seems crucial here: almost all of Ternikar's Muslim interviewees who approved of interethnic/racial marriage had renegotiated their Islamic perspectives in light of the American context and moved away from the more traditional conservatism of South Asian Islam; conversely, all of Ternikar's traditionally conservative Muslim interviewees disapproved of interethnic/racial marriage. Most of the Muslims we interviewed—of any generation—expressed modernist Islamic views of intermarriage.

"What if your daughter wanted to marry an Arab Muslim or a black Muslim?" we asked a 1.5-generation Indian woman at Islamic Foundation. "I would be absolutely okay with it. I would look at the person, I would not look at his race. . . . [But] if he was not Muslim, then, oh boy!" This leads us to the second religiously based view of intermarriage that emerged from our interviews—namely, that Islam rejects interreligious marriages. There is one exception to this prohibition: Islamic law allows a Muslim man to marry a Jewish or Christian woman, although a Muslim woman cannot do likewise.[3] The key legal assumption here has to do with the differing marital roles of the spouses and the implications for religious practices in the home. Islam assumes male headship of the family; thus the husband determines the religious practices of his wife and children. Under the Qur'anic principle of no compulsion in religion, a Muslim husband should allow his Jewish or Christian wife the freedom to practice her own religion, but this freedom may or may not be accorded a Muslim wife by a Jewish or Christian husband, who would be expected to convert to Islam. A Muslim husband should ensure that the children be raised as Muslims no matter the religious identity of his wife.

Of course the ideal arrangement between a Muslim husband and a non-Muslim wife does not always work out smoothly in practice. One second-generation

Indian woman from Islamic Foundation estimated that in only two of the ten marriages she knew of between Muslim husbands and Christian wives did the wife pay proper attention to the children's Muslim training, and these two wives eventually converted to Islam. It is difficult to quantify the total number and types of intermarriages at the two mosques in this study. We received inconsistent estimates of the number of intermarriages at Islamic Foundation, but a far more consistent sense that there are a significant number of intermarriages at Islamic Cultural Center, perhaps due to this mosque's much longer history.

### Overview of the South Asian Case

Ternikar (2004) argues that all second-generation South Asian Americans are negotiating their ethnic/racial and religious identities. Although intermarriage rates remain relatively low at this time, "marriage patterns among South Asian second-generation immigrants are changing to reflect their status as American immigrants. Second-generation *desi* [South Asian American] identity is a construction that reinforces pan-ethnic Asian identity and lends itself to facilitating interethnic marriages" (108, 116–117). She summarizes regarding all groups: "Low rates of interfaith marriage indicate that it is religion more than race and ethnicity that continues to matter for South Asian immigrants" (84).

Second-generation South Asian Muslims, more so than their Hindu and Christian counterparts, are creating a pan–South Asian religious identity in which interethnic marriages, especially between Indian and Pakistani Muslims, will be accepted more readily than by the immigrant generation. But Ternikar also reports that significant numbers of her Hindu and Christian interviewees also hold a presumption in favor of religious identity over ethnic/racial identity. On the whole, Hinduism will likely encourage a pan-Indian ethnicity, but it will contribute little to larger ethnic/racial amalgamations. Only groups like ISKCON and Gayatri, which deemphasize ethnic identity markers, will break out of the Indian ethnic/racial boundaries. With regard to an emerging pan–South Asian ethnic group in America, most Hindu groups will form a religious subgrouping while South Asian Christians and Muslims will expand according to their respective larger religious identities. As Ternikar notes, out-marriage between South Asians and non-South Asians is more common among Christians and Muslims than among Hindus. When South Asian Christians marry white Christians or South Asian Muslims marry Arab Muslims, for instance, religious identity is preserved at the expense of ethnic/racial identity.

## Major Ethnic/Racial Groupings

Many observers see an emergent reordering of the major American ethnic/racial categories—white, black, Hispanic, Asian—in which intermarriage plays a key role in redefining group boundaries and identities. In a section titled "Will the Descendants of Today's Immigrants Become 'White'?," Nancy Foner (2000, 229) states that "High rates of intermarriage—and the growing number of multiracial offspring—are also an indication that we are moving toward a new kind of racial order." Foner and others (e.g., Jacoby 2004; Lee and Bean 2004; Sanjek 1994; Smith and Edmondston 1997) lay out several possible scenarios for the future, including a true melting pot where all racial distinctions fuse into brown, or perhaps a new black/nonblack divide that will replace the historic black/white divide, with African Americans and other blacks (e.g., black immigrant groups) on one side and, on the other side, whites, Hispanics, and Asians who are willing to marry among themselves but not with blacks (cf. Fu 2003). Asian American intermarriage trends have also attracted scholarly attention. The two most important directions here are Asian-white intermarriages, which may be around 40 percent among younger couples (Smith and Edmondston 1997; cf. Saenz et al. 1995), and pan-Asian marital trends, including cluster groups of East Asians and South Asians (Fu 2003; Lee et al. 1998; Min 2002). Asian American youth seem particularly prone to adopt pan-Asian identities over either an "American" label or their immigrant parents' national identities (Portes and Rumbaut 2001).

As reconfigured ethnic/racial boundaries emerge, religion will no doubt have an important influence, given the impact of religion on marriage and family formation. The content and intensity of religious sectarianism will be especially pertinent.

### Sectarian Groups

We detected the least resistance to exogamy at our two Buddhist temples, both of which represent sectarian expressions of Buddhism and emphasize individualist notions of identity. No one at Ling Shen Ching Tze Temple, the Chinese True Buddha School affiliate, expressed any reservations about the issue. "That's their choice, that's really their choice," said a key female lay leader about dating across religious traditions. "If they can get along well, you know, to me as a Buddhist, I don't think there will be any conflicts at all because we feel that there's no need to, how to say that, we do not force anyone, okay? Everyone is in here because they want to come here."

As to interreligious marriage, the temple is not proprietary. If a prospective couple is Buddhist and Catholic, "those two have to make the decision where they want to be married, okay. If they want to be married in this temple, we will help them, we will have the [spiritual] master in here do the service for them. If they want to do it in the Catholic church, if we are their friends and they invite us, we are more than happy to be there." This member described her own marriage to a Catholic husband. She feels that her soul belongs to the Buddha, but his soul belongs to God, and that this is so for others as well. Their son alternates weekly in attending the temple and a Catholic church, and they will grant him the choice of which to identify with as he gets older and which to send his own children to. Buddhists accept Christianity because it teaches people to be good, she explained. The temple must do the same and help others to be good. If everyone is good, then society will not have any problems.

One member, a Taiwanese man whose Christian wife attends Ling Shen Ching Tze, noted that the most common intermarriage in the temple is between Buddhists and secular individuals. But that is "Okay, because our master teacher says, 'If you trust the teacher, yeah, go ahead [and marry].' So we don't say, 'Oh, that's no good and we are bad, we're not doing that.'"

At the Korean Buddhist site, HanMaUm Zen Center, some interviewees expressed their own or others' concerns about intermarriage, but every one of them followed up with positive evaluations. All Buddhist parents are probably sad when their children marry non-Buddhists, one religious leader speculated, though some deal with it better than others, especially through Buddhist teachings. "Buddhism doesn't really restrict you from having other religions per se, or practicing, but it just helps you to understand the universal principle of the world and the universe per se." Families should attend a church or a temple, but whichever they choose, they should "believe in a more general principle." As to interethnic/racial marriages, "go for it, because they love each other." After all, "it's America, you know."

"It will be nice if they have the same religion," said a female temple member of HanMaUm. Barring that, they need only share understanding and respect, and "try to understand that ultimately the goal is the same for every different religion." If the couple are "really religious, selfishness and ego are not existing." She challenged the conventional wisdom about cultural compatibility and marriage: "Doesn't matter, ethnic groups—I married a Korean but I still got divorced."

We asked a white man from HanMaUm who married a Korean woman for his thoughts on intermarriage. "From the Buddhist perspective, the only difference is that of form. The essential nature of all living beings is identical. It's just that things are manifested in different ways. . . . The thing about Zen is that it's all about the state of your mind, you know. And often they're willing to either make or break rules and do whatever it takes to change your consciousness. So, what I like about Zen is usually there aren't a lot of rules at all. There's not a lot of prescriptive stuff, 'Oh, you have to do this, you have to do that, you can't do this, you can't do that.'"

In other words, proscriptions against intermarriage do not stem from Zen Buddhist teachings, although they may stem from ethnocentricity. But even that seems to be weakening in America. "I think that they are well accepted," one Korean woman said of mixed couples at HanMaUm. "Especially where we live here, we live in America. We are from Korea—it's not like you're living in Korea, seeing the inter-religions or different ethnic people getting married. So it's more open and well accepted [here in America]." Earlier we noted the social pressures against immigrant groups maintaining their specific complex of Old World religious and ethnic/racial identities in the new American context. These Korean Buddhists draw upon Buddhist teachings that, in principle at least, sever the link between Korean-ness and Buddhism.

Buddhism will likely contribute to a white-Asian intermixture given its lack of doctrinal support for endogamy and the relatively large number of white Americans interested in this religion (see Perreira 2004 for a provocative study of one California Thai temple). Although beset by racial tensions throughout its history (Numrich 2003), Buddhism in America has turned a corner in self-awareness and seems ready to honor shared Buddhist identity over ethnic/racial distinctions (Tanaka 2001).

At Victory Outreach Church we encountered no mention of ethnicity or race in our conversations about intermarriage. Here the primary importance of Pentecostal identity came through in the language used to answer our questions. "We are not a religion," a second-generation Mexican man clarified for us. "What we are is just Christians. We are Bible believers." Rejecting the notion that Christianity is just one religion among other religions, a human creation rather than a revelation from God, is common in conservative Christian circles. This interviewee continued: "Okay, now, as far as people marrying other religions from here [Victory Outreach Church], you know, if they are really faithful members, they would not even consider marrying a person from another sect."

A religious leader of Victory Outreach agreed that interreligious marriage is scripturally unacceptable:

> No, because we teach [that] the Bible says for us not to be tied to the unyoked, you know, to marry of the same kind because if you try to marry with a different religion, they would bring a lot of controversy, a lot of disputes into the marriage, they would not have nothing in common. This person will believe this way, and this person will believe that way, and they won't have like nothing in common. There would be a lot of controversy, you know. So we try to tell the people to marry their own kind, not culturally wise, no, no, no, to marry as far as their religion, if you want to call it religious background. I mean Christian marries Christians. No, a Christian will not marry a person from other religions, you know what I mean?

Another Victory Outreach leader specified what being a Christian means in familiar conservative language: "We have never married anyone that is not serving the Lord, or that doesn't know the Lord. This is the way we are working." Thus marriage preferences here can extend well beyond the Hispanic identity of the congregation to Pentecostals (and other conservative Christians) of any ethnic/racial group.

Synagogue FREE is affiliated with Lubavitch Hasidism, a sectarian branch of Orthodox Judaism centered in Russia. The preferred marriage hierarchy here moves out from Russian Lubavitch Jews, to other Russian Orthodox Jews, to Orthodox Jews of other ethnicities—in other words, across Orthodox Jewish ethnic boundaries but not beyond. Here we see a strong collectivist expression of Orthodox Jewish identity.

Several interviewees emphasized the invalidity of out-marriage according to Orthodox Jewish law. Asked whether there had been any interreligious marriages performed at Synagogue FREE, one woman replied, "That can't be in the Orthodox synagogue." Another woman explained, "If they are Jews marrying non-Jews, their marriage is not valid according to the Jewish law. There is no marriage as such. I am not going to say how it is called in the Jewish law because it is not a very flattering name."[4] She noted that marriage between Ashkenazi and Sephardic Jews "poses some difficulties, but nevertheless it works." We assume she had only Orthodox spouses in mind.

Several interviewees used the word "national" when referring to what we would call "ethnic" Orthodox Jews. "I have a negative attitude toward that," a female Russian immigrant in her fifties said about intermarriage, "because, [as if] there are not enough problems in marriages in general, if it doubles with national problems, the marriage will fall apart. I am against mixed marriages." She was willing to grant the legitimacy of interreligious involvement only between older individuals who would produce no offspring as a result. Romantic liaisons will happen at any age: "Of course, we are all living people," she quipped. But if young people are involved, then it is definitely both "sad" and "negative."

"There are those who think that since the Jews have suffered so much, their marriages should be mono-national in order to replenish the Jewish population," an elderly immigrant opined. The concern about exogamous marriage is heightened in an America immigrant context. An elderly Russian couple referred to the Lubavitch community enclave in this country: "[Wife:] It is because of our closed circle. [Husband:] It has to do with that, as our son says, he lives not in America but in the Jewish community that is located in America." It was different for them in Russia: "[Wife:] The fact is that when we were in Russia, it didn't make any difference to us. And now he wouldn't do that. [Husband:] Yes, that's right because it has changed with our conversion to Judaism, both in our heads and in our hearts." This couple had been secular Jews in Russia but became interested in Lubavitch Hasidism after their son joined a Chabad center in Italy. They affiliated with Synagogue FREE upon coming to Chicago in order to become more religious, the conversion they referenced.

No one from Synagogue FREE expressed resignation about the inevitability of exogamous marriage in American society. There was a good deal of hand wringing over the number of Jewish out-marriages, but, at the same time, we detected a clear resolution to address and "correct the situation," as one religious leader put it. This can occur through the conversion (*giyur*) of a non-Jewish spouse.

"Judaism forbids its followers to marry people of different faiths," explained a lay leader of the synagogue. For such unions to be legitimate, the non-Jewish spouse must convert through "a special ritual that has always existed in Judaism, from antiquity—it is called giyur." Mixed families that come from Russia present "a very difficult problem," according to this person, since their marriage is not recognized by Jewish law, yet, even so, no rabbi would ever counsel the Jewish partner to dissolve the marriage. The non-Jewish spouse must do giyur, and, if it is the wife, so must the children since they are not considered Jewish. "By no means is there any element of chauvinism or racism [in this]. It is just a law of the religion. Judaism deeply respects all nations and all faiths . . . but the law with regard to the Jewish family is very clear too."

According to this source, Synagogue FREE conducts few giyurs because of the complexity and commitment involved. He contrasted the practice among Orthodox Jews with that in Reform Judaism, where little more than a statement of intention before a rabbi is required.

> As for Orthodox Judaism, it is not quite so easy to do giyur because a person who wants to convert to Judaism must study quite seriously with a rabbi. And sometimes, essentially speaking, this newly converted Jew must have perhaps even deeper knowledge of Judaism than a Jew by birth. . . . Once those people have done giyur, they are called *ger*, and they are enormously respected in the community. By no means are they treated as a second-grade people. On the contrary, they are Jews with all the rights who are very much respected.

One woman provided an interesting theological insight into such Jewish converts and the respect they command: "The opinion of Torah about people going through giyur is known. Jewish souls got into non-Jewish bodies for some sins, they were born in a non-Jewish family, and that soul constantly seeks realization as a Jewish soul, seeks returning into Jewishness. This is how Torah explains the origins of *giyum,* that is, non-Jewish people who convert into Jewishness. So, how do I treat those people? There is a law that prescribes how to treat them. One has to support them, help them as one can."

Out-marriage has concerned Jewish leaders for many years. Jonathan D. Sarna (2003) cites compelling evidence of diminishing Jewish identity, including a survey of the Boston Jewish community in which only one-third of unmarried adult respondents thought it was very important to marry someone Jewish. But as Dashefsky, Lazerwitz, and Tabory (2003) suggest, the decision of whether or not to raise the children as Jews may be more important to the perpetuation of Jewish identity than the fact of intermarriage per se. In any event, overall Jewish marriage patterns will likely remain within the parameters of the white population. Orthodox Jewish trends are worth watching since this branch of Judaism stresses endogamy to a much greater degree than other branches (Dashefsky, Lazerwitz, and Tabory 2003; "Poll: American Jews Accept Intermarriage"). Only intermarriages between Orthodox Jews of Ashkenazi (European) and Sephardic (non-European) ancestries would cross relatively wide ethnic/racial boundaries.

Conversion is also emphasized at Holy Virgin Protection Cathedral, a sectarian Russian Orthodox congregation, especially for the sake of raising the children of a mixed marriage as Orthodox Christians. "We try and demand that if the other side is not Orthodox, they should at least agree that their children would be Orthodox," said an elderly religious leader of the congregation. As to intermarriage, he continued, "Generally, it is not desirable, because then a family is broken apart." According to this interviewee, several intermarriages with Americans had occurred in the congregation, and several immigrant members had entered into intermarriages in Russia before coming to America—for instance, with Jews, Armenians, and Georgians. But they should all baptize their children in the church, he said. And the non-Orthodox spouses should convert—that way the parish will grow, he said with a chuckle.

An immigrant layperson thought that, for most of the intermarried couples at Holy Virgin Protection, the non-Orthodox spouse had converted or at least had adopted Orthodox practices. "In fact, there are practically no such conflicting couples [here]," he claimed. "Those who come, they live according to the Orthodox canons. And nobody ever asks them what religious background they have. There are ethnic Jews whom nobody even asks who they are, who their parents or grandparents are. They come to church, they are Orthodox people." Pointing to two interethnic marriages in the congregation, one Russian Serbian, the other Russian American, he contended that their shared Orthodox identity has overcome any ethnic contradictions and problems they might have had. Other intermarried couples may behave differently, but they have left the church, "and I don't see them, therefore I can't say."

This interviewee bemoaned the effects on the Orthodox spouse and the children when a non-Orthodox spouse takes a "negative attitude . . . , because a person must keep their faith, he must have an opportunity to live in his tradition. By the way, I have the same position with regard to the children. If their marriage doesn't interfere with observing their religious tradition and partaking of its wisdom and grace in the church language, then one can bless such a marriage despite all difficulties. But if it leads to rupture, to tearing apart from their religion, then it is not good."

Others agreed that affinity at least, if not official affiliation, is key. A second-generation woman, whose father remained Catholic for many years of marriage before converting, summarized the feeling of the congregation: "I think much depends on the potential or actual conversion of the non-Orthodox spouse. If the non-Orthodox spouse seems to be absent from our church completely—that is, takes no interest in an important part of his spouse's or her spouse's religion—it would be evaluated negatively. If we see at least some interest, I think it is valued more positively."

An immigrant woman told of a female relative who had married an African and then moved to Africa. After some difficult initial adjustments, the couple has now been happily married for more than fifteen years, due in large part to the fact that she has kept her religion. But such unions would seem uncommon in Orthodox Christian circles. Like our other Russian congregation, Synagogue FREE, ethnic/racial boundaries at Holy Virgin Protection are expanding as the Russian ethnicity at the heart of the group's identity erodes and the religious aspects of their respective identities come to the fore. In both cases, it is likely that marital choices will not extend far beyond the white population group.

### Mainstream Groups

We introduced the Roman Catholic and Muslim cases above in discussing South Asians. In both cases strong liberal or modernist views support interethnic/racial marriage within the respective religious boundaries. Yet we also picked up indications of a number of marriages with non-Catholic Christians in our Chicago sites—for instance, with Protestants at Five Holy Martyrs. One St. Lambert member, herself of Greek and German ancestries, explained that her family had no objection when some relatives married Egyptian Copts since "they're all Christians." Rita George Tvrtkovic (2001), a Chicago Archdiocese staffer married to a Bosnian husband of Catholic-Muslim heritage, cites an estimate that approximately 40 percent of all American Catholics are married to non-Catholics, mostly Christians of other denominations. Marriages beyond that, says Tvrtkovic, such as Christian-Muslim, present more challenges to the couples, draw more disapprobation "from their families, ethnic group and/or society at large," and thus require "especially sensitive and informed pastoral care."

Trends among most second-generation Muslims point in a postethnic or cosmopolitan direction wherein the ethnic consciousness of their immigrant forbears will weaken over time (Leonard 2003b). An emerging American Islam may well include a large pan–South Asian subgroup, as noted above, but it will likely expand to include other ethnic/racial groupings as well. There are already some notable intermarriage trends in this regard—namely, between Muslim immigrants and white and black Americans, in both cases often leading to the conversion of the non-Muslim partner. The intriguing growth in the number of Hispanic Muslims also suggests increasing intermarriage in this direction as well (Smith 1999).

One significant factor mentioned at both of the mosques we studied is the influence of the American context on spousal choices. A white lay leader from Islamic Cultural Center who converted after marrying her Muslim husband described what she sees around her: "Usually it's an American and another, like an American and an Egyptian, or an American and a Bosnian or a Palestinian. Once in a while you'll see a Bosnian and a Palestinian. I guess, because this is America, that's what we'll see mostly [namely, intermarriage with Americans]."

Thus both Catholics and Muslims will contribute to the breakdown of the boundaries between the major ethnic/racial groupings in America. Protestants likewise have this potential, as with Naperville Church of the Brethren. The members of Truth Lutheran Church, the Chinese Protestant congregation, tend to look down upon marrying non-Christians. This generally means either Chinese Buddhists or secularists raised on the communist Chinese mainland. "We pray hard for the husband" if he is not a Christian, said one Truth Lutheran member. "We want to convert them," said another. This interviewee finds Catholic spouses much more acceptable than Buddhists because Catholicism is similar to her own brand of Christianity: "If you count Christian and Catholic as separate, we have that kind of families. And some of the Catholics convert to Christian. But overall we have the same Bible, the preaching and teaching, the practices are the same, so I don't think that they are separate. For the others, if it is a Buddhist, it is hard." The perceptive reader will note the common evangelical distinction between "Christian" and "Catholic" in this statement, but that does not diminish the point that this woman has expanded the boundaries of what counts as acceptable religious endogamy. It is a short step then toward ethnic/racial exogamy within Christianity.

As to the ethnic/racial marital preferences of Truth Lutheran Church, most members, especially "the older, more conservative, the grandmas and grandpas and stuff, you know," as one person put it, prefer marriage to Chinese. One woman, herself married to a white man of mixed European ancestry, said she would be a little unhappy if her daughter married a Japanese man but very unhappy if her daughter married a man who "doesn't believe God. I will insist, tell her 'No,' because I think that's serious." She described a video shown recently at the church, from which she drew the lesson that belief in God is necessary for peace and good fortune at all levels: "It's really so true now, no peace because they don't believe God. I think the important thing is the need to believe God. . . . [I]f you believe God you are lucky, if you have whole family believe God, whole family lucky, whole city, whole country believe God, lucky, just like America. God bless America because a lot of persons believe God, they are lucky." Of course, many such Americans are not Chinese.

How does Truth Lutheran Church respond to mixed marriages? One of the congregation's religious leaders said, "I think we are open to it." "Most important is to have the same faith. Yeah, so a different race is not a big issue. . . . [W]e encourage them to have the same faiths, we believe that's the main factor to having a happy marriage." Given overall Asian American intermarriage patterns, we expect Chinese Protestants to contribute to intermarriage with white Christians.

We also considered the Greek Orthodox case earlier. We have no doubt that most members of St. Demetrios prefer marriages to remain within the Greek Orthodox fold. "You see, most Greeks believe that you should marry someone who is from the same country and the same religion," a thirty-year-old second-generation woman explained. "They have that belief, usually older people. And they don't agree if somebody married someone with a different religion. Personally, it doesn't bother me."

This interviewee alludes to the breakdown of the immigrant generation's preference in later generations. Another second-generation woman expressed her preference for a practicing non–Greek Orthodox spouse over a non-practicing Greek Orthodox one: "To me it's more important to be Orthodox as opposed to marrying somebody that's Greek that doesn't believe in the religion for whatever reason. So, religion, in my opinion, is more important." Here the boundaries of acceptable religious identity have expanded from Greek Orthodoxy to Orthodoxy generally. As one religious leader put it, "The one common bond that we share is not our Greek identity, but our Orthodox religion. That's what comes first within the [Orthodox] churches." But as we noted earlier, intermarriages at St. Demetrios have moved significantly beyond Orthodox boundaries to include Catholics, many of them Mexican. This contributes to the breakdown of the boundary between whites and Hispanics.

### Overview of Major Ethnic/Racial Groupings

As noted earlier, many observers of American demographic trends see an eventual reconfiguration of the major white, black, Hispanic, and Asian ethnic/racial categories, especially through intermarriage, resulting in what Nancy Foner (2000, 229) calls "a new kind of racial order." Proposed eventualities include a true melting pot where all racial distinctions fuse into brown, or, alternatively, the so-called black/nonblack divide. Religion has the motivational power to bridge deep ethnic/racial divides, even though this has occurred relatively infrequently in American history (Emerson and Kim 2003; Jenkins 2003).[5] Based on our analysis of immigrant marriage preferences and patterns, the following religions possess the doctrinal resources to cross current white/black/Hispanic/Asian group boundaries as well as the potential black/nonblack divide of the future: Roman Catholicism, Protestantism, Islam, Buddhism, and some expressions of Hinduism.

## Implications for Group Identity and Social Distance

"Trends in exogamy are significant because social scientists conceive of racial/ethnic intermarriage as a measure of decreasing social distance, declining racial/ethnic prejudice, and changing racial/ethnic group boundaries" (Lee and Bean 2004, 228). Scholars of both ethnicity/race and immigration often ignore or underappreciate religious factors that might help to shape the contours of America's emerging new ethnic/racial order. For instance, in their chapter on immigrant marriage patterns, Bean and Stevens (2003) make no mention at all of religion, not even when discussing social factors that affect spousal choices. Likewise, Portes and Rumbaut (2001) do not include religion in their analysis of factors that shape ethnic identities in second-generation immigrant children.[6] Others pay too little attention to religion, hardly moving beyond the Protestant-Catholic-Jew triple melting pot discussion (e.g., Lee et al. 1998; Lieberson and Waters 1988; Spickard 1989). Even here scholars too often ignore obvious questions involving religious factors. One wonders, for instance, whether the intriguing growth in Asian-Hispanic marriages reported by Lee et al. (1998) might be due in part to pairings of Catholic spouses from each group, not merely to geographic propinquity and shared immigrant experiences as the authors speculate.

The literature on recent immigrant religions has a slightly better record with regard to religious factors in intermarriage and implications for group identities (Alumkal 2001; Chai 1998; Chong 1998; Kurien 2004; Perreira 2004), but more systematic analysis is needed. Insightfully, Ebaugh and Chafetz (2000b) note that marital partner preferences provide one indication of how immigrant congregations prioritize their ethnic/racial identities vis-à-vis their religious identities. A strong majority (nine of thirteen) of the immigrant congregations in their Houston study emphasized the importance of religious identity over ethnic/racial identity, consistent with our assertion that religion becomes increasingly more salient than ethnicity/race as immigrant group identity evolves in the American context. As we have seen across the sixteen research sites in Chicago, marrying within the faith remains important even as the boundaries of the faith shift, especially as the acceptable ethnic/racial boundaries of the faith expand to varying degrees from group to group.

Implications for the civic engagement patterns of immigrant religious groups are significant. Intermarriage decreases social distances between groups and affects the evolving contours of group identities, in turn contributing to the reconfiguration of American society. Immigrant groups tend to be pulled outward from themselves, but in what directions and to what extent depends in large measure on religious factors within each group and in the larger society as well.

# 8

## Language in Immigrant Congregations

RELIGIOUS AND CIVIC
CONSIDERATIONS

*[The word] is an act, an attitude, a taking one's stand
and an exercise of power, and in every word there is
something creative.*

—Gerardus van der Leeuw (1938)

For their first field assignment, each member of our project team visited a different immigrant Buddhist temple in the Chicago area. They knew none of the non-English vernaculars spoken at the temples, such as Vietnamese, Japanese, or Thai, nor the nonvernacular ritual languages, such as Pali or Sanskrit. Moreover, they knew precious little about the specific Buddhist identities or civic engagement patterns of these temples. By the end of the project, we expected our research team to know how religious identity can structure language usage in an immigrant congregation and how such language usage can reflect or shape an immigrant congregation's relationship with outside groups.

The facade of the oldest Korean Buddhist temple in Chicago featured unpretentious signage in both Korean and English, the latter reading simply "Buddhist Temple," the only indication that the facility, a converted apartment building, served a religious function. Throughout our visit, including the social time after the religious service, a number of members spoke to us about the temple's history and current operations, and also translated ritual and conversational speech into English for our benefit. We talked to the lay founder of the temple, the current abbot, and second-generation members of the temple, all of whom shared their impressions of the pulse of the congregation. During the service, two members, a Korean woman and a Hispanic woman who had converted to Buddhism, teamed up to translate the abbot's "sermon" (their term) for us, passing handwritten notes back and forth between themselves, then between themselves and us, the whole process generating some interesting exchanges about Buddhist doctrines. Clearly the two women were not simply translating the monk's words but interpreting them as well, adding their understandings of Buddhism to his in presenting us with a meaningful explanation. A printed manual available in the

Immigrant congregations negotiate language boundaries in multiple ways. Photo by Jerry Berndt.

pews contained both vernacular Korean and English translations of the ritual elements of the service.

How does an immigrant congregation present itself publicly through linguistic channels? Who represents the congregation to the outside world and how? What audiences, internal and external, does an immigrant congregation address, and how in each case? How are issues of translation resolved, particularly regarding traditional religious terms, doctrines, texts, and rituals? In sum, what linguistic choices do immigrant congregations make, to further what religious ends, and with what civic consequences? Such considerations guide the present chapter, informed by the religious distinctions discussed in part 1.

## Language Usage in Immigrant Communities and Congregations

The immigration literature, both classical and recent, places language "at the core of the immigrant experience," to quote the introduction to a collection of seminal essays on post-1965 trends. "Language signifies identity and social relations and is structured by power relations. Therefore, it is not surprising that language matters are the focus of many debates over immigration, especially in the United States" (Suarez-Orozco, Suarez-Orozco, and Qin-Hilliard 2001, ix). America's historic assimilationist expectations make language the key to the cultural evolution of immigrant populations and organizations, as Portes and Rumbaut (2006, 207) explain: "Unlike many European nations, which are tolerant of linguistic diversity, in the United States the acquisition of nonaccented English and the dropping of foreign languages represent the litmus test of Americanization. Other aspects of immigrant culture (such as cuisine, community celebrations, and religion . . .) often last for several generations, but the home language seldom survives." Immigrant transition to English usage is as rapid today as always. Despite some variation across groups—for instance, less English adoption by Latinos than by Asians—Portes and Hao (1998, 288) can generalize, "English is alive and well among second-generation youths, but the languages their immigrant parents brought with them are not."

Its institutional prominence makes the congregation an important venue for the language evolution of the larger immigrant community. The "language question," wrote one historian of classical American immigration, "had its greatest impact upon the life of the immigrant churches" (Jones 1960, 76). The predominant model has been that of straight-line assimilation, often entailing conflict within congregations—moving from the primacy of the Old World vernacular during the first generation, through bilingualism with the rise of the second generation, to English-only usage by the third generation (e.g., Dolan 1975; Jick 1976; Nyholm 1963; Saloutos 1973). Niebuhr (1957, 212) stressed the inexorability of the process: "The choice between accommodation [assimilation] and extinction finally became a forced choice. Though churches may delay the moment of their surrender few elect to perish with their mother tongue."

The larger language question for immigrant congregations has become significantly more complex in the post-1965 period for three main reasons. First, the multiplicity of languages and dialects has reached remarkable proportions in many immigrant congregations, for instance in Catholic parishes serving several immigrant groups, Chinese Protestant churches with members from various territories of China and the Chinese diaspora, and Hindu temples that accommodate the diversity of Indian regional/linguistic identities. Second, post-1965 waves have constantly replenished the immigrant generation, unlike in the classical period of American immigration when that generation was virtually terminated by the 1924 immigration act. Today, Old World vernacular speakers keep arriving, even as English speakers are born and raised here. Third, social acceptance of multiculturalism, and thus multilingualism, is higher today than at any time in the nation's history. Assimilation still exerts tremendous power, but in a segmented fashion in immigrant lives (Portes and Zhou 1993), meaning that straight-line evolution toward English usage may be circumvented or stretched out in immigrant congregations (Yang 1999).

Ebaugh and Chafetz (2000a; cf. 2000b, chap. 20) discuss three language dilemmas found in recent immigrant congregations, dilemmas they characterize as having no optimal solutions. One revolves around retaining the second generation. In attempting to re-create the cultural ambiance of their homeland, including language patterns, the immigrant generation risks alienating their American-acculturated offspring. A second dilemma involves accommodating the language needs of multilingual congregations. Should one language prevail as a symbol of congregational unity, or should separate, language-specific programming be instituted or tolerated, jeopardizing the ideal of unity by creating language-based special interest constituencies? A third dilemma concerns the status of a ritual language that may not be understood by some or all of the members of the congregation. Should this language be translated for the sake of understanding, or should it remain unintelligible while presumably retaining its sacred qualities?

Like most scholars of recent American immigrant religions, Ebaugh and Chafetz (2000b) are primarily interested in congregational language usage as part of the broader dynamics of cultural reproduction, ethnic consolidation, and immigrant adjustment. Nonetheless, they broach a few topics concerning specifically religious language and religiously motivated language usage. The use of a ritual language is the most obvious, although this topic has drawn only minimal attention from scholars, and that more descriptive than analytical (e.g., Numrich 1996; Warner and Wittner 1998). Ebaugh and Chafetz also note that some congregations, from evangelical Protestants to mission-minded Buddhists, institute English programming in order to proselytize outside groups. Along these lines, Stevens (2004) reports on a Ghanaian Pentecostal church in Chicago where debate arose over whether the church's institutional purpose should be evangelism or consolidation of ethnic identity. In the end, evangelism prevailed, leading to English programming in order to attract outsiders.

Our analytical task in this chapter is more focused than the usual treatment of the larger language question about immigrant life, yet it promises further insight into the issue of immigrant engagement with American society. Surprisingly, even those few scholars who have devoted significant attention to language usage in immigrant congregations have not explained its relationship to civic engagement patterns, perhaps due to an unexamined assumption that English adoption necessarily increases interaction with the larger society.

We will examine language usage in the social behavior domain of religion, as found in immigrant religious associations (congregations). Sociolinguistics points out that language usage in any social domain, including the religious, reflects the motives and understandings of the speakers, who in this case use linguistic means to further religious ends (Samarin 1976). Here again, religion matters to America's newest immigrants as they make choices of self-expression that can lead in various directions vis-à-vis the larger society.

## What's in a Name

One of the first decisions an immigrant congregation must make is choosing an official or legal name. This will become the congregation's primary linguistic channel for public representation, both to its own clientele, actual and potential, and to outsiders, including government bodies (e.g., when applying for tax exempt status, city permits, or parochial school accreditation), utilities (e.g., in listing a phone number), businesses (both among co-immigrants and in the larger society), other religious groups (whether considered allies or rivals), and neighbors (regardless of whether the congregation advertises itself).

Name selection is anything but a random process for congregations, yet scholars have paid little attention to it. Wilbur Zelinsky's (2002) seminal study of church names in Cook County, Illinois, documents the present dearth of knowledge. Although Zelinsky's primary interest is to compare naming patterns in white and black Christian congregations, many of his observations can be applied to immigrant congregations of all religious identities.

We analyzed the naming patterns found in our small research sample of sixteen immigrant congregations of various religious affiliations, plus all immigrant Muslim (N = 50), Buddhist (N = 33), and Hindu (N = 27) congregations known to us in the six-county Chicago region, for a total pool of 126 immigrant congregations. The Muslim, Buddhist, and Hindu congregations represent the three largest non-Christian religions in recent American immigration (in that order), religions largely bracketed out of Zelinsky's study.

We begin with a fact that appears unsurprising at first: all but one of the congregations in our total pool include at least one religious term in their names. This appears unsurprising since these are, after all, religious organizations. But a congregation must choose to express this aspect of its organizational identity—contrast the reluctance of many faith-based social service agencies to self-identify as religious (Ebaugh et al. 2003). Religion clearly provides the primary organizing principle for immigrant congregations no matter what nonreligious functions they also serve. A common institutional trajectory moves from an initial cultural or ethnic association (that may offer religious activities) to an eventual religious center (that also offers cultural or ethnic activities). A name change and consecration rituals often mark this shift, and the continuing mix of religious and ethnic/cultural activities sometimes leads to internal congregational conflict (Numrich 1996). The Turkish American Cultural Alliance, the one site in our pool that does not include a religious term in its name, exemplifies an immigrant cultural association that has become a de facto religious center with an appointed clergy but has not changed its legal name to reflect this new institutional status.

Even more significant than the inclusion of a minimum of one religious term is the frequency of such terms in immigrant congregational names. Zelinsky notes that nearly two-thirds of the aggregate total of terms in his sample had religious connotations. Our pool of all Muslim, Buddhist, and Hindu immigrant congregations in Chicago showed a comparable tendency, with 58 percent of the aggregate total of terms being religious. Some of the religious sentiments in these names are quite fetching, such as Wat Khmer Metta (Buddhist: Cambodian

Temple of Loving Kindness), Manav Seva Mandir (Hindu: Temple Serving Humanity), and Masjid Noor (Muslim: Mosque of Light/Illumination).

Again, the notable presence of religious terminology is no trivial fact. Congregations are important voluntary associations in immigrant communities, and they do not mask their religious identities with secular or ambiguous terminology. The content of an immigrant congregation's name depends on an internal/external calculus of factors, including assimilationist pressures to employ English terms or to avoid drawing attention to one's differentness or foreignness. Immigrant congregational naming patterns share much in common with individual naming patterns among immigrants (Lieberson 2000), but it appears that congregational naming is more resistant to assimilationist pressures than individual naming. This may be due partly to the historic American norms of religious freedom and tolerance for religious differences (Mead 1963; Numrich, forthcoming a). Still, the historic realities have been uneven in this regard. Buddhism and Islam have relatively long histories in this country, in both cases fraught with prejudice and confrontation (Haddad 1986; Kashima 1977), whereas Hindu immigration is a largely post-1965 phenomenon evidencing comparatively less tension with the dominant society. This may help to explain certain commonalities in Buddhist and Muslim congregational naming patterns, and overagainst Hindu naming patterns. Buddhists and Muslims tend to favor congregational names with a preponderance of English words (defined as 50 percent or more of the name) far more than Hindus. Buddhists and Muslims also show less propensity than Hindus to use religious terminology in congregational names.

The same internal/external calculus obtains in the choice of architectural facade, wherein an immigrant congregation decides how much of its religious identity to reveal to the larger, sometimes unsympathetic society. Mosque architecture in North America, for instance, has tended to downplay recognizably Islamic elements, which, by definition, clash with the cultural landscape (Khalidi 1998). Buddhist temples in the United States blend into the American cultural landscape even more (Numrich 1996; 2000b). Immigrant congregations are much less likely to downplay the religious terminology in their names, although it is significant that Muslims and Buddhists have done so more than Hindus in Chicago (47 percent of the aggregate total of terms are religious in mosque names, 60 percent of Buddhist temple names, and 70 percent of Hindu temple names).

The larger American society has shown less tolerance historically for Old World national/ethnic distinctions than for religious distinctions among immigrant groups. In a well-known passage, Will Herberg (1955, 40) explained that all other traces of ethnic distinction must give way, "but such was the shape of America that it was largely in and through his [the immigrant's] religion that he, or rather his children and grandchildren, found an identifiable place in American life" (cf. Warner 1998b, 15–18). This may account for a marked reticence to feature nonreligious Old World identity markers in immigrant congregational names. Only two of the sixteen research site names reflect any kind of Old World national or ethnic identity, and these simply by implication: Five Holy Martyrs, a Catholic church named after Poland's first canonized saints, and St. Demetrios, a Greek Orthodox church. Chicago's immigrant Buddhist, Hindu, and Muslim congregations likewise express little of their national origins or ethnic identities in their names. Only one Hindu congregation does so explicitly, Sri Venkateswara (Balaji) Temple of Greater Chicago (Balaji indicating a south Indian identity), although a few other names imply regional specificity—for example, the Swaminarayan temples, which represent a Gujarat-based movement. Only three of the fifty Muslim congregational names express Old World national/ethnic identity, but even then all three are balanced with American national terms: Albanian American Islamic Center, Nigerian Islamic Association of United States of America, and Turkish American Cultural Alliance. Chicago-area Buddhists employ a comparatively larger number of Old World national/ethnic terms (nine of thirty-three congregations, or 27 percent), only one of which is balanced with an American national term (Korean American Buddhist Association of the Midwest). Despite this minor penchant of the Buddhists, the overall dearth of Old World national/ethnic terms in immigrant congregational names is surprising. We expected more public expression of this group identity marker and attribute the reticence to assimilationist pressures.

Another notable fact that might be pertinent here is the relatively large number of immigrant Buddhist, Hindu, and Muslim congregations in Chicago that indicate their immediate locality in their names—46 percent overall, a far higher percentage than in Zelinsky's study (8 percent). Zelinsky found locality terms unsurprising given the obvious place-based context of local religious organizations. But in immigrant circles such terms signify an American societal context, not merely a local address. The Islamic Cultural Center of Greater Chicago, for instance, may have been founded by Bosnians and may now be supported by a variety of immigrant groups, but it is located in Greater Chicago, not in any of the home countries of its constituents. Of course locality terms often merely indicate the territorial range of an immigrant congregation's actual or potential clientele—for example, Islamic Foundation North, which distinguishes itself thereby from the Islamic Foundation located in the western suburbs.

One trend not seen among any of the three major non-Christian religions is the extreme Christianization (read: assimilation) of congregational names that occurred in Japanese American Buddhism in the early twentieth century, whereby many temples adopted the name "Church" and an entire denomination changed its name from the Buddhist *Mission* of North America to the Buddhist *Churches* of America in 1944. Only one congregation in our pool of 110 Buddhist, Hindu, and Muslim congregations makes occasional use of such a name today—Chicago Nichiren Buddhist Church, also known as Chicago Nichiren Buddhist Temple. In all three religious groups a less extreme assimilationist trend can be seen: choosing familiar English terms or equivalents over unfamiliar, religion-specific terms—for example, Temple instead of Wat (Buddhism) or Mandir (Hinduism), and Center or even Mosque instead of Masjid (Islam). Such choices appear comparable to the dynamics of symbolic contamination/enhancement found in personal naming patterns, whereby a name can either lose or gain popularity depending on a larger cultural image associated with it (Lieberson 2000).

A major distinction can be made between congregational names that indicate a larger institutional affiliation and those that carry more generic religious meanings. Zelinsky notes the denominational specificity in Christian church names only in passing, but we see this as an important choice point in the congregational naming process which can indicate the level of separation/tension between an immigrant congregation and outside groups. Although "denomination" is too tight a concept for certain religious contexts, the principle is transferable beyond Christianity: some congregations adopt names signifying affiliation with or adherence to a larger institutional entity (denomination) or traditional lineage. Such names are sometimes inherited by, bestowed upon, or imposed on an immigrant congregation; in any of these scenarios, the decision is not completely the prerogative of current congregational leaders and members.

As with personal naming patterns (Perl and Wiggins 2004), certain names connote specific religious identities. But unlike personal religious name preferences, which face potential usurpation by other groups or by society as a whole, denomination/lineage names retain their specificity. Personal names that once carried Protestant or Catholic connotations may have been co-opted by others, but that hardly occurs with religious group names. The key issues here are whether an immigrant congregation has a specific denomination/lineage identity, and whether it advertises that identity in its name. Based on our analysis of Chicago immigrant congregations, it appears that denomination/lineage identity is far more important to Hindus (74 percent of their temple names indicate a denomination/lineage affiliation) than to Buddhists (30 percent) and Muslims (20 percent).

The Muslim case is particularly illuminating for its larger implications about group dynamics. Examples of denomination/lineage markers among Muslim mosques include Sunni, Shia, and Ismaili, while generic markers include the ubiquitous Islamic and Muslim, as well as Mosque and even Masjid (Arabic for Mosque). The preponderance of generic religious names among Muslim mosques in Chicago (nearly 80 percent) is striking. Both of our Muslim research sites chose names featuring a generic marker of their religious tradition, Islamic Foundation and Islamic Cultural Center of Greater Chicago. Here "Islamic" reflects a key religious ideal of the mosques—namely, to embody the *ummah,* an inclusive community based on a spiritual unity that transcends ethnic and sectarian distinctions among Muslims (Numrich, forthcoming b). The choice of the generic word "Islamic" also implies the modernist or progressive theological perspective of most of the leaders of these mosques (see Esposito 1998; Khan 2003). In the case of Islamic Cultural Center of Greater Chicago, the choice of an inclusive name in the early 1970s expressed the mosque's intended multiethnic Islamic unity, in distinction from the ethnic specificity of its parent organization, the Bosnian American Cultural Association. Internal ethnic contention over institutional control of the mosque led to litigation before the Cook County Circuit Court, which was resolved in 1992 in favor of the inclusiveness signified by the mosque's name (Numrich, forthcoming b).

Thirteen of our sixteen research sites in Chicago fall under the denomination/lineage category. Three of these thirteen inherited their names from an earlier and different time of congregational identity. The demographic and theological shift at Naperville Church of the Brethren (est. 1855), for instance, has been so great that key Indian leaders have adopted an unofficial name—Gujarati Christian Fellowship—that both distances themselves from the liberal tendencies of the predominantly white denomination and signifies their adherence to generic Indian evangelical Protestantism in India and the United States. All of our Hindu and Buddhist sites reflect a denominational/lineage identity within their larger religious traditions: BAPS Shree Swaminarayan Mandir (followers of the Hindu holy man, Sahajanand Swami or Swaminarayan), Gayatri Pariwar Mandir (devotees of the Hindu goddess, Gayatri), International Society for Krishna Consciousness (devotees of the Hindu god, Krishna), Ling Shen Ching Tze Temple, Chicago (name shared by the home temple of the True Buddha School, followers of the Chinese Grand Master Sheng-yen Lu), and HanMaUm Zen Center (followers of Master Dae Haeng Kun Sunim, head of the HanMaUm movement within the Chogye Order of Korean Seon or Zen Buddhism).

Such denomination/lineage markers indicate some degree of tension or separation with a larger religious tradition. We wondered which elements in an immigrant congregation's name might indicate degrees of tension or separation from the larger society. Relying on our research in the RICSC Project, previous research by coauthor Numrich (1996, 1997, 1999, 2000b, 2000c, forthcoming b), and expert informants, we assigned a somewhat crude measure of "high" versus "low" levels of civic engagement to each congregation in our pool of 110 Buddhist, Hindu, and Muslim immigrant congregations in the Chicago area.

"High civic engagement" entails sustained institutional involvement with organizations, associations, and institutions outside of an immigrant congregation's own ethnic and/or religious community. For instance, Muslim Community Center (MCC) on Chicago's north side participates in neighborhood and citywide social advocacy initiatives, maintains excellent relationships with local government officials, and opens its facility for use by community groups. MCC is also a leading participant in interfaith activities and was the only local mosque to cosponsor the historic Parliament of the World's Religions in Chicago in 1993.

"Low civic engagement" entails minimal institutional involvement beyond one's own ethnic and/or religious community, little more than maintaining existence as an organized entity in society, serving the needs of its own constituents, and conforming to minimum legal requirements. Several small neighborhood mosques in the vicinity of Muslim Community Center fit this description and look to MCC for advice when they must interact with the larger society in unfamiliar ways or for extended periods of time (Livezey et al., forthcoming).

We identified few high-engagement congregations in our pool (30 percent), Muslims having the greatest number (40 percent). We then looked for correlations between high civic engagement and name characteristics, both overall and specific to each religion, hypothesizing that high engagement would correlate with (1) low frequency of religious terms per se, (2) use of generic religious terms rather than denomination/lineage markers, (3) preponderance of English words, and (4) absence of national/ethnic terms. Hypothetically, such characteristics seem to indicate openness to the larger society and reluctance to portray a narrow identity, whether religious or national/ethnic. We hypothesized no correlation between civic engagement patterns and locality terms since we felt that use of the latter usually signals the territorial range of an immigrant congregation's actual or potential clientele and thus carries little significance with regard to openness or closed-ness to the larger society per se.

Our hypothesized correlations held across the board with regard to preponderance of English words and absence of national/ethnic terms. High-engagement congregations from all three religions tend to have these two name characteristics. The other hypothesized correlations held for some religions but not others. Frequency of religious terms in congregational names seems to hold little relevance for civic engagement, but the distinction between denomination/lineage and generic identity markers appears more relevant, though in a complex way. Nearly all of the high-engagement Buddhist and Muslim congregations use generic religious terms rather than denomination/lineage markers in their names, whereas nearly all of the high-engagement Hindu congregations use denomination/lineage markers in their names rather than generic religious terms. This may be due to the simple fact that generic self-designations like "Hindu" do not have the wide acceptance that "Islamic" has among Muslims and "Buddhist" has among Buddhists. Islam and Buddhism have strong universalistic tendencies, both being "world" or "global" religions in a way that Hinduism is not, at least not yet.

Thus, openness to engagement with the larger society cannot be predicted from either a denomination/lineage or a generic religious marker in a congregation's name. Denomination/lineage markers may indicate separation from co-religionists more than separation from society. Even among Buddhists and

Muslims, where a generic religious name tends to indicate civic openness, Rissho Kosei-kai Buddhist temples or Ahmadiyya mosques, both of which usually signify their denomination/lineage identities in their names, can also be highly engaged because of an emphasis on civic engagement in their respective denominations/lineages. The key here is that civic engagement (or lack thereof) stems from the teachings of both a congregation and its larger religious tradition, whether that be a particular denomination/lineage or the religion as a whole. If civic engagement is part of an immigrant congregation's religious heritage, it will be civically engaged no matter its name. This is part of the internal/external calculus of congregational name choice.

## Printed Materials and Programming

Its name is one linguistic channel through which an immigrant congregation represents itself publicly. Other linguistic channels include printed materials and programming, which may be aimed at multiple audiences both inside and outside of the congregation. Outside audiences include potential constituents as well as larger publics that may be congenial, hostile, or indifferent to the congregation.

Printed materials can be found at virtually every immigrant congregation. The volume and quality of these materials vary widely, as well as the languages in which they are written, but the congregation's religious priorities and target audiences show through clearly. Recall the Buddhist temples our researchers visited at the outset of our project. One serves a multiethnic and multilingual constituency that functionally divides into parallel congregations of culture Buddhists (a mix of Southeast Asian immigrants) and convert Buddhists (a small group of non-Asian attendees) (Numrich 1996, 2000b). The temple's official name includes a multisyllable phrase that carries linguistic and religious significance only for its Asian members, identifying the temple with the Theravada branch of Buddhism native to Southeast Asia. Largely for the benefit of its non-Asian clientele, the temple parenthetically supplies another name in its English printed materials, "The Buddhist Temple," which gives no indication of a Theravada affiliation, a minor consideration for most of these constituents.

This temple's English printed materials present a modernist Buddhism that emphasizes a rationalist philosophy and ethics, with a strong emphasis on meditation as the sine qua non of Buddhist practice. The primary handout for non-Asian temple visitors is a booklet titled *Buddhism: A Layman's Guide to Life,* a compendium of ethical duties taken from the ancient Pali scriptures and meant to help individuals reach Buddhism's ultimate goal of enlightenment or Nirvana. The author is identified by name only, no publisher or distributor is listed, and only an astute reader could determine that the booklet represents a Theravada version of modernist Buddhism (on modernist Buddhism generally, see Bechert [1984]).

The booklet refers readers to the temple's Web site, which acknowledges the temple's Theravada affiliation but also ranges widely within modernist Buddhism in its features and Internet links. The temple's top institutional objective, as posted on the Web site, is missiological, "To propagate and promote the teachings of the Buddha," the implication being that non-Asian non-Buddhists are the target population. Another objective identifies the needs of the temple's traditional ethno-Buddhist constituency: "To assist and promote educational and cultural activities in Thai, Laotian and Cambodian communities in Chicago and surrounding areas." The abbot promotes modernist Buddhism, which he calls "purified Buddhism," in his interaction with both of these constituencies. This entails some critique of the cultural Buddhism practiced by his Southeast Asian members, consistent with modernist Buddhism's dismissal of popular Buddhism in Asia. But modernist Buddhism serves well in the public representation of the temple to outsiders, which is slowly bringing this temple into the orbit of civil society, especially through membership in the Buddhist Council of the Midwest (Numrich 1999, 2003, 2005).

Contrast the English printed materials at this temple with those at one of our Buddhist project sites, Ling Shen Ching Tze Temple, Chicago. Here the visitor receives booklets and periodicals produced by the temple's parent organization, the True Buddha School (TBS), and prominently featuring its founder, Grand Master Sheng-yen Lu. These materials often include a list of more than two dozen TBS local chapters throughout North America, plus the home temple in Redmond, Washington, after which the Chicago temple is named. The content reflects the syncretic nature of the True Buddha School, which combines elements of Tantric Buddhism and indigenous Chinese religions and claims psychic and healing powers for Master Lu.

Perusal of the True Buddha School's Web site reveals the strong sectarian identity of the group.[1] All features and links are TBS related, with Master Lu's teachings prominently displayed. One anonymous essay, "The Importance of Lineage Transmission," stresses the authority and ritual efficacy of Master Lu and his particular Tantric Buddhist lineage. If anyone outside of the True Buddha School should intone its sacred mantras, they will not experience the empowerment promised a true follower. True followers "take refuge" (a Buddhist phrase identifying adherence to a teacher or master) only in Master Lu, otherwise they forfeit their empowerment. Looking elsewhere is unnecessary, for "True Buddha School's lineage transmission is the greatest."

This form of Buddhism is far different from the modernist Buddhism of the temple described above. In fact, a modernist Buddhist would denounce the type of empowerment promoted by the True Buddha School as nonrational, even superstitious. This group's sectarian expressions of Buddhism do not have the same appeal to non-Buddhist inquirers as modernist Buddhism. Ling Shen Ching Tze Temple has not moved very far in its civic engagement. The temple is not affiliated with the Buddhist Council of the Midwest and it has only recently explored a working relationship with the local affiliate of Tzu Chi Foundation, a Chinese Buddhist relief organization. The temple's civic engagement is limited to activities in its Chinatown neighborhood.

Immigrant congregations represent themselves through programming in addition to printed materials. Specifically religious programming usually divides into two broad categories, nurture and mission. All congregations, immigrant and nonimmigrant alike, invest heavily in nurturing the spiritual well-being of members/attendees. This is, after all, their primary raison d'être—whatever other reasons it has for existing, spiritual nurture distinguishes a congregation from other immigrant associations.

Even so, much of the literature on recent immigrant congregations focuses on what might be called nonspiritual nurturing programs, covering the familiar territory of cultural reproduction, ethnic consolidation, and immigrant adjustment. Formal instruction in English and immigrant vernacular languages occupies a great deal of scholarly attention, but little thought is given to religious motivations that might underlie programming decisions in these areas. We were struck by the fact that only three of our sixteen research sites formally teach the English language, while less than three-fourths do so for immigrant vernacular languages, rather low numbers for such ostensibly important topics in immigrant congregations. Of course, in some of these cases, such instruction may be considered unnecessary—for instance, members may already have English proficiency or they can obtain needed English instruction outside of the congregation, or they can enroll in vernacular language classes at an immigrant community center. Sometimes a congregation might wish to offer such instruction but cannot mount the human and material resources necessary to do so.

But specifically religious reasons can also play a part in an immigrant congregation's decision whether or not to provide formal language instruction. This may simply entail a feeling that a congregation should focus more on spirituality than practicality, as interviewees from Holy Virgin Protection Cathedral told us. Or the spiritual and the practical can coincide in complex ways. Ling Shen Ching Tze, the Chinese Buddhist temple, offers Mandarin classes to its children for primarily religious reasons, first so they can understand the religious texts and rituals of the True Buddha School for themselves, and second to assist the immigrant generation in expressing the teachings in proper English. Cultural benefits accrued in learning Mandarin are a secondary consideration for this temple.

In the Chicago Ghanaian Pentecostal church mentioned earlier (Stevens 2004), the strong emphasis on evangelism led to the initiation of English-language programming in the first generation, contravening the conventional wisdom that intergenerational conflicts create a straight-line evolution from the first-generation immigrant vernacular to English accommodation of later generations. This finding surprises only if one overlooks religious motivations. The Indian members of Naperville Church of the Brethren share the theological perspective of the Ghanaian church. Over the years, these Indian evangelicals have steadfastly declined their non-Indian pastors' periodic offers to institute bilingual elements in the Sunday morning services (a monthly Sunday evening service is held in Gujarati). Moreover, they have never taught Gujarati language or culture in the Sunday school program. When asked why this is so, one leader explained that the immigrant generation wants their children to learn English and assimilate quickly into American culture.

But that is not the whole explanation. Leaders at the BAPS Swaminarayan Hindu temple—and most Hindu temples in the United States—also want their children to learn English and assimilate quickly into American culture, yet these temples typically provide Indian language and cultural programming for them. The difference is in the religious identities of the respective groups. For Swaminarayans and other Hindus from Gujarat, religion and ethnicity are nearly coterminous. Not so for Gujarati Christians, whose religious identity is at odds with their ethnic/regional identity. The surprised reactions from Indian peers they meet who have never heard of Gujarati Christians led the youth of Naperville Church of the Brethren to coin a new name for themselves, "Guju Christians." For them, the religious half of this neologism trumps the ethnic half.

In its latest hiring, Naperville Church of the Brethren chose a Jamaican Baptist pastor, showing no interest in even considering an Indian candidate. The key here? Evangelical Christian identity trumped both ethnic identity and denominational affiliation. The new pastor talks the evangelical talk and moves in evangelical circles. This congregation is a major node in a network of Indian evangelical Protestantism that stretches from Chicago, to other Indian communities in the United States, to India. Guest preachers and touring groups, most of them not Brethren, regularly visit the Naperville church. English serves as the default vernacular language when these diverse Indian groups gather together, while the default religious language of evangelicalism binds them together as kindred in the Holy Spirit. Their new pastor can represent the congregation quite well in such contexts even though he is not Indian.

Unlike spiritual nurturing, which is always a major programming component in immigrant congregations, the importance of mission programming varies widely, some congregations showing little interest in anyone outside their doors. Mission-minded immigrant congregations may distinguish various target audiences—for example, co-immigrants who are "congregation-less" (equivalent to the narrowly construed term "unchurched") or potential converts from the larger society. Larry Poston's (1992) study of Muslim *da'wah* (propagation of the faith generally, including missionary activities) makes some useful distinctions that can be generalized to other religious groups.

Poston identifies two broad understandings among North American Muslims, the distinction hinging on where they direct their da'wah.[2] Passivist Muslims turn inward to the Muslim community, "concerned primarily or solely with the retention and maintenance of their Islamicity," whereas activist Muslims turn outward, "desirous of transforming the non-Muslim society of which they are a part at both the individual and communal levels so that it will reflect Islamic values and beliefs" (31). Poston grudgingly accepts the passivist approach, which he says characterizes most North American mosques, as a legitimate form of da'wah if it includes exhortation of nominal Muslims, but he finds no evidence of this in the mosques. Dissatisfied with this state of affairs, according to Poston, a host of activist paramosque organizations have emerged that adopt one of two basic strategies in pursuing their mission to the larger society—either the direct approach of activistic preaching or the indirect approach of lifestyle evangelism.

Poston points out that activist Muslim organizations are more civically engaged than passivist ones. As suggested in the previous section, more Chicago-area mosques seem to fall in the activist camp than Poston's generalization about North American mosques would suggest. Whatever the precise tally, the implications of Poston's analysis bear consideration, with regard both to Muslim mosques and to immigrant congregations from other religions. Even in a religion with a strong doctrinal impetus for missionary activities, like Islam, Christianity, or Buddhism, the decision to act on that impetus must be made by congregations. Moreover, once that decision has been made, a strategy must be chosen, whether to preach or to let lifestyles do the preaching, or a combination of both strategies. Activist immigrant congregations will be more civically engaged than passivist ones, and, no matter what strategy they adopt, their ultimate goal is to influence the larger society with their particular religious values. Given what we know about the moral projects of religious groups, we can predict whether their respective missionary endeavors will take individualist or collectivist strategies. Groups with collectivist moral projects will more likely engage other collectivist religious groups around questions that affect larger social structures and processes. We see this in the mosques of our Chicago project, both of which promote a modernist version of Islam quite compatible with liberal interfaith initiatives to create a harmonious multireligious America.

## Religious Language Brokering

Religious language brokering is a kind of congregational representation that involves more than mere translation of words. Here we expand on the general notion of language brokering between different linguistic and cultural groups, where individuals act as intermediaries who "influence the contents and nature of the messages they convey, and ultimately affect the perceptions and decisions of the agents for whom they act" (Tse 1995, 180). A religious language broker acts as an intermediary between his/her congregation and outside audiences, serving as a spokesperson who represents the congregation's religious ideas, practices, and identity, contributing his or her own understandings and perspectives to the representation, and affecting the ways in which the congregation is perceived both by outside audiences and by itself. These perceptions then form the basis for interaction between the congregation and outsiders.

Who performs this important task of religious language brokering for immigrant congregations? That depends on a variety of factors. Sometimes serendipity enters into the picture. The person closest to the telephone answers it, someone greets the unannounced visitor at the door or in the pew. Such brokers often lack the requisite dual vernacular language competency (i.e., English and the immigrant language) to field queries adequately. As researchers of recent immigrant congregations have learned, it may take several phone calls to reach a competent broker, and a site visit may entail shunting among several people before such a person is found. We recall the first Buddhist temple that we approached to join our project. After assurances by several lay brokers that the temple would surely sign on, the priest informed us that that would not be the case. Unfortunately, we could not understand the reasons given by the priest, due to a language barrier.

Dual vernacular language competency and at least a modicum of biculturalism constitute the minimum requirements for religious language brokering. One must know enough English and enough about American culture to make the transfer of knowledge understandable. Some of the widely reported frustration of the second generation stems from their elders' unwillingness to allow them to broker for the congregation, or indeed to take on much meaningful leadership generally. Although many of these young people possess the requisite English facility and American cultural savvy, their elders do not recognize their religious credentials to serve as official brokers for the congregation. Ironically, in some cases this leads to the designation of nonimmigrants to fill this role, individuals who may know the congregation, and even the congregation's religious heritage, far less well than the second generation and who may thus offer a significantly skewed representation to outsiders.

Lay religious language brokers are common in recent immigrant congregations, sometimes merely by default, often deliberately. One of our research sites in Chicago had a religious leader prior to our project who was adept in all three requisites for the brokering role: he was bilingual in English and the immigrant vernacular, familiar with American culture, and trained in the religious tradition. This combination also made him very effective in reaching the second generation. When one of the project principal investigators first met this person some years ago, he noted the leader's fluent and compelling use of American colloquialisms. Perhaps second only to native humor, such linguistic peculiarities are very difficult for nonnative speakers to learn. The congregation's "denominational" headquarters transferred this religious leader to an affiliated branch in another city before we began research at the site. The current leader has impeccable religious credentials but limited competency in English and American culture, necessitating a translator for extended conversations or interviews. Of course, translators impose their own interpretations and understandings in brokering the broker's communication in such contexts, adding yet another layer of meaning to a message.

In many immigrant congregations, religious specialists perform very narrow ritual functions and wield little or no institutional authority. The real control of the congregation may be vested in a lay board of directors or its equivalent, some of whom may broker for the congregation. This reflects what R. Stephen Warner (1994) calls the de facto congregationalism of American religion, and it may lead to lay/clergy tension in immigrant congregations (Numrich 1996).

Religious language brokering in immigrant mosques is a particularly interesting case. An oft-cited study reports that nearly 20 percent of the mosques surveyed do not have an imam and that the imams in only about half of the remaining mosques serve as the institutional leader (Bagby, Perl, and Froehle 2001, 46). The lack of imams per se, and of imams with the requisite qualifications and/or authority to serve as religious language brokers, has created a special group of what Garbi Schmidt (crediting John Esposito) calls "professional Muslims," who are now "so prominent that they have a noticeable effect on the present constitution of knowledge and authority within the community, in particularly how this community is presented to the non-Muslim surroundings" (Schmidt 1998, 189). Schmidt sees these professional Muslims as institutionally unaffiliated, but in fact they often serve as designated brokers for immigrant mosques. They are professionals in the sense of being Western educated and trained in high status occupations like medicine, engineering, and education. They are not religious professionals, in the usual sense of that term, as trained clergy. They may possess a great deal of religious knowledge, but it is self-acquired and not credentialed by any recognized religious authority outside of the mosque.

These professional Muslims typically hold a progressive or modernist understanding of Islam characterized by appreciation for many aspects of Western culture and knowledge, and by a desire to find points of agreement between Western and Islamic worldviews (on modernist Islam, see Esposito [1998]). Findings from the mosque study cited above suggest that a large majority of U.S. mosques can be classified as modernist: 71 percent make Islamic decisions by taking into account modern circumstances and the contexts of authoritative texts and traditions, rather than following a more traditional and literalistic approach (Bagby, Perl, and Froehle 2001). As Karen Leonard (2003a) points out, traditionalists criticize the modernist Islam promoted by these spokespersons, creating a rift in Muslim leadership in this country. Traditionalist and modernist brokers vie with each other to be the authoritative representatives of Islam. For the most part, the modernists have triumphed to date, and thus their version of Islam has penetrated American society to a greater extent than the traditionalist version. The latter may still be relatively strong among Muslims, but modernist Islam is more visible to outsiders, especially through media coverage and interfaith activities. "Professional Muslims," to use Schmidt's term, are in demand in a way that traditionalist Muslims are not, and also to an extent that imams of any perspective are not.

Of course, imams and so-called professional Muslims can share religious brokering responsibilities, as has been the case for years at Islamic Cultural Center of Greater Chicago (ICCGC).[3] For ICCGC (and mosques like it), the notion of professional Muslims must be expanded to include high status businessmen and corporate executives in addition to laymen with high education and skill levels.

Since the 1970s, ICCGC has been served by religiously trained imams respected by Muslim and non-Muslim groups in the United States and internationally. ICCGC's first imam, Kamil Avdich (1975–1979), was a founding member of the Council of Imams in North America (established circa 1972) and served as editor for its periodical, *Path of Righteousness*. He was well known for his modernist Islamic perspective, as the following excerpt from ICCGC's written history reveals (Behlim 1994, 29): "His views on Islam and the role of Muslims in American culture were impressively progressive for his time. He had a vision for the Muslim community to incorporate themselves into the western world, and he shared his sentiments with the members of his congregation." Imam Avdich was a tireless advocate of pluralist harmony, both among Muslims and between Muslims and adherents of other faiths. As a biographer (al-Ahari 2001, 75) puts it, "He continued to work for inter-ethnic Muslim dialog and inter-faith dialog until his dying breath."

ICCGC's succeeding imams have been no less prominent brokers of modernist Islam. Mustafa Ceric (1981–1986) completed a doctorate at the University of Chicago under the tutelage of the well-known modernist Islamic scholar Fazlur Rahman. Imam Ceric is remembered in the following way in a commemorative booklet published by ICCGC (Zvizdich 1988, 11): "As Imam of the Islamic Cultural Center, he spoke out and represented us in a variety of different religious circles around Chicago. His teachings, his tolerance, and his love of all peoples has not been forgotten." Imam Ceric returned to Yugoslavia in the late 1980s and today serves as Reis-ul-Ulema (Supreme Authority) and Grand Mufti for the entire Muslim community of Bosnia-Herzegovina.

Imam Senad Agic (1989–present) presided over ICCGC during the internal ethnic turmoil that nearly closed the mosque in the early 1990s, eventually helping the membership reiterate ICCGC's founding ideal of embodying a multi-ethnic Islamic ummah. In the heat of the civil unrest in the former Yugoslavia in the mid-1990s, Imam Agic gave an interview to the liberal Protestant periodical *The Christian Century* (August 2, 1995), in which he repudiated militant Islamism and characterized the heart of Islam as that of love, coexistence, and respect for others, found at its best in the Sufi way: "So let Sufism and the Islam of love help communicate the message of the prophet Muhammad, peace be upon him." Imam Agic is an active member of the local interfaith clergy association.

ICCGC's first imam, Kamil Avdich, is the only imam to date to have served as ICCGC's president as well. The presidents since his time have all been laymen, including a businessman and two corporate CEOs. Talat Othman, a financier and banker who served multiple terms as president, was instrumental in shepherding ICCGC through the difficult early 1990s. The Circuit Court judge who heard the litigation singled him out for praise, saying, "Mr. Othman, you have done a Lincoln-like job in keeping this place of worship open and functioning."

The judge's reference to Abraham Lincoln is apt in capturing the high level of civic engagement that characterizes this congregation. ICCGC draws from a modernist Islamic perspective in seeking to create a multiethnic Islamic ummah that contributes positively to American society. In the words of Talat Othman, upon the completion of ICCGC's facility in 1988, "Since our membership consists of Muslims from many different ethnic origins, it is incumbent on all of us, as members of society, to contribute toward enriching the American culture by introducing the best that our respective cultures have to offer." At ICCGC, imams and lay leaders have shared in brokering a modernist Islam—as opposed to other kinds of Islam—to both the Islamic community and the larger society. Clearly, religious language brokering involves far more than mere words, as immigrant congregations broker their religious identities in engaging outsiders.

## Translating the Sacred

Two languages can be heard regularly at Naperville Church of the Brethren—Gujarati, the first language of Indian immigrants and the second language of their American-born offspring, and English, the immigrant generation's second language, their offspring's first language, and the white members' only language. One interviewee commented about language usage in the context of doctrinal fault lines within the membership: "The Indian group, theologically, is at a very different place than the white group. Fortunately, we have two different languages, so we never get into a lot of that. . . . In many congregations theology can be a unifying thing, but it can [also] be a thing people fight over. Here we haven't gotten to that point because in order to talk theology, you've got to have a real good grasp of language."

This person understood some of the complexities of religious language usage in an immigrant religious organization, where matters both mundane and transcendent are expressed through one or more tongues. As our interviewee intimated, the languages spoken in an immigrant congregation can either unify or divide the faithful.

In this section we consider the broad topic of translating the sacred. This concerns far more than the use of a ritual language, which we will discuss, but also a range of religious elements that require translation in an immigrant context. Throughout this discussion, we also explore the correlations between sacred translations and civic engagement patterns of immigrant congregations.

We do well to begin with insights from the fields of history of religions, psychology of religion, and ritual studies in order to understand what is at stake in translating the sacred. Gerardus van der Leeuw, Rudolf Otto, and Mircea Eliade identified the origins and manifestations of the basic religious experience throughout human history and across cultures. That experience centers around perceptions of transcendent realities invested with sacred powers that evoke strong feelings in human beings. Despite legitimate criticisms that have been raised regarding their essentialist views of religion and methodological issues about understanding the religious mind, these classical theorists nevertheless help to explain the motivating force of religious worldviews.

Van der Leeuw (1938) opened his *Religion in Essence and Manifestation* with a discussion of the object and power of religion. The object of religion's attention is "*a highly exceptional and extremely impressive 'Other,'* " wrote van der Leeuw, and "this Object is a departure from all that is usual and familiar . . . , the consequence of the *Power* it generates" (23). In *The Idea of the Holy,* Otto (1950) coined the term "numinous" (from the Latin word for "divine majesty") to refer to the "unnamed Something" at the heart of all religious experience: "There is no religion in which it does not live as the real innermost core, and without it no religion would be worthy of the name" (6). Otto suggested that human beings experience the numinous as at once Holy and Wholly Other than themselves, a *mysterium tremendum* ("overwhelming mystery") that nonetheless fascinates. Eliade (1958, 1961), like Durkheim, distinguished the notions of sacred and profane. Acknowledging his debt to Rudolf Otto, Eliade studied the manifestations of the sacred in time and space, which he called "hierophanies" (from the Greek words for "sacred" and "appear"). "It could be said," Eliade (1961, 11) wrote, "that the history of religions—from the most primitive to the most highly developed—is constituted by a great number of hierophanies, by manifestations of sacred realities."

Sacred perceptions and demands must be communicated through language, for instance in doctrines, scriptures, myths, ethical and legal prescriptions, and rituals. Words, phrases, and texts may partake in the sacredness of the transcendent realities they purport to convey—a deity's name, a mantra, or a holy book do not represent ordinary words to the faithful. Consider the statement printed on pamphlets produced by the True Buddha School, indicating this group's reverence for the words of its founder and current head, Grand Master

Shen-yen Lu: "Please place this text in a clean place. If you no longer want this text, please return it to the temple, burn the text with respect, or recycle the paper. Do not throw it in the trash."

Sometimes a religion deems an entire language sacred (Wheelock 1987), like the nonvernaculars Sanskrit (Hinduism and Buddhism), Pali (Buddhism), Latin (pre–Vatican II Roman Catholicism), and Old or Church Slavonic (Slavic Orthodox Christianity). Arabic, the vernacular of the founding Muslim community, took on sacred connotations by its link to a hierophany, the revelation of the Qur'an to the Prophet Muhammad. "Being the language of the Qur'ân, which is the first source of Muslim theology, law and ethics, and the vehicle of the fulfillment of the ritual obligations, Arabic has occupied a fundamental place in Muslim religious life right up to the present day" (Wiegers 1995, 304). Arabic words invested with Islamic sacred meaning have functioned as markers of Muslim space, from greetings among the faithful to calligraphy in Islamic architecture (Metcalf 1996).

In the end, however, to religious minds, the essential otherness of the sacred renders any language, even sacred language, woefully inadequate to the task of representing it, or even conveying the feelings evoked by it. All the phrases and nomenclature used to describe the object of religion's attention, according to Rudolf Otto (1950), are at best ideograms of transcendent realities that can only be understood through direct experience. This leads to nonlinguistic means of expression, like symbolism, art, architecture, music, and performance. Language usage in ritual performance differs in style and pattern from language usage in other contexts and intends some kind of sacred transformation of ritual participants (Samarin 1976; Wheelock 1987).

Religious language creates group identity and thus establishes boundaries vis-à-vis others. "For every [religious] speech community, whether it be a whole denomination on a national scale or the congregation of one church in this denomination, there are taken-for-granted expectations for the way language will be used and for what purposes" (Samarin 1976, 5). The demarcation function of religious language is especially evident in doctrines and rituals. Ironically, the importance of group demarcation increases as the similarities with outsiders increase, since a group must distinguish itself from its closest rivals and competitors (Snoek 1995; also, Platvoet and van der Toorn 1995).

Given this background, we see the significant risks involved when an immigrant congregation translates religious language, risks only partly illuminated by the usual considerations of immigrant adaptation dynamics or by the mere fact that longstanding cultural practices resist change (Lieberson 2000). First and foremost, translations risk dilution of sacred power. This helps to explain the intensity of debates over substituting vernacular equivalencies for the ritual language of a formal religious service. "Religious traditions have often held the position that synonymy does not preserve sacrality" (Wheelock 1987, 440). This sense of sacrality inheres through more than the sense of mystery created by the unintelligible sounds of a nonvernacular language like Sanskrit or by ritualized usages of a vernacular language like Arabic. These particular sounds or usages express the "unchanging, eternal validity" of a cumulative religious tradition (441). Arbitrary sounds or language usage will not evoke the same feelings in ritual participants, and translations come off as weak substitutes, at least initially. It may take years, even generations, for a congregation or its larger religious tradition to recapture spiritual satisfaction in vernacular equivalencies of a ritual language, as in the Roman Catholic experience. The classic lament of the second generation, intoned by a Thai Buddhist teenager during a Pali ritual activity, "I don't even know what we're saying!" (Numrich 1996, 106), is not merely another symptom of generational disaffection. Often, their immigrant parents do not know what they're saying either, especially where an unintelligible ritual language is involved. But for the parents, these particular sounds and language usages symbolize a sacred heritage that cannot easily be put into other words. The usual generational disaffection is compounded here by religious disaffection.

Translating doctrines and key religious concepts is also risky. Scholars of classical American immigration noted how intertwined theology and language could be. "Opposition to the use of English, or extreme caution regarding it," wrote one historian of immigrant Lutheranism, "was rooted in the belief of many that its introduction would result in an erosion of the Lutheran doctrinal position and adoption of non-Lutheran practices" (Nelson 1975, 350). For these immigrants, faith and word were inseparable, so that something sacred would certainly be lost, or perhaps a foreign sacredness added, in translation. An opposite theological judgment was pronounced by one nineteenth-century Swedish Lutheran pastor who criticized German Lutherans for not adopting English, preaching "their language rather than the Gospel" (in Lund 1954, 63).

The difficulty of finding equivalencies of key doctrines and concepts may lead to multiple translations, or to no translation at all. When a religious group decides that too much would be lost in translation, and thus simply transliterates a term into English, they have identified the doctrinal core of their religious tradition. The word *dharma* functions in this way for some Buddhist and Hindu groups—it can mean anything from "duty" to "teaching" to "religion," per se, and each group or subgroup invests the word with its own peculiar content. These specific investments of meaning can serve as points of contention between rival religious groups, as well as barriers of understanding in interactions with outsiders. In an attempt to overcome barriers with outsiders, sometimes quite a bit of meaning is given up—perhaps lost—in translation. A media report of a dispute within a local Lao Buddhist temple quoted one member who referred to the monks as "the ones who carry God's word" (Osterman 2004). The phrase "God's word" is surprising in this context, probably intended to translate

*Buddha dharma,* or "Buddha's teachings," for American readers. To equate Buddha dharma with "God's word" in this way may solve a problem of translation in one sense, but it also creates potential problems of meaning and understanding between groups.

Translating the sacred also risks transgressing religious identity boundaries. Groups often resist ritual modification because of ritual's effectiveness in social demarcation. Rituals can distinguish subgroups within multiconstituency immigrant congregations, as in Hindu temples that honor various gods, each served by its proper ritual specialists. In many Catholic parishes, groups observe ethnic-specific holy day feasts or celebrate mass in their own vernacular languages. Filipino expressions of Catholicism have been fully integrated into the ritual life of St. Lambert Catholic Church, including Simbang Gabi (an Advent novena), the Santo Niño (Holy Infant) mass, and the mass for the national martyr of the Philippines, San Lorenzo Ruiz de Manila. At Five Holy Martyrs, the Górale Highlanders, a Polish subethnic group with a distinct dialect and cultural traditions, regularly celebrate their own feast days. This parish offers five Sunday masses, three in Polish, two in English, but none in Spanish, despite its growing Spanish-speaking membership. Confession is also offered in Polish and English but not Spanish. Unlike nearby Euro-ethnic parishes that have instituted Spanish-language rituals, Five Holy Martyrs recently decided against doing so.

The group demarcation function may make rituals the most difficult area of immigrant congregational life for intergroup interaction, both within a congregation and between a congregation and other religious groups. We might imagine a ritual distance scale, comparable to the well-known Bogardus social distance scale, where ritual marks the last boundary crossed in relating to other religious groups, as marriage is for social intimacy. Immigrant congregations that interact ritually with other religious groups, or that allow nonadherents to participate in their rituals, do not perceive those others as religious threats or competitors (cf. Snoek 1995). Modernist or liberal religious groups, for instance, have more in common with liberals of other religions than with traditionalists in their own religious families, as evidenced by the myriad interfaith prayer gatherings after September 11, 2001. We attended one such gathering sponsored by Gayatri Pariwar Mandir on the birthday of their guru, Pragyavtar Gurudev, and attended by Buddhist, Christian, Jewish, Muslim, and Sikh representatives. The hosts strongly encouraged everyone to participate in the Hindu rituals performed for the event, guiding guests through the unfamiliar motions, in effect bestowing temporary Hindu status on them and thereby eliminating the religious boundaries represented in the gathering.

We can profitably conclude this section with a comparative analysis of ritual language usage at the sixteen research sites, looking at religious motivations and possible correlations with congregational civic engagement patterns. More than half of the sixteen congregations employ a language that carries special status in ritual contexts. Often these ritual languages are either unintelligible or only partially intelligible to the participants, like Church Slavonic for Russian Orthodox Christians, Hebrew for Jews, Sanskrit for Hindus, and Sanskrit in Sino-Korean transliteration for Korean Buddhists. Arabic represents a special case because of the overlap of Qur'anic and ritualized usages with vernacular usage by some mosque members.

For all of these ritual languages, immigrant congregations must decide whether to translate the meaning for the benefit of some or all of its members. Most of our congregations do so, either through real time translation or formal instruction at other times, pointing up the importance vested in intellectual comprehension of sacred teachings. At the same time, there is little interest in these congregations in vernacular substitutions for the ritual language usage. A move in this direction contributed to a rift in the Russian Orthodox Christian congregation. Ling Shen Ching Tze provides an interesting case in this regard. The ritual chanting at this Chinese Buddhist temple is a Mandarin translation of Tibetan Sanskrit texts that are considered too sacred for use by the uninitiated. "What if we did it wrong?" asked our key informant, rhetorically. Writes Grand Master Sheng-yen Lu, founder of this temple's lineage, the True Buddha School, "the merit of reciting a mantra in its Chinese translation is, of course, not the same as reciting the mantra in its original form" ("How to Quiet the Mind and How to Recite Mantras," 9). In other words, even though a congregation or its denomination/lineage might acknowledge the importance of comprehending the teachings embedded in a special ritual language, they may not consider direct translation the best means to accomplish this goal.

The two predominantly Russian immigrant congregations in this project are alike in many respects. Both represent sectarian expressions of their larger religious traditions: Holy Virgin Protection Cathedral is affiliated with the Russian Orthodox Church Outside of Russia (ROCOR), a split-off from the Russian Orthodox Church or Moscow Patriarchate; Synagogue FREE is part of the Chabad Lubavitch movement, a predominantly Russian branch of Hasidic Orthodox Judaism. The memberships of both congregations speak multiple vernaculars, including Russian (predominant at both), English, and several minority ethnic languages (Yiddish at the synagogue, Armenian, Bulgarian, German, Polish, Serbian, and Ukrainian at the church). Both congregations employ a ritual language that is at best partially intelligible to untutored participants: Hebrew at the synagogue, Old or Church Slavonic at the church. Both congregations have collective identities that combine Russian ethnicity with a strong religious component: Orthodox Judaism at Synagogue FREE, Orthodox Christianity at Holy Virgin Protection. But here they differ significantly—in the coupling (or uncoupling) of the ethnic and religious components of their respective identities. As we shall see, this is reflected in the language choices at each congregation and produces differing civic engagement patterns in each.

Synagogue FREE cultivates a Lubavitch form of "Jewishness" (*Yiddishkeit*) that includes a strong emphasis on Hebrew language usage and instruction for both children and adults. As one interviewee put it, "Hebrew is from God." As another answered when asked why he joined Synagogue FREE, "Personally, I wanted to improve in learning how to pray in Hebrew, not just in Russian." Others attested to the importance of ritual usage of Hebrew in synagogue services because of its inherent sacredness as well as the lessons about Jewishness expressed in Hebrew in the Torah, the first five books of the Bible. A key congregational leader explained that, "naturally, God himself commanded us to study the holy language in such an organization as the synagogue." For this leader, the Hebrew school is Synagogue FREE's highest programmatic priority because "it provides the Jewish future for our Russian Jews." Note that this does not preclude Russian and English language usage and instruction, but it clearly places these in a religiously subsidiary position. Russian and English translations of Hebrew ritual language are provided in the prayer books, and Hebrew-literate members translate for others during services, but Lubavitch Hasidim would not think of replacing the Hebrew text with Russian and English equivalents, as occurs in some Jewish settings. Synagogue FREE offers Russian language instruction, but Jewishness is not inherently tied to Russian, as it is to Hebrew or even, derivatively, to the Hebrew-influenced Yiddish. The synagogue offers English language instruction as part of its extensive social and vocational services programming for Russian immigrants and refugees, but for practical ends. English is not the language of Torah.

Synagogue FREE's cultivation of a distinctively Lubavitch Jewishness based on the authority of the Hebrew Torah creates a limited organizational ecology, although its ecology is still wider than non-Lubavitch Hasidic groups. FREE relates to some public institutions, like city government offices and public schools, but mostly in order to protect its Hasidic interests. FREE moves largely among other Jewish organizations, Orthodox and non-Orthodox, that are compatible with Lubavitch religious understandings and goals, especially in supporting the nation of Israel, a position that puts them at odds with Satmar Hasidism, for instance. Like the Chabad Lubavitch movement overall, but unlike Hasidism generally, Synagogue FREE engages in outreach to nonobservant Jews, primarily Russian Jews, following the teachings of their founder, Rebbe Menachem Mendel Schneerson. Synagogue FREE's Russian-language newspaper, *Shalom*, reaches a readership of perhaps fifty thousand in more than twenty-five states. For its members, Synagogue FREE creates a network affectionately called *mezhpuha*, from the Yiddish *meshpucha* or *mishpucha* ("extended family"), that "embraces not only religious but also cultural, social, professional, and economic aspects of a person's life," writes Dimitro Volkov (2003), our primary on-site researcher. Those members whose business or other contacts necessarily take them outside of this extended family network are encouraged to establish a firm foundation in Lubavitch Jewishness through the synagogue's educational and religious programming.

Holy Virgin Protection (HVP) Cathedral creates both a different language usage and a different civic engagement pattern than Synagogue FREE. According to Volkov, our primary on-site researcher there as well, HVP has uncoupled Orthodox Christianity from Russian culture in a way that places institutional primacy on the spiritual enlightenment of its members. Many of the usual activities found in immigrant congregations are quite limited at HVP because members do not consider these to be "essential elements of the church life," Volkov (2003) reports. "The central position of spiritual matters in their experience as members of HVP has been a recurrent theme in my interviews. . . . HVP members portrayed their parish primarily, and often solely, as a spiritual impetus [in their lives]." Liturgies at Holy Virgin Protection Cathedral are conducted exclusively in Old or Church Slavonic, a sacred language familiar, though largely undecipherable, to Slavic Orthodox Christians no matter their national origin. The importance of this language has more to do with inspiration than literal comprehension. HVP does not provide a translation of the liturgy, while formal instruction in Church Slavonic has been limited to minimal offerings in the parish education program (a brief experiment in adult instruction was discontinued). Several members who favored an English-language chapel left HVP in 2000 to establish an independent parish, but the remaining members generally find the ritual language inspiring and integral to the church's core mission of spiritual enlightenment. As one member explained, "There's something about listening to the singing in Slavonic that, in English, it's different. . . . Maybe that's because I grew up with it and it goes back to my childhood, but I am more comfortable hearing it in Slavonic than in English. Because, I think, then I don't listen to every word, I don't understand every word, and I can then pray more. But if I hear every word in English, I begin to listen to each word instead of worshiping and praying."

Holy Virgin Protection Cathedral has uncoupled the sacred from Russian culture in a way that allows its members to embrace American society, just as the coupling of the sacred and Lubavitch Jewishness leads Synagogue FREE's members in the opposite direction. As Volkov (2003) notes, the Russian Lubavitch members of Synagogue FREE value America since it offers them the freedom "to rediscover their Jewishness" and "allows their religious and ethnic community to exist in a secure self-contained space." They can live autonomously in their extended Lubavitch family, "in isolation from the *goyim* [Gentile] ways." For Synagogue FREE, the Hebrew language symbolizes Jewish separateness, both ethnically and religiously. As a lay leader explained in discussing the synagogue's Sunday school program, Americans generally make a distinction between ethnic and religious identities, but these are inseparable for Jews.

The Russian Orthodox Christian members of Holy Virgin Protection Cathedral, on the other hand, value American society because it offers them the opportunity to make a Russian cultural contribution to the larger multicultural mosaic. They are proud of the recognition they receive from the larger society in this regard. Commemorative certificates from two Illinois governors are prominently displayed at the church, the one from Gov. George Ryan honoring a Russian cultural festival sponsored by the church, reading (in part): "Your dedicated effort to uphold and continue the Russian culture and heritage is outstanding. Holy Virgin Protection Cathedral is a vital part of the community and you should be proud of its contributions and achievements. On behalf of the citizens of Illinois, please accept my best wishes on this special occasion." By being true to their Russian heritage they can become "good Americans," as one interviewee put it. This is the underlying purpose of the Russian language instruction in the Saturday school—to educate the children about their Russian-ness, but as Russian Americans. Importantly, this is divorced from religious concerns per se. Spiritual enlightenment is shared by participants in the liturgy, which is expressed in Church Slavonic, not in Russian or any of the other vernaculars of the congregation. Like the Russian Orthodox Church Outside of Russia overall, which shows little interest in mission work or larger ecumenical interaction (Krindatch 2002), HVP relates to a small circle of Slavic Orthodox groups. This is comparable to Synagogue FREE's small religious circle of Jewish groups. However, unlike Synagogue FREE, HVP encourages its members to engage a wider civic circle separate from its religious circle. At HVP, civic openness coexists with spiritual enclavism; at Synagogue FREE, enclavism is both ethno-religious and civic.

## Religious and Civic Aspects of Language Usage in Immigrant Congregations

Of all the areas of immigrant congregational life discussed in part 2 of this book, we considered language the most challenging to analyze, largely because researchers of American immigration seemed to have run out of interesting things to say about it. In this chapter we examined how religious identities structure language usage in immigrant congregations and how such language usage in turn reflects or shapes immigrant congregations' relationships with outside groups. We considered the linguistic choices immigrant congregations make in furthering certain religious ends, and we noted the civic consequences of those linguistic choices. In other words, we shifted the usual analytical perspective on immigrant language dynamics, from treating language primarily as a dependent variable shaped by society's demands or contingencies to treating religion as an independent variable that shapes not only congregational linguistics but also congregational agency in society. Clearly, much more is involved in the language dynamics of immigrant congregations than issues of cultural reproduction, ethnic consolidation, and social adjustment, important as these are.

If, to some degree, all immigrant congregations serve a quasi-sect function for their marginalized constituents who live "on the religious and social periphery of society" (Tomasi 1975, 105), then we need to know what prompts an immigrant congregation either to draw closer to the center of society or to withdraw further toward the periphery. As we have seen, congregational choices of linguistic self-expression can lead in either direction. These choices are exercised in or channeled through various aspects of the everyday life of congregations, and we have highlighted four: naming patterns, printed materials and programming, brokering self-representation, and translating the sacred. Recalling the insights of Gerardus van der Leeuw in the opening epigraph for this chapter, we have seen that immigrant congregations take a stand in society through their words, thereby exercising their power and creativity as religious actors.

# PART THREE

## CIVIC ENGAGEMENT

# 9

## Individual Engagement

CITIZENSHIP IN IMMIGRANT
RELIGIONS

*America is a society that has successfully combined
religion and social participation throughout its history. The rules of American religion are that one
does not have to stop enjoying the fellowship of secular society to please God; nor must one stop being
religious to be a citizen.*

—R. Stephen Warner (1988)

Maricel Awitan, an immigrant from the Philippines, came to the United States as
a nurse in 1968. A year later, her husband, also a nurse, joined her. They now live
in Skokie, a suburb just north of Chicago, where they raised their six children. At
first acquaintance, Maricel seems to be a shy soft-spoken woman, but she is an
important lay leader at St. Lambert Roman Catholic Church. She directs the Filipino Families of Skokie Choir and is active in various civic affairs. When Maricel
and her husband first settled in Skokie, they were the only Filipino family in a
neighborhood that was almost entirely Jewish. They were preoccupied with
work and children and involved themselves little in church or neighborhood
affairs. Maricel's transformation from quiet homebody to actively engaged community member was a gradual transition, and the St. Lambert congregation had
much to do with it.

Maricel began to be more civically engaged when she sent her children to
school. She and her husband chose the public school over the parish school because
it had a stronger music program, and they became active in neighborhood school-
related activities. The Awitans' involvement at St. Lambert began in earnest when
their oldest daughter had her first communion. Until then, they had been only
sporadic attendees. "You know, when you have so many kids, you say, 'Oh, gosh.
I don't have time. I'm so *busy*. I need to work.'" But she went on to explain, "My
oldest one, when she had the first communion, she didn't want to receive communion if we did not receive communion. So, okay, we should go to church."

At about this time, St. Lambert parish was experiencing a growing ethnic
diversity. The priests were supportive and drew the Awitan family into the

community. She and her husband were invited to participate on occasion as readers in the liturgy or as altar servers. Maricel had begun directing a community Filipino choir, and it used the church basement to rehearse. Before long, they were being asked to sing occasionally in a mass, and even to present a full concert in the church for a Filipino cultural evening. Eventually, the St. Lambert parish began regularly celebrating the ethnic religious festivals of its various ethnic groups. The Filipino festivals of Santo Niño and San Lorenzo became major events in the life of the parish and the Skokie Filipino community. In addition to the masses, there were dinners, dancing, theatrical presentations, and processions through the neighborhood streets. The Chicago Archdiocese invited Maricel to help plan citywide multicultural religious services, and her choir was increasingly in demand for interfaith and community events.

As Maricel's civic engagement increased, it was not limited to church-related activities. For several years, she helped teach English-as-a-second-language (ESL) classes in the local public school's after-school program. She began leading a smaller musical group that rehearsed in her home and performed in weddings and other community events. Before long, she was invited to be part of community cultural events so often that she began to turn some of them down.

Maricel's experience of growing civic activity was not an unusual story among our interviewees. Others also told of being drawn into public activity via their congregation, even though the form and content of that activity varied across religious groups.

In part 2, we examined specific topics or social domains to see how religion might have an impact on immigrants' engagement with others. In part 3, drawing on the particular findings of part 2, we will be discussing more generally how immigrant congregations and their members engage civic issues in the public arena. The very word "civic" is based on the Latin word for "citizen" and connotes the actions or attributes of citizens, denizens of a city. While "civic" is often used in reference to local or municipal institutions and actions, it has been broadened in common usage to refer to larger publics as well. People can be citizens of a nation or even of the world, in addition to being part of local civic associations or communities. The congregations we studied participate in civic life across the local-global spectrum; but like most congregations, they operate primarily as local institutions focused on local concerns. All the congregations we observed, even those that were quite sectarian, practiced civic engagement of one sort or another. Interacting with others in the public arena is a fact of modern life, especially in complex diverse urban settings.

Not all congregations, however, engage the public in the same way. Engagement can occur at various levels of social action, and the strategies of engagement can also vary significantly. In our research, we focused on two broad types of civic engagement—actions taken by individual citizens and actions taken by congregations as a group in cooperation with or in opposition to other groups in the public arena. Strategies of engagement can vary in a number of ways. They may be progressive or conservative. They may attempt to promote or extend a group's influence, or they may be more defensive in nature. Such strategies are likely to be shaped by a group's conception of their moral project, and thus may be either more focused on individual rights and problems or more collectively oriented toward larger structural concerns.

Let us be clear at the outset that we are defining citizenship broadly. We do not limit ourselves to legal issues of whether one is officially a citizen or not, though of course immigrant congregations need to deal with citizenship concerns in this narrower legal sense. Nor do we limit our observations to formal political actions of citizens such as voting or party participation. People may participate as citizens, as members of a public, in many different ways. They may belong to the local school's PTA. They may participate in social or political activism in less formal ways. They may even act as citizens within their own congregations, serving on committees or boards or informally engaging concerns within the public arena defined by their congregation's self-proclaimed boundaries. Our primary concern is with how religion matters for the whole gamut of possible citizenship actions by congregational members.

We are of course not the first observers to note that congregations affect how congregants behave as citizens. (See, for example, Warner [1999] or Chaves [2004].) In the particular case of immigrant congregations, the religious communal setting can be a training ground for broader citizenship—helping members develop the organizational, communication and/or democratic skills necessary for influencing decision making in the public arena in the American context. As Ammerman (1997, 364) notes, "every congregation that asks its members to teach classes and chair committees provides opportunities for the development and exercise of civic skills." Our contribution to this conversation is to articulate in greater detail precisely how religion matters in this process.

## How Religion Might Matter

How does religion matter for citizens' actions in the public arena? The religious variables that have framed our analysis thus far are helpful in considering this question. It seems reasonable to suppose that members of congregations with individualist conceptions of moral authority and/or moral projects would behave differently as citizens than would those who come from congregations with more collectivist notions. The moral authority variable seems especially important to us. Congregations that give significant moral authority to individuals are likely to affirm and empower autonomous individual action in the public arena. Congregations that expect individual members to submit to the authority of the collective religious tradition or community will likely have a significant influence over whether and how citizens practice civic engagement. Such engagement will likely be in support of the agenda and interests of the religious tradition. That is not to say that such communities will necessarily produce conservative citizens. The agenda and interests of the collective religious tradition may well be progressive in their political orientation—as in the Catholic support of action for workers' rights and participation in labor unions.

Sectarianism is also likely to influence the orientation of individual acts of citizenship. We would expect highly sectarian groups to engender citizenship activities that are largely internally oriented. Individuals may behave as citizens largely within the confines of their religious community, as when members of Synagogue FREE produce a Russian-language newspaper targeting a Lubavitch Hasidic readership. Even when members of sectarian groups act as citizens in the public arena, the purposes of the action may be largely internal to the group. Thus, members of Synagogue FREE may engage the public when they distribute literature or strike up conversations on the street. But such engagement is primarily oriented toward attracting others into the synagogue community.

Mainstream (i.e., nonsectarian) groups, on the other hand, should produce acts of citizenship that are more externally oriented, addressed to issues that are of concern to the public writ large. When the St. Lambert Catholic parish encourages its members to engage in interfaith or cross-cultural activities (within the church or without), it supports the civic engagement of its members around issues significant for the diverse Skokie community as a whole. Thus, sectarian and nonsectarian congregations alike produce civically engaged citizens, but the content and orientation of the engagement is likely to vary.

This brief treatment of how religion might matter conveys some of the questions and expectations we brought to our data on the citizenship involvement of immigrant congregants. Clearly, once we try to specify more precisely how religion's influence is exerted, the analysis becomes more complex, with more nuances to consider. We hope to make some sense of the complexity in the discussions to follow—looking first at citizenship issues that have been predominant in earlier work such as immigrant status or political behavior, then considering how citizenship defined more broadly is practiced within the congregation and in the larger public arena. This will not only allow us to explain in greater detail how religion matters for acts of citizenship. It will also permit some speculation about what the future may hold for an American civic life characterized by religious diversity.

## The Citizenship Status of Immigrants

Citizenship status can be considered in multiple ways. There is the narrower legal sense in which immigrants must deal with U.S. government functionaries to gain or maintain their visa status or earn official U.S. citizenship. Our respondents often told stories about their trials and tribulations related to legal status. There is also a broader sense of citizenship status that is more closely tied to identity. With what nationality will an immigrant identify in their acts as citizens? Will they identify primarily with their nation of origin and act as citizens with that identity in mind? Or will they act as citizens within the public arena in the United States or their current locale with American concerns in mind, drawing on their identities as immigrant *Americans*? Respondents also frequently spoke of citizenship in this broader sense.

Most of the congregations we studied, in the course of their everyday business, had to deal with citizenship issues in the more narrow legal sense. When recent immigrants face uncertainties or problems related to their legal status, many of them turn to congregations where they find an organized community of people who share their language and national background. But how congregations respond to these concerns varies in ways related to the individualist-collectivist distinction.

Individualist congregations are likely to deal with status issues on an ad hoc basis, focusing on ways they can support or empower particular individuals in addressing their particular problems. For example, one leader of the Gayatri Pariwar Mandir described the temple's response as "we have to enlighten them and lead [them] to the good path." Leaders we interviewed frequently spoke of themselves as referral agents, helping individuals with problems to connect with other agencies or people who might be able to help. Some congregations, for example, mentioned pointing people toward lawyers who were willing to do pro bono service on immigration issues, but the actual contact was usually left to the person to initiate on their own. Other leaders spoke of assisting with writing letters and helping members to navigate the immigration bureaucracy. Beyond such informal material help, congregations (and especially the individualist ones) were likely to identify ways that their religious mission could empower people to deal with the exigencies of immigrant life. At the ISKCON temple, for example, we were told the following:

> We do seminars [about] what spiritual life is about, who is God, you know, can we really be happy in this particular world? . . . And then we have programs when a new devotee comes, we just show him around and just try . . . to make a good relationship with him. . . . Spiritual love, the basis of spiritual love is love and care, so that's what we try to do most of the time.

Collectivist congregations, on the other hand, were much more likely to have programmatic responses to legal status issues. For example, a congregation might have an organized program to assist with legal status or offer citizenship or ESL classes. Leaders were prone to talk about immigrant status in structural terms rather than individual ones—focusing on how immigrant status problems contributed to poverty, economic exploitation, or domestic violence. As a nun at Maternity BVM Catholic parish told us, "Without those blessed documents, they are confined to being poor." She went on to recite a litany of problems that follow from poverty—access to health care, access to education, and domestic violence. Solutions were often targeted at these structural issues rather than individual empowerment. Maternity BVM, for example, hosted occasional immigration workshops where the local congressman or service agencies could meet with recent immigrants to disseminate information about legal status concerns and to mobilize support for legal amnesty for undocumented immigrants.

Citizenship status in the second broader sense of national identity also appeared frequently in our interviews. Questions about citizenship status were as likely to evoke a listing of a congregation's ethnic groups as they were to prompt comments about legal issues. We found this to be especially true for congregations with collectivist religious orientations. Such congregations seemed to instinctively respond in terms of collective identities. Individualist groups were more likely to downplay the importance of such categories—sometimes having difficulty in even identifying who was immigrant and who was not. At the Ling Shen Ching Tze Buddhist temple we were told, "In here we don't track who's newly immigrant. The temple's door is open for everyone. [Anyone] willing to become a member could do that, so it's really—immigrant or nonimmigrant, to us, is not important."

Thinking of citizenship status in terms of primary and secondary identities highlights several challenges that immigrant congregations must face. The question of which nationality is primary has an impact, of course, on how members will behave as citizens. It also has implications for how a congregation can create an effective identity, particularly when many different ethnicities may coexist within its membership.

Congregations employ different strategies for dealing with this sort of status question. Some treat it as a potentially conflict-generating problem that needs to be solved. One respondent at Five Holy Martyrs Catholic parish, for example, described how different identity emphases could lead to divisions within families. "Sometimes . . . only one of them wants to live here, and another one only dreams to go back. And then it is very, very hard for both of them to live like that."

More often, however, congregations in our study find ways to embrace diverse identities within their walls, helping different groups to coexist, collaborate, and learn from each other. Their primary purpose in doing this seems to be to build a stronger religious community or congregation. But, perhaps less intended, these strategies also provide experimental proving grounds for testing methods of addressing racial and ethnic pluralism in the larger society. Congregational members can develop skills that are transportable into their neighborhoods, schools, or workplaces, which are also increasingly diverse.

St. Lambert Catholic Church is exemplary in this regard. The parish, located in the ethnically diverse suburb of Skokie, mirrors the diversity of its surroundings. The pastor, rather than trying to meld all the various ethnic groups into a single "least common denominator" congregational identity, has chosen to embrace the diversity within the parish by giving each ethnic group the freedom to celebrate its own particular way of being Catholic. The congregation celebrates feast days of local saints in the members' countries of origin and supports prayer groups and home-based religious practices when these are important to congregational subgroups. The San Lorenzo and Santo Niño festivals of the large Filipino contingent are particularly important congregational events. Although the strategy of choosing pluralism over assimilation met with some initial resistance from old-timers, members today express appreciation for the vitality and variety of congregational life.

St. Lambert's strategy of supporting and celebrating immigrant status within the congregation influences how its members behave as citizens in their local setting outside the church. The congregation supports ethnic festivals in Skokie, encouraging members to learn about the many cultures that are present in its town. It sponsors Buddhist-Christian dialogue events that bring citizens from different traditions together to discuss their differences. Its parish school, open to all members of the community, claimed that more than fifty different languages were spoken in the homes of its students. PTA meetings thus became a public arena where members were required to engage in acts of citizenship on a common ground shared by many different groups.

Thus, many immigrant congregations serve as settings where individuals can learn to manage the competing demands of multiple citizenship identities—how to know which identity is an appropriate basis for action in which setting and how to move easily between one identity and the other as situations demand. How particular individuals make these choices may, of course, vary significantly by language or by generation. Bilingualism is a useful skill in navigating identities, but Spanish is more likely to be useful for this in the U.S. context than, say, Mandarin. First-generation immigrants are more likely to think of themselves primarily as citizens of their country of origin, while second- or third-generation immigrants are more likely to think of themselves as Americans first and something else second.

Language and generational variation can have an important impact on *where* members exercise their citizenship. Those whose primary citizenship identities are with their countries of origin are more likely to act as citizens within the context of their congregations, while those for whom country of origin is secondary are more likely to act in public arenas outside the congregation. We saw this at work in Naperville Church of the Brethren. The congregation was made up largely of Gujarati Indians. The core activists within the congregation were first-generation immigrants from the Gujarat state in India. They thought of themselves as Gujarati and Church of the Brethren members, based on their origins in Church of the Brethren missionary-founded congregations in India. There was also a significant group (about 25 percent of the congregation) of American-born members whose Gujarati identity was still important, but less central. They more readily embraced the mainstream Protestant denominational identity than many of their immigrant parents. Their citizenship activities were oriented toward a public that lay outside the congregational setting. As one older respondent told us, "There are quite a few of them, but you don't see them because they all work." Of course, the fact that they worked did not distinguish them from the first generation, but their work led them to invest their time and energies outside the congregation rather than inside.

## Political Activism

Another common question for observers of immigrant congregations is how they behave politically, both in routine political action such as voting, or in nonroutine action such as engaging in protest, dissent, or movements for change. Nearly all the data we collected on this sort of political activism came from congregations whose religious ideas and practices were collectivist in orientation. More individualistic congregations tended to treat politics as a matter of individual choice and even intentionally distanced themselves from political action. At the Ling Shen Ching Tze Buddhist temple, for example, we were told in no uncertain terms that Grand Master Lu, their founder and leader, eschewed political involvement of any kind. This was confirmed in an unattributed pamphlet given to us at the temple, "Questions and Answers on the True Buddha School."

Members at Naperville Church of the Brethren, and at many other immigrant congregations, made their U.S. loyalties explicit, especially after 9/11. Photo by Jerry Berndt.

It quoted Grand Master Lu from a 1992 press conference in New York: "If we become partial to any particular political party, it will create more disputes. That is why we look upon all sentient beings and all political parties with a mind of equanimity and we do not place any restrictions on the political consciousness of the students."

With collectivist religious groups, it was a different story. Political activism was viewed as a natural outgrowth of a group's collective identity. Even individualistic actions like voting were articulated as obligations resulting from group membership. A leader at the Islamic Cultural Center, for example, told us about his efforts to encourage his people to vote and to get involved in public activities like postdisaster relief efforts. "This is part of our job as an American," he said. "You are American. You are a citizen. . . . I really feel strongly about that because this is our country, and we love this country, and we care for this country, and we should show our love and affection for it. That is the way I feel, really."

When it came to actual participation in election politics, the congregations we studied varied in their response. Catholic parishes, steeped in American assumptions about separation of church and state, adhered to the Chicago Archdiocese policy that campaigning should not take place on church property. During a local election in Skokie in 2001, the following notice appeared in the weekly church bulletin, signed by the pastor.

> It came to my attention that a candidate for the office of Trustee locally, who is a member of the Skokie Community Vision Party, **without the pastor's knowledge or approval**, addressed St. Lambert Seniors' Club. **It is against parish policy to endorse candidates or parties or to allow candidates to give campaign speeches or distribute literature on parish property**. As a parish, we encourage you to know issues and candidates and to vote. Our position is consistent with the policies of the Chicago Archdiocese and good citizenship.

Note that, as we would expect when a religion locates moral authority in its collective tradition, voting and good citizenship is encouraged, but political activism is to occur within the parameters of church policy and pastoral approval.

Other congregations also supported involvement in election politics within the parameters of their own religious tradition, but some of these traditions were less squeamish about keeping a wall of separation between religion and the state. Both the BAPS Swaminarayan Hindu temple and the Islamic Cultural Center hosted local candidates who gave public addresses to the congregation. Some congregations also hosted guest speakers who were political figures in immigrant members' countries of origin, and who spoke about political issues in their homelands.

Beyond election politics, political activism may also address current events or hot political topics in the public square. The congregations we studied, especially the collectivist ones, support this type of activism as well. The focus of such activism is nearly always on issues that are rooted in a congregation's religious commitments or that are of immediate interest to the lives of its members. Five Holy Martyrs Catholic parish houses an active Right to Life group. Synagogue FREE supports pro-Israeli activism. Maternity BVM, a Catholic parish where the influence of liberation theology is evident, sponsors events promoting the rights of day laborers or addressing concerns of undocumented immigrants.

Thus, congregations provide organizational and material resources—an infrastructure—that enables members to mobilize effectively in pursuit of political interests. Those interests are rooted not only in material concerns, but in religious commitments as well. Congregations whose core religious ideas and actions draw on collectivist assumptions seem particularly well suited to provide a supportive context for political activism. This, of course, is not a new phenomenon on the American scene. What is new is the fact that many immigrant congregations exist outside the Judeo-Christian tradition that for so long has been the sole franchise for legitimate religiously based political action in the United States.

## Citizenship within Congregations

Thanks to religious disestablishment and the individual rights enshrined in the U.S. Constitution, congregations are a ubiquitous form of voluntary association in the United States. It is not surprising, then, that congregations depend so heavily on volunteer support. Congregations are places where people behave as citizens of a common polity, investing their time, money, and emotions in pursuit of individual and collective interests. We saw ample evidence of this sort of citizenship within all the congregations we studied. There were, however, significant differences in *how* citizenship occurred, particularly between the categories of individualist and collectivist groups.

Individualist congregations were settings where participants could engage with each other and the outside world in collective activities. For example, the Gayatri temple, small as it was, produced a periodical, *Learning Torch,* and a weekly Gujarati-language thirty-minute radio program. But these things were done in a largely ad hoc way, without the help of formal structures and bureaucratic procedures. One of the core participants at the temple told us, "Oh, yes. I always write down articles. Every Sunday we have a special radio program. . . . And in that radio program, we give the knowledge about our Gayatri . . . what events we have done, what events are coming, announcement of schedules, and so on. . . . Sometimes we go to the radio station also, me and Kusum will." But when we asked what station was broadcasting the program, she couldn't remember.

This kind of off-hand laissez-faire approach to voluntary citizenship activities was typical of nearly all the congregations we coded as individualist. Paid staffing was extremely rare. Instead, participants just seemed to look around, see what needed to be done, and do it. One of the men involved at Gayatri said the following:

> I like to go and do some free service. I decided to do that. I said, "Why not go to the temple and help them out?" She [the temple leader] needs a lot of help. Yeah, she's all alone, running all over the place, trying to do things. . . . Whatever she wants me to do, I do it. . . . Like you saw me at St. Henry that day, I was climbing up on the ladder, and hanging things, taking pictures, all that stuff. Even in the temple, I do the same thing. Sometimes, whenever we have special functions in the temple, some of these Indian restaurants on Devon Avenue, they offer their services. They offer free food. I go pick it up, and take it to the temple, and then it's served.

At the HanMaUm Korean Zen Buddhist temple, we were told that the *sunim* (the Buddhist nun who was the temple's spiritual leader) was also responsible for all the administrative work. We pressed our informant, "Does she have somebody who helps with that?" The answer: "If needed, there are people who can help, but not in terms of a set responsibility or declared position or something like that. Like, if someone knows something about computers that she doesn't know, then that person can sometimes lend a hand, [but] in terms of set structure, there's really only her and the other sunim." He went on to explain that all the nitty-gritty everyday work of congregational life—organizing postservice lunches, doing clean-up, giving people rides, organizing the library—was done by individuals who volunteered for a year at a time with minimal coordination or supervision (also done by volunteers).

Such unstructured volunteer work is the lifeblood of most of the individualist congregations, especially the smaller ones. In fact, it is often this very fact that attracts people to the congregation in the first place. Individuals who are activists in their countries of origin, even those who are not particularly religious, find congregations in the United States to be a welcome outlet for their activist impulses. For example, the yoga classes offered at Gayatri were established almost by accident. The volunteer instructor was someone who had a passion for yoga, but only occasionally dropped in to the storefront temple for worship. She spoke to a few other Gayatri members about her interests in yoga, and they said "Why not do it here?" She began offering group and individual yoga instruction on an ad hoc basis. This soon developed into one of Gayatri's services to the community, and the instructor became a more active participant in the temple's activities. Any fees paid by students went into the temple's coffers.

Acts of good citizenship are not only good for the congregations who benefit. They also provide the volunteers themselves with a chance to develop important social and civic skills. Unstructured volunteerism gives congregational members a chance to try their hand at a range of tasks, perhaps developing or discovering skills of which they had been unaware. The pastor at Truth Lutheran Church told us, "For example, some people, if they are willing to serve as a council member, they might learn how to work with other people. And we have quite a few people, their job is computer programmer. When they go to their office, they don't work with other people a lot. They just sit the whole day before the computer, before the monitor, and do their job. But when they become a council member, they need to learn to communicate with other people and then to work with other people. So that's partly a benefit for them, too. They can serve and also learn to work with other people."

For congregations who are more collectivistically oriented, voluntary citizenship is also important, but it is much more structured and formally organized. The BAPS Swaminarayan Hindu temple reported having thirty volunteer departments engaged in everything from kitchen duty to stage management to legal services. Rather than the ad hoc "whatever there is to do, I do it" attitude noted earlier, volunteers are matched with departments according to expertise. As Jay Desai said, "Each volunteer has to be suitable . . . , has to have the skills necessary to competently perform a function, and if that's not there, obviously that's a problem. Not that there's anything wrong with the individual, but the volunteer opportunity has to be a good fit and a match with the volunteer and the volunteer skills."

In these more structured congregations, the role of leadership in organizing citizenship duties is much more prominent. Leaders not only ensure that suitable individuals are given appropriate tasks, they also make certain that the programmed activities pursue the congregation's mission. The thirty departments at BAPS were primarily charged with facilitating the large Sunday services and the cultural/educational programs during the week. As Desai said, "A good volunteer is one who has a genuine willingness to do good to please Pramukh Swami Maharaj [leader of the BAPS global movement] in furtherance of his wishes and via the BAPS mission, which is one and the same, we feel."

One might plausibly argue that the highly structured character of BAPS voluntarism is as much due to its enormous size as to its collectivist culture or its strong leadership. However, Victory Outreach, a much smaller Protestant Christian congregation, shares BAPS's collectivist orientation and also has a striking range of volunteer ministries for such a small group. Likewise, informants there also highlighted the central role of leadership. As a key leader told us, "We have the nursery ministry, children's education ministry, the worship ministry. We have the evangelism ministry. We have the ushering department ministry. And I have my leaders in every ministry, and then my hand is in every ministry. They all call on me."

Collectivist congregations also differed from their individualist counterparts in how they viewed the relationship between volunteering and the individual volunteer. While more individualistic congregations highlighted volunteering as an opportunity for individuals to choose to follow their passions and exercise their skills, the collectivist groups were more likely to highlight the impact of communal activity on the volunteers. The congregation *called* volunteers to service and emphasized citizenship not only as a duty to the community, but also as an opportunity for personal growth and development. Jay Desai said, "We have an analogy in Gujarati that says if you put a whole bunch of utensils in a box, they're going to rattle, but if they rattle enough, pretty soon the outside of those utensils is going to be pretty smooth. So by volunteering, our aim is to become smooth. And the byproduct of that is that you're much more equipped to deal with problematic instances, people, and situations outside of this BAPS arena in your job, personal life, etc. But the main purpose is to learn self-control; and if you can do that, you're more disciplined and you're more likely to move further on the pathway to salvation, towards a higher body." The pastor of Victory Outreach put it another way. "They [first-generation immigrants] come here, they feel at home, you know. They want to participate. We have picnics. We have dramas. We get them involved in things so they won't feel lonely, and for their time to be occupied. So they won't have a lot of empty spaces in their life [that they would fill with] other things."

Not all congregational citizenship is volunteer activity, of course, especially in the more structured congregations. Structure implies formal offices, and officeholders may be paid employees. Maternity BVM Catholic parish has more than thirty paid employees operating parish offices, a school, and a counseling center. But even in large operations such as this, volunteering still plays a key, if secondary, role. As one priest said, "We have a theme of our parish here, that is *'Cada miembro un ministro,'*—every member a minister. That is the theme we bring out from time to time, the idea that the first focus of each member's ministry is their home, workplace, and community. And then, secondarily, if they have time to [give] this way, to take on some helpful and administrative work in the parish itself, maybe liturgy. There are many, many roles for the laity within the liturgy these days: reading the scriptures, ministry, ushering, chorus. But that is really, so to speak, *adentro,* focused within, in contrast to what their first focus is called to be: the world in which they live and work (and for the student, study)." The priest's comment highlights two things that are especially characteristic of Catholic parishes, even in comparison to other collectivist groups. First, there is a professional paid staff that carries out much of the work of the parish, assisted by lay volunteers who do their congregational citizenship on the side. Second, there is a blurring of the boundaries between the church and the world, especially for lay Catholics. Religious citizenship and worldly citizenship are one and the same.

The latter point was made especially clear by Maria, one of the catechism instructors. "I am always saying, 'Church is not Sunday only, you know.' Whatever I learn, I got to take it outside. If it means taking my catechism class on

Sunday, and I have to deal with an issue that happened in the neighborhood—somebody got shot, a kid got shot—that is my catechism that day, because the kids are all talking about the shooting. So catechism that day is not the book. Forget the book. We are going to talk about what happened, and that's the catechism for that day. . . . Until we start getting groups that are going to be working at some of these issues that are affecting our neighborhood, our church is not gonna be a living church, you know."

This blurring of the boundaries between inside and outside citizenship is a consequence of particular Catholic teachings about the contiguity of church and geographic place, the notion of a parish. Not all religious traditions, even collectivist ones, share that notion. Islam, for example, sees its mosques as houses of prayer for any Muslim who wishes to enter. They are not congregations in the same cohesive sense that Christians or Jews mean when they use the term. Mosques may have mailing lists, but they do not have formal membership rolls. The high point of a mosque's religious week, the Friday (*Jummah*) prayer service, is likely to include, beyond its core participants, a large and fluctuating collection of people who are there because the mosque is convenient to their place of work. These participants often live far away from the mosque and are thus unlikely to take part in any of its other programs or activities. This poses special problems for mosques in encouraging communal citizenship. As a leader of the Islamic Cultural Center said,

> This mosque doesn't have a Muslim neighborhood. But it is in Northbrook, and many Muslims with high education work in Northbrook and neighboring villages—doctors, engineers. So they take a break for Jummah prayer. We never see those people who come to Jummah on Saturday or Sunday. Even when we ask them to attend some of our functions on Saturdays or Sundays, they don't come because they live somewhere too far, and they don't take this mosque as their own mosque. They see this mosque as only a Jummah prayer mosque. So the people who come for Jummah prayer keep changing. They are not always the same people. Some come to this mosque constantly for a number of years, then they have to move to another company, then we don't see them.

Mosques address this dilemma in various ways. Most mosques have a lay volunteer board of directors that represents the core constituents of a mosque community and governs its temporal affairs. According to the Mosque Study Project (Bagby et al. 2001), about 95 percent of American mosques have such boards, and in about 60 percent of the cases the board holds final decision-making authority. The imam is the administrative leader of the mosque in less than half the cases, but he can use the moral authority of his office to encourage active participation of lay Muslims in the life of the mosque. Some mosques are also likely to collaborate with each other in organizations like the Council of Islamic Organizations of Greater Chicago to organize larger scale events and initiatives that require coordination of volunteer efforts. But Muslims cannot count as much as Christians and Jews can on member loyalty to a particular congregation to mobilize the citizenship of its participants.

Another kind of citizenship dilemma is faced by multiethnic congregations. How people behave as citizens and the kinds of activities that will capture their enthusiasm and commitment is often shaped by ethnic as well as religious identities. Thus, members of multiethnic congregations will often organize around ethnic identities to carry out particular activities. At the Islamic Cultural Center in Northbrook there is a strong identification with the Bosnian community, but there are also a number of Arab and South Asian participants. As a consequence, there are two women's groups in the mosque, the ICC Women's Group and the Bosnian Women's Group. The former is most interested in preserving Islamic identity, while the latter focuses on preserving Bosnian identity. The groups coexist peacefully and even worked together on fund-raising dinners to aid refugees of war in Bosnia, Kosovo, and Chechnya.

Thus, multiethnic congregations must manage the complexities and potential tensions related to multiple ways of being citizens within the congregation. Transition from one dominant ethnicity to another can be particularly difficult. As Naperville Church of the Brethren moved from a majority white congregation to a majority Indian membership, it saw the withering away of many programs that had been dear to former members but held little interest for the immigrant membership. Hiring a Jamaican pastor provided neutral leadership that facilitated the transition relatively painlessly.

But multiethnicity can also be a boon to a congregation's life. St. Lambert parish in Skokie, thanks at least in part to the visionary and open-minded leadership of its pastor, was able to successfully embrace the increasing ethnic diversity of its town. An ethnically varied congregation of more than 1,200 attends its Sunday services. The church's calendar includes feast days and holiday celebrations for a variety of ethnic groups, including not only the large Filipino group, but Cuban, Mexican, Chinese, Korean, and Sri Lankan as well. St. Lambert's annual Brat Fest, which dates back to its time as a predominantly German parish, retains its name, but is now an ethnic food fest with dishes from all over the world. There is also a resource benefit to the parish. Embracing the ethnic diversity increases the involvement of individual members because there are more choirs, more clubs, more seniors groups, and so on. Ethnic groups who use parish facilities for their events make donations to the parish. As one leader noted, "It is strange that our ethnic groups don't cost us anything. In fact, they bring home the bacon."

## Civic Engagement and Civil Religion

Engaged citizens in immigrant congregations also may direct their energies outward, engaging other groups and public issues outside the confines of their own intimate community. All the congregations we studied supported the external engagement of their members in one way or another; but the form, content, and extent of such engagement varies across religions. Once again, the distinction between individualism and collectivism matters.

Contrary to the concerns raised by Bellah et al. (1985), individualistically oriented religion does not necessarily squelch public civic commitments or engagement. In fact, locating moral authority within individual reason and experience may even facilitate interchange with others. Individualism allows for cultural relativism and usually embraces the notion of multiple perspectives on truth, a foundational assumption for dialogue and interchange between religious and ethnic groups in a pluralistic public arena. The individualist congregations we studied demonstrated this in their activities. For example, they were the congregations most likely to be actively involved with the Council for a Parliament of the World's Religions or to engage in dialogue with people of other faiths. Gayatri Pariwar Mandir encourages its members to participate in events organized by the Parliament or by Chicago's Interfaith Alliance. A devotee at ISKCON told us about their interchange and cooperation with the local Catholic parish:

> [The pastor] is a very nice person. It's like we have a mutual admiration society thing going on. It's nice that this happened, because I know Krishna Consciousness is still kind of a new thing to a lot of people in America, and to have that kind of nice relationship is a welcome thing. We try to keep all the channels open . . . sometimes to get something done, a mutual thing, like helping get the neighborhood cleaned up from drug dealers or something like that, it's a mutual kind of goal we have. So all the churches pitch in together. And then, in the same process, working together, we understand each other better—so we're not people with, well, Cyclops or two heads or . . . [laughs].

While individualism can, therefore, support civic participation, it does shape the form and content of such engagement in distinct ways. In comparison to the collectivist groups, members of individualist congregations are more likely to participate civically in informal ways, be less dependent on external resources for their involvement, and emphasize civic activity that advances their own particular religious and ethnic interests.

Informal civic participation took a variety of forms. At Gayatri Pariwar Mandir, members provided meals for sick or needy neighbors and organized health lectures and informal clinics that used Indian ayurvedic and homeopathic health practices to address needs of recent immigrants. But these services were provided in an ad hoc way rather than via a formal institutionalized program. As one member told us, "Gayatri temple is good. It gives us strength, [teaches us] how to purify our life, how to reach out and help people." When we asked how the temple did that, the response was somewhat vague and halting. "I . . . , I just, whenever people need some help, like with food or something, I try to do that. I try to cook. I try to do everything. Clothes or anything, I do that. Or sometimes, United Way, they need help, so I donate money, you know? I try to do whatever I can do to help other people. A little bit will help somebody." We followed up by asking whether Gayatri temple ever did these things as a group. "Um, I don't know about here, but I'll do my own somewhere else. I do that." Similarly, at HanMaUm Buddhist temple, members spoke of involvement in the PTA, local arts organizations, or neighborhood block organizations. But again, the activities were ad hoc rather than programmatic efforts of the temple itself. Members took their Buddhism to the streets as good Buddhists but did not necessarily view their civic participation as an extension of the temple to which they belonged.

Much of the civic participation we observed, especially in individualist congregations, was focused on individual religious or ethnic identity-based interests. At Naperville Church of the Brethren, for example, immigrants were unlikely to participate in activities that the previous white congregants had emphasized. As a (white) former pastor told us, "For years . . . we've had a project of buying Christmas presents for children that's taken out there [to Wayside Cross Ministries in Aurora, Illinois]. But, basically, [Indians] don't give [their] children Christmas presents, and that's just not part of their culture. And the white group year after year just can't seem to get that into their heads that that's not what [Indians] do. . . . I mean, they're not giving their own kids presents, and I know they feel like they're contributing to the commercialization of Christmas to do this. They don't see it as a mission. You know, American families think this is nice to give presents to poor kids. Indian families just don't see it that way." On the other hand, Indian immigrants in the Naperville congregation don't just stay at home sitting on their hands. They are active in the Indian Christian Federation of the Midwest and do things with them like marching in the Indian Independence Day parade. They are well connected to other Gujarati organizations and extended family networks and are quick to respond to crises such as sickness or death in the community or to problems in India such as the earthquake in Gujarat state. But note that these examples of civic engagement primarily occur within the context of Gujarati (mostly evangelical) Christian social networks. The Naperville congregation has been adamant about not cooperating with Hindu groups or events, even refusing to rent their space to Hindu groups for weddings or other celebrations.

Even for second-generation immigrants, we observe these patterns persisting. College or university contexts provide an opportunity for young adult children of immigrants to gain experience in civic engagement, but the pattern of ad hoc identity-based engagement remains. Ethnic student organizations are prominent and seem to be the primary channel for college students' engagement. As one Chinese Lutheran young adult told us, "In college, [my involvement] was more Asian. I think that was one thing that I kind of regretted. They swept me in, and I felt very comfortable in it. . . . I got to know people in my dorm better—those were all different people; but in terms of actual clubs, I felt kind of weird joining."

Another kind of civic participation that we looked for in our interviews was participation in civil religion. Individualist religion, of course, does not provide extensive symbolic or material resources for engagement in civil religion. Not surprisingly, we found very little evidence of it in our interviews with members of congregations in our individualist category. Occasionally, we noticed people wearing "United We Stand" pins or displaying flags, especially after September 11. Some congregations occasionally included patriotic music in their services or displayed the American flag, but this was not the norm, and it may have had more to do with the post-9/11 climate than with a serious interest in American civil religion.

In contrast to the ad hoc informal civic participation when moral authority or moral projects are viewed individualistically, collectivistic religious ideals produce more programmatic and formally organized venues for civic participation. When a religious group conceives of its primary moral projects in collectivist ways, especially in the absence of sectarianism, it facilitates the civic engagement of members. Civic participation may be seen as a duty, even above religious activity. The civic participation that occurs is also more likely to address a broader range of public issues, rather than being limited to the pursuit of particular private group interests.

On civic participation as a religious duty, Jay Desai, a lay leader at the BAPS Swaminarayan temple, explained how the temple's members were involved in a variety of social services: "Many ask 'How can you mix spirituality and social services?' We ask, 'How can you separate the two?'" As quoted earlier, a priest at the Maternity BVM Roman Catholic parish was even more emphatic: "the first focus of each member's ministry is their home, workplace, and community," where they "live, work, and pray and play."

This is not to imply that collectivist congregations view religious activity within the congregation as unimportant or irrelevant. Rather, they are more likely than are individualists to view civic participation itself as religious activity, and to think of their members' public participation as representative of the congregation's mission. Several of the key activists at Maternity BVM are leaders in outside social action groups, but they act as members of the parish and often hold public meetings or protest events within the parish grounds itself. They are the first talking heads that local television news crews are likely to contact, and televised interviews often occur with the church buildings in the background. Thus, members' individual civic participation also heightens the visibility and strengthens the collective identity of the parish as a community concerned about neighborhood public issues.

Another way collectivists contrast with individualists is in the form that civic participation takes. Collectivists are more likely to be engaged in organized, programmatic, institutional ways than in the informal ad hoc manner characteristic of the individualist groups. In our interviews, there was frequent mention of involvement with block clubs or of collaborating with civic institutions such as the mayor's office or the police department to address particular neighborhood issues. Maria, a key lay member at Maternity BVM, was particularly articulate on this.

> Now from the church I got involved in an organization that opened my eyes on how I can change a block, on how I can change different negative things that were happening in our block. This was a terrible block. Twelve years ago we were ready to move out, but they told us how we can move things, you know. And that's what I want other people to learn—that they can do things just like I do, you know. They think I am a politician. I am not a politician. I just find that I got to know who's who. If we have a problem with the light, I don't want to dial 311, I want to know who is in charge of the light in my block and I want to meet that person, you know. If I need to talk with the mayor, we'll have a meeting with the mayor. He comes to our block. He knows us because we are involved. We are involved in many meetings, in many things that he sees us, so he knows us. But you got to know who your aldermen are. You got to know who your street sanitation people are. You got to know who is involved in your area so that you could start partnering, because the thing is that we got to partner up with whoever . . . but using all the resource agencies and organizations that are in your neighborhood. Use them, because that's how we are going to make up a community village, a community village that is networking and helping each other. Like if I know Juan knows how to do this, well, let's get Juan. He knows how to work on the computer. Let's get him over here so he can help our kids. Juan knows another guy who knows how to do math. Let's get him to come in and help.

Note that when Maria thinks of addressing a public problem via civic participation, she moves immediately, seemingly instinctively, to collective solutions, drawing other individuals and agencies into collaboratively building a neighborhood "village" that will be able to tackle the problem at hand. Of course, not everyone we encountered was such an energetic organizer. But even our interviewees who participated less dramatically tended to do so via collectivities—groups like block clubs, the PTA, or other community organizations.

Thus far, we have focused on how the civic participation of people from collectivist congregations tends toward taking action in addressing issues in the neighborhood or larger community outside the congregation. This is particularly true of nonsectarian congregations like Maternity BVM. Sectarianism, however, can interact with collectivism to produce somewhat different patterns of citizen engagement. In sectarian congregations, the most relevant collectivity is usually the congregation or religious group itself. Individuals are still likely to participate in organized programmatic ways, but the groups via which they participate in civic life are often rooted in a particular religious or ethnic identity, rather than being broader, more pluralistic groups (like block clubs or PTAs). For example, members at Synagogue FREE produce a Russian-language newspaper that is distributed widely outside the congregation. Each month, between fifteen hundred and two thousand issues are distributed out of state, about half going to New York. The primary target audience is the Russian-speaking immigrant community, however, not the larger American public square. Any impact the paper has on broader public discourse is likely to be an indirect product of its impact on its Russian immigrant readers.

Turning to the question of civil religion, it is perhaps unsurprising that we found more evidence of civil religious activity in collectivist congregations than we saw in the individualist groups. It was not, however, a generic American civil religion that we found. Some, to be sure, involved standard symbols that one might find in many U.S. religious settings. The American flag, for example, was often prominently displayed, both inside and outside religious sanctuaries. At St. Demetrios Greek Orthodox Church, however, it appeared alongside a Greek flag. We found similar juxtapositions at other congregations, as well. Polish symbols were prominent in a large mosaic mural behind the altar at Five Holy Martyrs Roman Catholic Church. Apparently, civil religion in immigrant congregations can apply both to the host country and the country of origin.

This conjunction of civil religions in immigrant congregations may portend a shift in how civil religion will affect American public life and discourse. For immigrant religions, it is not likely to induce blind loyalty to U.S. actions and policies, nor is it simply a melding of civil religion into one generic stew. Rather, congregational leaders and members appear to hold multiple identities and loyalties in a dynamic tension. Participating in U.S. civil religion *and* in a foreign civil religion may produce loyal dissent within the U.S. context. On one of our visits to the Islamic Cultural Center, for example, we noted a bulletin board proudly displaying a local newspaper report on the imam's condemnation of U.S. sanctions against Iraq. Nearby was a window full of American flags made from construction paper by the children in the mosque's day school.

In our observations in congregational settings, we also noticed some signs of an emergent global civil religion, particularly in multiethnic congregations. At St. Lambert Roman Catholic Church, we observed the choir rehearsing "America, the Beautiful" for performance in a later service. At the same time, several women were taping flags to the choir balcony from the many countries of origin represented in the congregation. National flags from countries in North and South America, Europe, Africa, Asia, and the Middle East were on display.

Similarly, if on a smaller scale, the sanctuary of Victory Outreach displayed flags from many different countries in Latin America.

It remains to be seen how these trends in civil religion will play out in the post-9/11 climate in the United States. Certainly the congregations we observed turned up the volume on their claims to being loyal Americans after the events in 2001. But we did not observe a concomitant decline in displaying their connections to other parts of the world. If anything, the response of new immigrant religious groups to 9/11 brought individuals and groups of various national origins together in declaring their religion to be civil and appropriately public in contrast to the uncivil religion of the perpetrators of violence. This may very well hasten a trend toward a more globalized and multiethnic civil religion.

# 10    *Organizational Engagement*

THE ECOLOGY OF IMMIGRANT
CONGREGATIONS

> *We can think about the community in which a con-*
> *gregation is lodged as an ecology of resources and*
> *organizations in which people seek out social support*
> *for everything from the most basic survival needs to*
> *sociability, aesthetic pleasure, meaning making, and*
> *community improvement.*
>
> —Nancy Ammerman (1997)

In January 2001, a devastating earthquake struck the state of Gujarat in India. Official counts of more than twenty thousand fatalities and nearly sixteen million other people affected by the devastation generated humanitarian responses from governments and nongovernmental organizations from around the world. These relief efforts provided an early test of our ideas about how religion might matter for civic engagement locally, nationally, and globally. It was particularly illustrative of how new immigrant congregations can operate within networks connecting various religious, civic, governmental, and business organizations.

The response to the 2001 Gujarat earthquake mounted by the BAPS Swaminarayan Hindu temple in suburban Chicago stood out among all our research sites, even among the five sites with exclusively or significantly large Indian constituencies. The Chicago temple coordinated the local portion of a massive relief effort by the BAPS international organization. It allied with civic partners from both the Indian American community, such as the Indian Pharmacists of Chicago and various Indian American businesses, and the larger non-Indian community, like Swedish Covenant Hospital of Chicago and United Airlines. The DuPage County Board, with whom the temple had developed an amiable working relationship over the years, passed a resolution in support of the earthquake victims and encouraged county residents to contribute to the BAPS relief efforts.

Within a very short time, the temple was able to send a DC-10 loaded with relief supplies from Chicago to Bombay. A county official characterized the local temple as "one of most organized, detail-oriented groups I've ever worked with." The *Chicago Tribune*'s coverage of local responses to the disaster listed contact information for only two organizations, CARE and BAPS (Zajac and Hussain 2001). (Later that same year, the BAPS congregation mounted a similar relief effort for the residents of New York City following the devastating events of September 11.)

What aspects of BAPS Swaminarayan Hinduism motivated this group's impressive response to the Gujarat earthquake and created an organizational ecology capable of delivering a global response? We received our first clues in a talk given by a Swaminarayan dignitary at the Chicago temple several months after the earthquake. "What is the body and the soul?" he asked the congregation, employing generic Hindu theology as an entrée into the BAPS perspective.

> God created it all, body and soul, not just to enjoy, but to serve God. . . . You all have wealth, treasure, and knowledge. You have been given it by God, but you must use it properly. You must use your gifts for good causes, such as serving God. This can't be done just by *prasada* [a common Hindu ritual] and prayer. We also need to serve God. Through the *sadhus* [spiritual and moral leaders] we can reach God. Serving the needs of the world is serving God. . . . To learn what is good and bad, you need the guidance of the sadhus and the scripture. Without sadhus and scripture, we can't choose the right path.

The speaker then tied BAPS theology directly to the recent earthquake: "We have all the knowledge, but gurus [spiritual teachers] help us to use it, to operate it. That is the greatness of our gurus, to inspire us. The earthquake did unimaginable damage. Everyone has to do something. God appears in many forms and it is our duty to serve [them]. . . . We must serve the world and get inspiration."

According to Raymond Williams's (2001) authoritative treatment of Swaminarayan Hinduism, the ultimate moral authority for this religious group resides in *akshar purushottam* (the "AP" in BAPS), the Supreme Person in the realm of Ultimate Reality who incarnates in the group's founder, Sahajanand Swami or Swaminarayan (1781–1830), and his spiritual successors. "The akshar, as one of the succession of 'god-realized' saints, is the representative of god on earth; he gives the perfect example, speaks with the authority of god, and receives the reverence and worship of the devotees. He is accepted as the perfect ideal for emulation by all spiritual aspirants" (Williams 2001, 93). Swaminarayan Hinduism is known for linking sacredness and morality in these holy persons, unlike other Hindu groups whose holy persons are unfettered by moral considerations. BAPS sadhus provide ethical as well as spiritual models for the lay followers.

From its inception in nineteenth-century Gujarat, Swaminarayan Hinduism has been renowned for its central moral project, which stresses individual moral regeneration that leads to social improvement. The British colonial government was impressed with the Swaminarayan movement's force for civic good, and a case can be made that the two worked in concert to bring social stability and modernization to Gujarat. It is common today for Indian government officials to attend Swaminarayan festivals, indicating a continuing recognition of the movement's civic importance. Less than two weeks after the 2001 earthquake, the chief minister of Gujarat issued a public commendation of the BAPS relief efforts, noting that these were part of a legacy of civic good works by the group in India and elsewhere.

Williams sees Swaminarayan Hinduism as a case study in the powerful influence of religion's transcendent referent in adherents' lives. "The stated purpose of his [Sahajanand's] manifestation is the redemption of many souls and the establishment of moral and social order" (92). Theology and morality are integrally linked in Swaminarayan Hinduism, as the group's view of the sacred world motivates its reforms of the social world.

The Gujarat earthquake relief efforts typified the practical theology of the BAPS Swaminarayan movement. According to a local BAPS source, the other Hindu temples of Chicago chose not to join the BAPS project, although the local Jain temple did so. In some cases, the local Hindu reticence may have stemmed from sectarian differences in understanding the moral implications of Hindu theology, in other cases perhaps it was due to preference for their own relief efforts. Several other religious organizations were involved in the earthquake relief efforts generally. Some contributed to the efforts of the India Development and Relief Fund, an umbrella organization of Indian Americans that raises funds for relief and development projects in India. Other Hindu groups appear to share with BAPS a practical Vedantic theology with humanitarian imperatives. (Another example of such a Hindu group is the Ramakrishna movement. See Jackson [1994].)

Larger religious divisions within the Indian American community precluded other linkages. For example, certain conservative Muslim or evangelical Christian groups declined to collaborate with their co-ethnic Hindus in relief efforts. It is too simplistic to assume that immense tragedies like earthquakes will necessarily forge broad religious coalitions to respond to human needs, even when ethnicity is shared. For the majority of members in our Gujarati Protestant site, for example, throwing in with Hindus on any moral project would be unthinkable, for that would constitute a tacit approval of Hinduism's truth claims. Instead, earthquake relief efforts in this church were funneled largely through a network of evangelical Indian initiatives, virtually bypassing the channels used by the congregation's parent denomination.

Another major event that occurred early in our research was the 9/11 attack on New York's World Trade Center and the Pentagon in Washington, D.C. Our research sites responded to this tragedy as well, often motivated by their religious ideas, practices, and identities. As with the responses to the Gujarat earthquake, religion mattered in specific ways. The mosques responded to some extent out of their generic Muslim identity, but, more important, as particular kinds of Muslim congregations. The same with our churches, temples, and synagogue—they responded as Christians, Buddhists, Hindus, and Jews in a broad sense, but, more important, followed their particular perspectives within each religious tradition.

Internal congregational perspectives are not always uniform or unified, again illustrated by the suburban Gujarati Protestant congregation in the wake of 9/11. An initially German American congregation established in 1855, Naperville Church of the Brethren became predominantly Indian in the 1990s. The immigrant members bring a conservative missionary Brethren identity into the liberal Brethren territory of the United States. Most of the congregation's non-Indian clergy and lay leaders during the period of Indian influx have been liberal Brethren. Indian leaders have adopted an unofficial name—Gujarati Christian Fellowship—that both distances their membership from the liberal tendencies of the parent denomination and signifies their adherence to a generic Indian evangelical Protestantism. This congregation is a major node in an Indian evangelical network that stretches from Chicago to other Indian communities in the United States and back to the Indian homeland.

The difference between missionary Brethren and liberal Brethren perspectives surfaced on our visit to the Naperville church shortly after 9/11. We noticed two disparate items on the bulletin board in the foyer. The first presented the denomination's positions on the attacks, the subsequent retaliatory incidents across the United States, and the general topic of Christian relations with other religions. The document blended denominational emphases on social justice and active pacifism with a liberal Protestant interfaith agenda. Also on the bulletin board was a newsletter from Al-Bashir, an evangelical Christian organization in India, addressed to one of the congregation's Indian leaders. In Al-Bashir's view, 9/11 opened a door in India, offering the potential to "win many souls together for Christ from among the Muslims who definitely head towards a Christless grave." One Indian leader of the Naperville congregation explained to us that the Indian members did not support the Brethren denomination's stance against the subsequent war in Iraq. He suggested that, given incidents of Muslim persecution of Christians in India, they perceive Muslims as the enemy. They also see Muslims more as souls to be saved than as partners in interfaith dialogue. Such views differ from the liberal views of other congregational leaders and members, including many second-generation Indians nurtured in denominational Brethrenism by their Sunday school teachers and youth group leaders. Like many congregations, the Naperville church's response (or multiple responses) to social issues and world events often reflects internal religious differences.

In the rest of this chapter we will explore in greater detail how the civic engagement of immigrant congregations is influenced by their location in various important organizational networks and by the character of their relationships within those networks. We, like many others before us (e.g.,

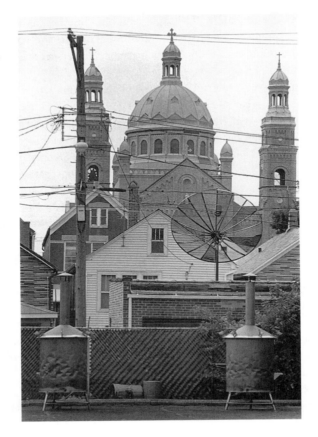

Immigrant congregations belong to local, national, and international social networks. Photo by Jerry Berndt.

Ammerman 1997; Eiesland and Warner 1998; Ebaugh et al. 2000; Eiesland 2000), find the ecological metaphor to be helpful here.[1] Congregations exist within dynamic webs of relationships that provide opportunities and constraints and define some as friends and others as enemies within a given historical, religious, or geographic context. When and how a group chooses to engage with others will be shaped by the social and organizational ecology webs to which they belong and which they help to create. We will examine multiple dimensions of ecological relationships: geographic ecology (relationships to other civic and political organizations in a congregation's locale), economic ecology (relationships to occupational niches, job markets, or other economic institutions), intra- and interdenominational ecology (relationships to other groups within the same broad religious tradition), and interfaith ecology (relationships to other broad religious traditions).

## How Religion Might Matter

What influence might religion have on how immigrant congregations connect to their organizational ecologies? The moral project variable we have employed throughout this book is likely to be particularly important here. Those who conceive of their primary moral projects in collectivist terms are more likely to view particular issues or problems in broader structural terms. They should thus be more likely to recognize their linkages to other groups and institutions and activate those linkages when they seek to engage public issues. We expect to see more readiness among collectivists to engage in collaborative efforts with others and, conversely, to identify other groups or institutions as targets in seeking to bring about some sort of social change. Congregations, on the other hand, who define their primary moral projects in individualist terms should be less likely to build strong ties with other collectivities in their environment and more likely to connect in informal or ad hoc ways. They may also be more likely to view other groups as competitors offering alternative solutions to individual problems, whether those be salvation or substance abuse rehabilitation.

Sectarianism is also likely to play a significant role in shaping a congregation's ecological connections. Strong sectarianism, especially around social or cultural issues (rather than specifically religious ones), will hinder the ability to forge collaborative links with others. To the extent that sectarians do build alliances, their most valued ecological networks are likely to be more homogeneous. We would expect groups that are both individualist and sectarian to have particularly tenuous ecological ties.

Finally, it may well be that these religious factors vary in their influence across the different domains of engagement explored earlier. Some issues or categories of activity, such as occupation, may be a relatively safe context within which to engage other groups. In another domain, such as education, linking up with external groups may threaten religious or ethnic identity. There, ecological ties may be more contentious than collaborative.

## Geographic Ecology

Congregations are located in a particular place. Religions of course vary in how they relate to their place, and that relationship will have an impact on how they engage with others in the same locale. Scholars distinguish between two broad types of congregations' connection to their geography. Ammerman has labeled these types parish congregations and niche congregations (Ammerman 1997; see also Livezey 2000; Livezey et al., forthcoming; Ebaugh and Chafetz 2000b). Parish congregations are closely tied to their neighborhoods. Historically, Roman Catholic parishes have been the archetype, viewing the church and the immediate locale it serves as essentially contiguous. But other religious traditions also tend to establish congregations that are closely identified with place, such as the Jewish *eruv* and Mormon wards and stakes. Niche congregations, on the other hand, serve a niche market of the population. For them, a location may be chosen on pragmatic grounds or for idiosyncratic reasons. Their members are usually not residents of the local neighborhood, but they may travel significant distances to participate in the congregation's activities, drawn by the particular services it offers.

Both types are represented among our research sites in about equal proportions. Significantly, there is a strong correlation between our individualist-collectivist distinction and the geographic type. Congregations who view their primary moral project in collective terms, focusing on building the right kind of community, seem much more likely to apply those instincts to the place immediately around them and to recognize the contiguity of religious and geographic community. On the other hand, an individualist approach to moral action is a good fit with the niche congregational form. A congregation can apply its moral influence to individuals independently of the geographic place where they live. It only requires that individuals be present in the congregation, whether they walk to services from their homes in the neighborhood or commute from many miles away.

Relating to geographic place is a front-burner issue for immigrant congregations. Immigration produces population change. Thus, immigrant congregations are very often located in places that are experiencing demographic change, whether in the central city, in the suburbs, or along the exurban perimeter. We observed four patterns of immigrant congregational connection to their changing environs. Most were present in both types of congregation, but the first two were more prevalent in parish or collectivist congregations, while the third and fourth were more common in the niche or individualist congregations.

The first pattern occurs when a congregation's demographic composition changes to reflect the changing composition of its neighborhood. This pattern is typical of congregations that are committed to the parish model. The Maternity BVM Roman Catholic parish, for example, is located in a neighborhood that for many years was populated almost entirely by residents from Puerto Rico. In recent years, many Puerto Ricans (especially the upwardly mobile) have been displaced by newer Mexican and Central American immigrants. The parish maintained its mission to its mostly poor or working-class Spanish-speaking neighbors. In the process the ethnic makeup of its congregants shifted to a much more diverse Latin American group. With the influx of new members from Mexico and Central America, there was an increased influence of charismatic/Pentecostal religion, and the parish established a charismatic prayer group whose regulars are predominantly Central American. Thus, in this collectivist parish congregation, a changing neighborhood produced changes in the congregation itself.

A second pattern we observed is when an immigrant congregation emerges alongside a new population. This can occur when a congregation chooses to locate itself where there is a residential concentration of its target population. Gayatri Pariwar Mandir, a storefront Hindu temple, moved from its previous location in the suburbs to Devon Avenue on Chicago's north side after that became, in the 1980s, an area with a very high concentration of Indo-Pakistani immigrants. It may also occur when immigrants choose to settle near a religious congregation of their tradition that is already located in a particular place. Further west on Devon Avenue, Synagogue FREE, for example, was established as a Lubavitch Hasidic congregation in 1973 in an old historically Jewish neighborhood. Its mission from the start was to serve immigrant Jews from Eastern Europe, especially Russia, and its presence in the neighborhood helped to attract Russian immigrants to the locale. In both these cases, the immigrant congregation and the immigrant population develop together, mutually reinforcing each other and helping to stabilize the religious and ethnic character of the neighborhood.

A third pattern is when the neighborhood changes around an older established congregation, but the congregation's demographics remain the same. Typically in such a case, the former neighborhood residents move out but continue returning to the neighborhood for religious services. This was the case, for example, at Five Holy Martyrs Roman Catholic parish. Its neighborhood, Brighton Park, had been a predominantly Polish neighborhood since the parish's founding in 1908. Beginning in the 1990s, the neighborhood gradually transitioned to being predominantly Mexican, but the congregation continues to serve new Polish immigrants, as well as second- and third-generation Polish Americans. It chose not to offer any Spanish-language masses, as many other formerly Polish parishes on Chicago's southwest side have done. In the process, Five Holy Martyrs, although Catholic, has shifted toward the niche congregational type. Its niche market is the population of Polish immigrants and Polish Americans, and it draws its congregants from around the city and suburbs. Perhaps as a consequence, Five Holy Martyrs is the only one of the three Roman Catholic parishes we studied to be coded as individualist in its conception of its primary moral project.

Finally, there is a fourth common pattern that may involve little or no intentional connection to a congregation's neighborhood. Many immigrant congregations choose their location for convenience (cheap land or proximity to major transportation thoroughfares) or for idiosyncratic reasons (avoiding hostile neighborhoods or developing in the neighborhood where its leader happens to live). The BAPS Swaminarayan Hindu temple chose to develop its complex in the far northwestern suburb of Bartlett because that is where it was able to acquire a large plot of land at reasonable cost. Islamic Cultural Center of Greater Chicago settled in Northbrook, even in the absence of a large concentration of Bosnian Muslims there, because their imam moved to Northbrook for personal reasons and was able to acquire a property for a mosque and Bosnian Cultural Center. After the fact, of course, these congregations may develop local connections for pragmatic or religious reasons. BAPS has of necessity maintained a close relationship with the DuPage County Board that facilitates its ambitious building projects, and the current imam of the Islamic Cultural Center has become very active in the local interfaith clergy association.

The patterns described here have a significant impact on the geographic dispersion of a congregation's members and thus on the possibilities for civic engagement. The first and second patterns are characterized by a locally concentrated membership. Combined with a collectivist parish model of congregational life, this supports a more concerted and intense engagement with a narrower range of local concerns. The third and fourth patterns are characterized by a widely dispersed membership whose individuals connect to a broad and diverse collection of social and institutional networks. This may not bode well for a congregation's active involvement in its immediate neighborhood, but it may support civic engagement across a larger variety of settings. And as Granovetter (1973) showed, such diverse and weak ties may be very advantageous indeed, providing a broad range of access to information and influence.[2] We turn now to a closer look at how these varying geographic patterns and the religious distinction between individualism and collectivism produce variations in the form and content of a congregation's engagement with its neighborhood.

The neighborhood connections of collectivist congregations, especially if they are of the parish type, parallel the patterns we observed when we considered collectivists' individual citizenship engagement. That is, such congregations' ecological relationships tend to be more programmatic and institutionalized rather than ad hoc and provisional. These sorts of congregations typically exhibit the first two geographic patterns discussed above—that is, older established parish congregations whose demographics change to reflect their neighborhood, or newer emergent congregations who develop alongside a new religious or ethnic population in a neighborhood. Their ecological connections are multiple, dense, and local.

The Maternity BVM Catholic parish joins alliances with other religious and civic associations to address neighborhood concerns such as immigration policies, rights of day laborers, or gang violence. (The only groups with whom they explicitly avoid collaborating are Protestant Pentecostal churches, because they distrust their motives, seeing them as more interested in recruiting converts from Catholicism than in addressing neighborhood problems.) Similarly, Synagogue FREE joins forces with other local social service agencies and community organizations (primarily Jewish, but not necessarily Hasidic or Orthodox) to provide for the needs of its members and neighbors.

While the form of ecological relationships—multiple, dense, and local—may be similar across the various collectivist parishes, the content of such relationships varies. Socioeconomic class appears to be particularly important here, even more than religion. While Maternity BVM and Synagogue FREE, located in poor or working-class neighborhoods, affiliate with others to address social and economic issues, St. Lambert Catholic parish in Skokie and the Islamic Cultural Center in Northbrook do so to address cultural issues. Both of the latter are located in middle- and upper-class neighborhoods, serving a relatively well-educated and well-off constituency. Their concerns run more toward increasing interreligious and intercultural understanding. They participate with other groups in organizing religious dialogues or participating in multicultural events of various sorts.

Within the class differences, however, religion still matters. As noted above, Maternity BVM is willing to ally itself with others, but only with certain others. It has a collaborative relationship with the San Lucas United Church of Christ congregation, but not with neighborhood Pentecostal congregations, because the latter have proselytizing ambitions, while the former does not. Victory Outreach, a smaller Protestant congregation, but one that also exists in a close parishlike relationship with its neighborhood, does almost no collaborative work with other groups. It prefers to confront others in a more evangelistic mode rather than to risk diluting its message by collaborating.

The parish or neighborhood form of geographic ecology was actually in the minority among the sixteen congregations we studied. More than two-thirds of our research sites (and nearly all of the individualist congregations) were of the niche type.[3] Niche congregations nearly all reflected the third and fourth geographic patterns identified above—either old established congregations whose demographics reflected an earlier neighborhood population, or congregations whose geographic location was somewhat accidental and based on pragmatic considerations. Particularly for the individualist congregations in this group, their neighborhood connections parallel the patterns noted in the last chapter for individualist citizenship engagement. That is, they tend to be ad hoc and impermanent, assembled for particular purposes but not forged for the long haul. Their ecological ties tend to be weaker and more broadly dispersed than the dense local ties of the collectivist parishes.

For example, the ISKCON temple in the Rogers Park community area of Chicago maintains friendly relations with the local Catholic church, using its parking lot for overflow at large ISKCON events. Its members participate in an annual interreligious festival in the neighborhood and join in parades with other groups on religious or ethnic holidays. There is very little, however, in the way of programmatic involvement in formal interorganizational alliances—that is, the sort of connections that would be stable and persist over time. We found this ecological pattern to be typical of other niche congregations we studied, particularly those, such as the Buddhist temples, who were more individualistic in how they defined their primary moral projects.

This is not to say, however, that such congregations have few ecological resources to exploit. Having a variety of weaker ad hoc connections means that in any given situation the congregation has a broad pool of potential collaborators. As one of the ISKCON leaders told us, "We try to keep all the channels open, because in this day and age, in order to sometimes get something done . . . like help get the neighborhood cleaned up from drug dealers or something . . . it's a mutual kind of goal, so all the churches pitch in together to achieve a common goal." Broad and shallow relationships are also more likely to be civil, even friendly. This is particularly valuable for religious groups like ISKCON that may be new in the neighborhood or that have controversial reputations to overcome. As quoted earlier, the same leader noted that, in the process of working together with other groups on particular projects, "we [come to] understand each other better—so we're not people with, well, Cyclops or two heads or . . . [laughs]. We find that our philosophies are pretty much alike."

## Economic Ecology

Congregations play a significant but varying role in the webs of economic relationships that help to form urban communities. Immigrant congregations, especially, often comprise a critical mass of individuals with particular occupational and economic needs, presenting a marketing niche for businesses and other economic entities. In our interviews and observations we noted that congregations took part in employment markets, engaged in symbiotic relations with local and transnational businesses, and occasionally were important economic actors themselves.

One of the most pressing concerns for new immigrants to the United States is their place in the employment market. Some immigrants, especially professionals, arrive with a job already in hand. But many others need to figure out how to navigate the American employment terrain after arriving here. Often, even if they do find work, they find themselves underemployed, working in jobs that do not make full use of their skills and training. In most of the congregations we studied, we found explicit concern for connecting new immigrants with employment opportunities; but how such concern is expressed varies significantly. Not surprisingly, the individualist/collectivist distinction matters.

Individualist congregations, likely to view employment as a product of individual choices and actions, depend primarily on informal networking and support for members facing employment difficulties. As an informant at the ISKCON temple told us:

> Sometimes members of our congregation that are new to America may approach the temple representatives for some type of job placement . . . And because our congregation is quite large with members coming from various walks of life, many that are business owners, we'll try to connect them with

someone from our congregation who perhaps has their own job and can hire that individual for some time or can assist them in some type of job placement. . . . Usually, just by linking these individuals with other members of our congregation, something can be worked out like finding a job for that individual or helping them with language differences or cultural differences.

Similarly, a key leader at Naperville Church of the Brethren told us that the congregation had no formal job training or placement programs but focused instead on informal encouragement and moral support for unemployed or underemployed individuals.

I think any pastor who comes here has got to be aware of that issue because how can you leave your country as a middle-aged professional earning a certain salary and you come to a church and you become a low-paid worker and the pastor is unconcerned? It concerns me because these people have given up a lot, you know, and it seems to me that any pastor would seek to at least encourage them, not force, because you can't force anybody, encourage them to explore options. "Look, you can get a better job if you do A, B, C. What about it?"

Note that in both these cases the onus is on individuals to take proper action, and the expectation is that other individuals will offer assistance. The consequence is that these congregations have little in the way of organized, programmatic, collective activities in the local employment ecology, but congregational members may have access to a broad range of individual linkages to a variety of job market locations. Again, the strength of weak ties comes to mind.

Collectivist congregations, on the other hand, are much more likely to be organizationally involved in the job market, a node in their own right in the local occupational ecology. Maternity BVM Catholic Church, for example, works collaboratively both with labor unions and the local Chamber of Commerce in addressing local development and employment concerns. The BAPS Swaminarayan temple has close relations with the Indian Pharmacy Association, collaborating with them in various activities, including organizing relief efforts for the Gujarat earthquake described earlier. Even Victory Outreach, a much smaller congregation with much fewer resources, keeps a permanent bulletin board with information about GED classes, current job postings, and information on the church's "Life Skills Ministry," where participants are taught how to build a résumé, interview successfully, and plan a workable personal budget.

Another related ecological system involves congregational relationships with business enterprises. These are often local relationships but may even extend internationally. We observed important symbiotic relations between congregations and businesses in both types of congregations, but most extensively in the collectivist group. The most readily apparent relationships are between congregations and food-related businesses. These were notable in our wind-shield survey of the neighborhoods surrounding the congregations we studied. Even if a congregation is not located within an ethnic residential enclave, it acts as a regular attractor of particular ethnic clientele, and, consequently, ethnic restaurants and/or grocery stores are likely to locate nearby. Such businesses may provide goods and services to congregations (sometimes donating food for support of clerics, sometimes catering special events for a reduced fee or gratis), and the religious leaders of congregations may provide blessings or other ritual services to the business owners. This is particularly noteworthy in the case of many immigrant Buddhist communities where the importance of the ritual interaction between laity and monastics around meals has created a complex network of temples and restaurants even beyond the neighborhood.

We found the most extensive relationships with businesses in collectivist congregations. Groups who instinctively think of themselves as a collective whole rather than a collection of individuals may find it easier to build linkages with other corporate entities. In any case, among the collectivist congregations, we observed extensive connections to local businesses—and this was true across the range of religious traditions. Bulletins and event programs in mosques, temples, and churches carried advertising for business enterprises. There is an obvious symbiotic relationship here where businesses help to support the activities of the congregation, and the congregation provides the business with an easily accessible market. Sometimes these relationships seemed surprisingly cozy. At the close of one Catholic mass, for example, the priest asked people to remain in their seats for an important announcement. The announcement turned out to be a presentation by the manager of a local pharmacy, who proceeded to tout his business's good services and discount prices. His business cards, which he distributed at the door, noted that the business was bilingual.

Congregations may also provide an opportunity for philanthropic activity on the part of large businesses. At Synagogue FREE, for example, much of the furniture and the cost of an extensive renovation were donated by a construction company whose owner was affiliated with the synagogue. Sometimes, these philanthropic relations may be more distant but still quite beneficial to congregations. One large corporation, which employs some of the members at St. Lambert Catholic Church, allows its employees to take paid days for community service. One of the very active lay members we interviewed was thus able to contribute time to organize special events at St. Lambert without giving up her income. This obviously benefits the congregation but also serves the corporation well in generating good will and perhaps a tax deduction.

Another type of economic relationship occurs when congregations operate businesses on their own. Of course, many U.S. congregations engage in small-scale businesses such as bookshops, rummage sales, or carnivals. But a few of the congregations we studied (and only within the collectivist group) were engaged in economic activity on a rather large scale. Synagogue FREE publishes *Shalom*, a Russian-language newspaper, with a large national and international circulation. In addition to about two thousand subscribers, it is distributed in local Russian-oriented businesses. Beyond providing employment for members, the newspaper helps Synagogue FREE to maintain relationships with Russian immigrants locally and to identify itself nationally and internationally as a destination synagogue in Chicago.

The BAPS Swaminarayan temple is also a significant economic entity in addition to being a religious congregation. Serving food to all guests and worshippers is a religious duty for the temple. Given that thousands attend the temple on a regular basis, food production is a large operation. The Chicago temple has its own subsidiary corporation that serves food free of charge at the temple but also operates as a catering business. In addition, it has a large snack-food production and distribution operation, providing packaged snacks that adhere to Swaminarayan dietary restrictions. Its goods are distributed nationally. The worldwide BAPS organization also has its own printing press, located in India. Via desktop publishing and the Internet, local temples such as the one in Chicago can produce their own literature for use within the temple and for distribution in their bookstore. The material is actually printed in India and shipped to the United States for distribution. The Chicago BAPS temple is also a distributor of the BAPS Amrut line of ayurvedic health care products manufactured in India. Thus, congregations may be important economic actors not only locally but also nationally and internationally.

All three varieties of occupational/economic relationships we observed in congregations provide important services to immigrant members. Services such as entrée to labor markets are provided by virtually all congregations, small and large, individualist and collectivist alike. Beyond that, congregations who develop extensive organized and sustained economic relationships (and here we are speaking primarily of collectivist congregations) contribute to broader development and stability within their locale, particularly when their relationships are primarily local. They generate economic activity and investment and, perhaps more important, build webs of interdependence and mutual obligation that help to form and sustain community.

## Religious Ecology

There are several different religious ecological systems to consider in the case of local congregations. First, there is the network of relationships between a congregation and the larger religious organization to which it belongs. "Denomination" is the term used by Christian churches, but other religions have more or less analogous forms (such as the lineages in Buddhism and Hinduism). We refer to these as intradenominational relationships. Second, there are networks of relationships between a given congregation and other religious groups within its broader religious tradition but outside its denomination. For example, an Orthodox synagogue may participate in a Jewish social service program that includes Conservative and Reform groups as well. We refer to these networks as interdenominational. Finally, local congregations may also belong to networks of relationships with groups in altogether different religious traditions, as when a Hindu temple collaborates with the local Catholic parish. We call these interfaith networks. Not surprisingly, the religious characteristics of a congregation influence how it relates to other religious bodies. We found, however, that the individual/collective distinctions that are so influential in other ecologies did not have a significant effect on religious ecologies. Of the religious variables highlighted in this book, sectarianism seemed to have the most influence on intra- and interreligious relations.

One of the most important characteristics of intradenominational religious ecologies is the flow of resources. Denominations are interdependent systems comprising varied relationships of exchange. The medium of exchange may be material, as in financial contributions or subsidies, or it may be a less tangible resource like religious authority or submission. We asked respondents in our research sites about their relationships with other bodies within their denomination. The relationships they described varied with respect to the direction that resources flowed.

Resources may flow upward from the congregation to larger or broader denominational institutions. For example, the Gayatri Hindu temple sends financial donations back to Gayatri Pariwar headquarters in India and promotes sales of magazines and literature published by Gayatri in India. Ling Shen Ching Tze Buddhist temple similarly sends donations to its world headquarters in Seattle, which then distributes it around the world. Naperville Church of the Brethren responds to world needs by sending funds to the Church of the Brethren denominational headquarters, which in turn sends contributions to Church World Service, an ecumenical relief and service organization.

Conversely, resources may flow downward from institutions above the congregation in the denominational hierarchy. Maternity BVM Roman Catholic parish, for example, receives significant subsidies from the Chicago Archdiocese supporting various religious and social services to its Humboldt Park neighborhood. Money is not the only religious resource that flows downward, of course. Religious resources may do the same. The ISKCON temple receives all its literature and teaching materials from its national headquarters in Los Angeles. The *sadhus* (religious leaders) at the BAPS Hindu temple are trained at BAPS headquarters in India and appointed in consultation with Pramukh Swami Maharaj, the religious head of the worldwide organization. Curricular materials for the many religious and cultural classes offered by the temple are produced by BAPS national headquarters in New York.

Finally, resources may flow laterally between congregations within a denomination. This was the most frequent kind of relationship mentioned by our interviewees. Most congregations relate to other similar bodies in activities like pulpit exchanges where a leader of one congregation is a guest speaker in another. Such exchanges not only strengthen religious identity but also serve as important sources of information flows across congregational boundaries. Such exchanges may even occur internationally. A leader of Truth Lutheran Church spoke of attending the Asian Lutheran International conferences. "There are other Lutherans from other countries and we come together. We meet in Bangkok. So the Asian churches, they know more how they can work with us. For example, if we have Filipinos here in Naperville, we can talk to the Lutheran church in the Philippines and [tell them] 'they need a pastor here, can you send someone here to be their pastor?' We work together in that case."

Congregations may also collaborate together to carry out mission or service efforts. St. Demetrios Greek Orthodox parish has a special relationship, via International Orthodox Christian Charities, with the bishop of Hong Kong. The bishop makes frequent visits to St. Demetrios and the congregation sends financial contributions and people for volunteer service activities in various Asian locations. They have also sent volunteers to an Orthodox parish in Tijuana, Mexico, donating labor and materials for construction projects there and participating in cross-cultural bilingual liturgies. But lateral relationships are not always instrumental and mission/service oriented. St. Demetrios is also very active in the Greek Orthodox Basketball League, competing with other Greek Orthodox parishes in Chicago.

Resource flows in religious ecologies are not necessarily symmetrical. Some congregations are donor congregations, while others are heavily subsidized. Some are relatively autonomous with respect to religious authority, while others are quite dependent. Both the direction and the content of resource exchanges varied widely across the congregations we studied. Size did not seem to be as significant a factor as one might assume. Some very small congregations were primarily donors (Gayatri), and some very large congregations were heavily subsidized (Maternity BVM). We also observed similar variations on both sides of the individualist-collectivist distinction. The only one of our variables that did have some correlation with intradenominational resource flows was sectarianism. Both mainstream and sectarian congregations spoke frequently of lateral relationships with likeminded congregations, but the upward-downward distinction varied systematically between mainstream and sectarian groups.

Most of the eight congregations we coded as mainstream mentioned relationships where resources flowed upward. These were often financial resources in the form of contributions to denominational agencies and institutions. (The only exception among the eight mainstream groups was Maternity BVM Catholic church, a large but poor parish that depends on external subsidies to maintain its various religious and service programs.) But resources can also take the form of time and energy, as when members volunteer in denominational programs or leaders serve on denominational boards. Several of the congregations we studied described relationships and activities of this sort. If immigrant congregations continue and increase their involvement in denominational institutions, this may have a significant impact on the character of the religious institutions that most of us commonly think of as mainstream.

None of the five congregations coded as strongly sectarian (ISKCON, BAPS, Synagogue FREE, Victory Outreach, and Holy Virgin Protection) mentioned relationships where resources flowed upward. They did, however, discuss the downward flow of resources, particularly religious teaching and authority. It appears that maintaining a strong sectarianism in the contemporary world requires the firm exercise of religious authority. Local congregations do not speak particularly negatively about this, but they clearly feel its effects. Given that the highest religious authority for these groups often (but not always) comes from outside the United States, and to the extent that these congregations are civically engaged (and most of them are), this pattern may have interesting consequences for American civil society, in that it is yet another channel of international influence in an increasingly multicultural public arena.

Interdenominational ecologies often involve themselves in religious and service activities similar to those internal to denominations. Interdenominational activities, however, are usually more publicly and civically oriented. One of the most common of such networks is a neighborhood clerical association. Typically, these are dominated by Christian denominations, although recently many have opened themselves to clergy of other traditions as well. Many of the religious leaders we interviewed mentioned participation in such local interdenominational associations. Such associations may involve themselves in local political or social issues. They may also provide social services such as food pantries or homeless shelters. Most often they engage in religious activity such as interdenominational Thanksgiving services, pulpit exchanges, or theological dialogues.

An analogous kind of network, but one that is regionally rather than locally based, is the interethnic interdenominational association. Both Naperville Church of the Brethren and Truth Lutheran Church belong to metrowide associations of Indian Christian churches and Chinese churches, respectively. Such associations engage in activities similar to any interdenominational clergy association, but here religious activity is overlaid with ethnic interests as well. Congregations may collectively celebrate ethnic or national holidays as well as religious ones.

Interdenominational clergy and congregational associations have a long tradition in American Christianity, so it is not surprising to see immigrant Christian churches participating in them and developing new ones. But this form of association is also being adopted by other immigrant religious traditions. The Council of Islamic Organizations of Greater Chicago coordinates joint activities of Muslims and mosques across the Chicago metro region. These include large public celebrations of major Muslim holidays, as well as less visible activities, such as producing newsletters and event calendars, mobilizing to provide prayer space for Muslim students in public schools, or working to support the civil rights and physical safety of cab drivers. They can also serve as a public mouthpiece, speaking for the Muslim community as a whole. This makes them an important voice in the civic arena. For example, the council was one of the first organizations to issue a public statement denouncing the attacks of September 11. Similarly, but somewhat less visibly, the Buddhist Council of the Midwest functions as an interdenominational association for area Buddhists. It coordinates regular inter-Buddhist meetings in various temples, as well as a large joint celebration of the Buddha's birthday. The Hindu community has not as yet developed a similar institutional inter-Hindu association, but frequent participation of individual worshippers in multiple temples may help to link area Hindus in a web of personal relationships.

Many of the congregations we studied mentioned participation in such interdenominational associations and activities. Conspicuously absent, however, were the sectarian groups. None of them spoke of participating in a local or regional association. Only one, Victory Outreach, mentioned occasional pulpit exchanges with other likeminded Protestant groups. As we will see, sectarian congregations do participate in at least a limited way with other faiths. It would appear, however, that holding to a particular and bounded version of religious truth makes it difficult for them to collaborate with co-religionists outside their group. Since interdenominational associations are a primary avenue for religion to enter public life, sectarian groups may thus be working at a disadvantage.

Finally, there are also interfaith networks. They participate in similar social and religious activities, but at an even broader and more abstract level than do interdenominational associations. In order to succeed over time, such associations need to focus on similarities more than differences. This necessarily means that they must be cautious in dealing with controversial public issues, about which religions may be in disagreement. Still, they do offer a legitimate platform, especially for new religions, whereby groups may engage with others in public conversation.

One of the most important such networks, especially since its headquarters are in Chicago, is the Council for a Parliament of the World's Religions. They coordinate interfaith activities and religious dialogues for their members. Several of the congregations we studied were involved with Council activities. The Interfaith Alliance of Chicago offers a similar venue for dialogue and conversation. Such networks are especially attractive to new immigrant religious groups who may not have well-established networks in their own religious tradition.

Another, albeit less institutionalized, form of religious ecology is the pattern of neighborhood interfaith relationships that often emerge around instrumental issues as mundane as sharing parking lots for overflow crowds on religious holidays. In fact, we were surprised at how often parking lots were mentioned when we asked about cooperation with other religious groups. Given the premium on parking in an urban region like Chicago, we should not have been so surprised. But seemingly mundane cooperation such as this can lead to personal relationships between clergy and laypeople of different faiths—relationships that may have consequences beyond the immediate quotidian need. For example, one of the parking lot friendships was between the ISKCON temple and the neighboring St. Jerome's Catholic Church. The friendship blossomed to the point that the parish priest wrote a letter to the local alderman, recommending the temple for "The Excellent Contribution to Rogers Park" award for cleaning up the front of neighborhood apartments, providing food for the homeless, maintaining the temple, and "vigorously praying for peace in the community." Later, the ISKCON temple was invited to provide the food for a daylong "Pathways to Peace" festival organized by twenty-five Rogers Park churches, temples, and mosques. Thus, sharing a parking lot developed into ISKCON's legitimate place at the neighborhood interfaith table and a voice in neighborhood affairs.

As the previous anecdote shows, sectarian groups like ISKCON are not as averse to interfaith relations as they are to interdenominational networks. Particularly for a conversionist group like ISKCON or Victory Outreach, relationships with religious others are required as part of the group's mission, and, no doubt, relations with exotic others are less threatening to a sectarian identity than relations with close others such as co-religionists of other denominations. Not all sectarian groups are conversionist, however. For example, Holy Virgin Protection, a Russian Orthodox cathedral, is not conversionist in its religious outlook. It not only avoids interdenominational and interfaith relations, it is actively averse to them.

While the institutionalized interfaith organizations are important venues where immigrant religions can gain a public voice, it is likely that the local interfaith ecologies are even more important for civic engagement. Relationships that are based on mundanities like parking lots or attendance at each other's celebrations grow over time into something more—a relationship where each feels some loyalty and responsibility for the well-being of the other. This enables a rapid response to public events like September 11 or the earthquake in Gujarat. Islamic Cultural Center, the mosque in Northbrook, had a somewhat improbable relationship with a local orthodox synagogue to which the mosque had loaned worship space while the Jewish congregation was still without a building. This history of close relations with other faiths meant that immediately following the events of September 11, there was a strong expression of interfaith support for the mosque in Northbrook and a series of interfaith events to solidify relations between Christians, Muslims, and Jews in the wake of the tragedy. Similarly, the BAPS Hindu temple had built a relationship with the local

Catholic parish (again, beginning with shared parking lots) that could be tapped when BAPS was organizing its massive relief efforts for the Gujarat earthquake. Its friendly relations with local religious (and political) organizations gave it legitimacy and easy access to the bureaucratic machinery necessary to launch such a campaign on short notice.

## Conclusion

We have discussed three different types of organizational ecologies, or webs of relationships to which immigrant congregations belong. Such ecologies are not static. They are dynamic and shifting, activated at some times and quiescent at others. In our observations they were most visible during special events or for special purposes.

One type of special event, present in nearly all the research sites, is the fund-raiser. There is, of course, a long tradition of fund-raisers in religious communities of all sorts. The rummage sale is a congregational cliché. In Chicago, many Catholic parishes organize neighborhood festivals that include music, food, games, and carnival rides. New immigrant religious organizations have quickly adopted this sort of activity. One of the first events we attended at Islamic Foundation was a weekend bazaar that attracted many South Asian customers, along with a smattering of other ethnicities, who shopped for clothing, crafts, and food. Apart from the obvious fund-raising purpose, such events also help to build relationships between a congregation and its neighbors. For exotic religions such as Islam or Russian Orthodoxy, fund-raisers allow congregations to educate others about their culture, reducing fears or prejudices and paving the way for other kinds of cooperative activity.

We also observed other kinds of special-purpose events more directly and explicitly structured as organizational network events. One that was often mentioned in our interviews is the interfaith event, whose purpose is to engage in interreligious dialogue or to increase interreligious or intercultural understanding. For example, St. Lambert Catholic Church and Islamic Cultural Center told of their involvement in multiple interfaith events in their communities. Both the Gayatri and ISKCON temples were active in Pathways to Peace, a large interreligious festival in the Rogers Park neighborhood on Chicago's north side. It was part of a series of events facilitated by the Council for a Parliament of the World's Religions, responding to a spate of religiously and racially motivated hate crimes in the area. The festival, involving dozens of different religious congregations, included rituals, cultural demonstrations, lectures and dialogues, and balloons and face-painting for the children. ISKCON catered the food for the entire event.

Interfaith events such as these were not as universally present in our research sites as were fund-raisers, because participation in them is somewhat dependent on a group's religious worldview. Sectarian groups, particularly those with an exclusivist view of religious truth, were less likely to participate. Victory Outreach, for example, had few ecological connections in general, but it was particularly wary of relationships with other religions. As one leader there said when asked about cooperating with other religious groups, "As far as other religions, . . . the only thing we got in common is that we both love God. But there is no way I could live his style, you know. The only way I could help him is to let him know that Jesus is Lord, to repent or meet his doom." He must have realized that this was not a widely accepted approach, because he immediately followed up with "I'm not offending you in any way? You're not from a religious sect, are you?" Such avoidance was not limited to conservative Protestants. When we asked the same question of a leader at Holy Virgin Protection, a Russian Orthodox cathedral, the response was "No, absolutely not. The Orthodox Church does not have relationships with any other religious organizations, or with any other movements. It is only engaged in the Orthodox Christian church life."

Another sort of special-purpose activity that frequently activated ecological networks centered on the provision of social services. Most (but not all) congregations see such service to others as part of their mission. Many of them, however, do not have the financial or personnel resources to provide significant service on their own. Consequently, collaborating with others becomes a necessity. Among our research sites, such collaboration was common. Synagogue FREE collaborates with a number of Jewish service agencies to serve its refugee population. Arguably the best example is Maternity BVM Catholic Church. Although they are a relatively poor congregation, they provide a large range of services to their neighborhood. They are able to do so by drawing on their linkages to the archdiocese, other neighborhood churches, community organizations, and city agencies. They serve as an important node in a network of organizations, providing space and visibility and facilitating conversation and collaboration in addressing a variety of neighborhood needs. But, as noted earlier in this chapter, religion remains an important factor in shaping such relationships. Maternity BVM is happy to collaborate with other Protestant congregations who share their collectivist approach to social problems, but they are not nearly as open to cooperation with the many smaller Pentecostal congregations who are more individualist in their approach (and more likely to proselytize).

Finally, it is important to note that crisis events are particularly significant in activating latent organizational ecologies, strengthening preexisting relationships and developing new ones. During the time we were in the field, two events were of particular importance—the earthquake in Gujarat, India, and the September 11 attacks. More recently, of course, the Asian tsunami in late 2004 and Hurricane Katrina in 2005 called for similar responses from congregations. We observed that congregations that already had formed connections to other religious and civic organizations were able to respond very quickly to crisis needs by catalyzing a collaborative response. The ability of the BAPS Hindu temple to rapidly collect and deliver massive amounts of aid to India (and also to New York City after September 11) is the best example of this. Following September 11, both Islamic Cultural Center and Islamic Foundation were able to quickly generate their own responses and participate in collaborative statements denouncing the attacks, not only as a human tragedy, but as a violation of basic Muslim principles. They were also the recipients of widespread interfaith support. Large interfaith assemblies were held to express solidarity and to forestall retribution from vigilantes. The religious ecologies to which they belonged organized vigils to protect mosques from vandalism and to help shape local opinion about American Muslims.

Crisis events thus draw on preexisting organizational relationships, but they can also strengthen and develop these relationships going forward. The immediate aftermath of September 11 had the ironic effect of strengthening the voice of American Muslims and giving them a more prominent place at the public table. Because of this enhanced integration into the American religious system and civil society, Muslims have been able to criticize the ensuing war in Iraq without fear of significant retribution. The point here is that organizational ecologies are dynamic. What may begin as simply an exchange visit or sharing a parking lot may (especially given the catalyst of a special event) develop into significant collaboration. These strengthened networks can have a significant impact on the well-being of communities and on the vitality of public debates.

# 11

## When and How Religion Matters for Immigrant Civic Engagement

*Recognizing that diverse religious traditions hold incommensurable beliefs is, it seems to me, a valuable step forward, at least compared with the kind of social science that not only tries to float above these truth claims as a methodological strategy, but also implicitly assumes that such truth claims matter so little that religious communities can be treated like so many social clubs or athletic teams.*

—Robert Wuthnow (2004)

The epigraph above revisits sociologist Robert Wuthnow's (2004) comment cited in the introduction. Wuthnow makes his point in a section entitled "The Meanings of Diversity" in his 2003 presidential address to the Society for the Scientific Study of Religion. Wuthnow compliments the political philosopher John Rawls for "acknowledg[ing] that modern societies are characterized by a diversity of groups and traditions that fundamentally hold what he [Rawls] refers to as 'incommensurable' moral and epistemological claims" (161, 163). This is the context of Wuthnow's critique of the kind of social scientific analysis that ignores or underappreciates that which distinguishes religious groups from other types of associations.

We expand upon Wuthnow's critique in two ways. First, we include more than beliefs or truth claims in our understanding of what distinguishes religious from other types of associations. Hence our more encompassing phrase "religious ideas, practices, and identities," as well as our focus on three key variables or factors that play significant roles in congregational civic engagement— sectarianism, moral authority, and moral projects. Second, we implicate other observers of recent immigration trends in addition to social scientists for their lack of attention to what makes a religious group distinctive and how that distinctiveness informs the group's civic engagement. We find much to celebrate in the growing body of research on religious communities and groups in the social scientific literature on recent immigration, even as we have challenged the field

In the everyday life of immigrant congregations multiple groups can engage the challenge of diversity. Photo by Jerry Berndt.

to greater analytical sophistication. We make the same challenge to other scholarly disciplines and various audiences that have a vested interest in understanding these religious groups and their place in American society.

## Recommendations to Scholars

Early in our project we made the methodological decision to study the role of congregations in the civic engagement patterns of recent immigrants. As noted in the introduction, we chose congregations as our unit of investigation because of the congregation's continuing central role in the organized expression of religion in the United States, including the immigrant context. The intervening chapters have shown the powerful influence congregations and congregational leaders exert on their members and affiliated constituents. We agree with critics of the congregational method that its focus on organized religious life may render other important aspects of immigrant lived religion relatively out of focus. "It is necessary to augment congregational approaches with analyses of ways in which lived religion is intertwined with the politics of daily life, analyses that explore the 'diffuse' but not less intense or valid religious life of immigrants beyond visible assemblies and well-organized, territorially bound associations . . . [that is,] religion as it is lived in kitchens, clinics, social service centers, plazas, bars, restaurants, and other quotidian sites" (Vasquez 2005, 234–235).

Of course, this is not necessarily an either/or methodological decision—the interplay of institutional and quotidian aspects of immigrant lived religion can be examined in the same study, as we have done in the chapters on occupation, marriage, and citizenship, for instance. We believe that a congregational focus makes good methodological sense when the research question addresses civic engagement patterns. As Vasquez admits, "the congregational approach will likely continue to yield valuable insights into the ways in which religious organizations mediate the formation of collective identities among immigrants" (234).[1] In the American socioeconomic political system, collective identities matter greatly, and thus the religious factors that help to shape immigrant collective identities matter greatly as well. Congregations remain a major shaper and representative of immigrant collective identities vis-à-vis American society.

A congregational approach brings religion into both local context and institutional focus, important ways of grounding theories about the civic implications of America's evolving religious diversity. *Taking Religious Pluralism Seriously: Spiritual Politics on America's Sacred Ground* (McGraw and Formicola 2005), for instance, provides an intellectual service by assessing the philosophical compatibility of multiple religious voices in America's historic public forum (McGraw 2005); but these voices remain largely ethereal and unconnected to organized lived religion on the civic landscape. For example, we learn a great deal about Hindu doctrines, texts, and ethical prescriptions, but nothing about how local Hindu temples actually apply these civically (Rambachan 2005). We cannot assume that all Hindu temples adopt the same civic stance because they are somehow generically Hindu. As we have seen, BAPS Swaminarayan, ISKCON, and Gayatri represent sectarian variations on large Hindu themes, all of which differ significantly from other Hindu groups.

Similarly with America's Buddhists. If Buddhism, like any religion, "is a tool for transformation of both oneself and society," then how is this tool used by local Buddhist temples and centers, especially with regard to transforming American society, or at least affecting it in some more limited way (Gross 2005, 225)? In *Taking Religious Pluralism Seriously*, Rita M. Gross addresses a number of contentious public issues, including gay rights, abortion, and school prayer, arguing a civic position as a Buddhist scholar-practitioner. On the civic ethics of the "under God" clause in the Pledge of Allegiance, Gross generalizes that American Buddhists resent having "a foreign religious ideology forced upon them if they wish to pledge allegiance to their country out loud, formally, and publicly" (219, cf. 228).

Upon close inspection, however, only certain Buddhists resent this ideological intrusion or even consider the "under God" clause an issue at all. The amicus brief filed in conjunction with the well-known Newdow case in 2004 ("Brief Amicus Curiae") represented twenty-three Buddhist parties, only two of them recent immigrant groups (two Thai temples). It is unlikely that the two Buddhist temples in this Chicago study would find any interest in this issue either. The question is not why Buddhists get involved (or not) in public issues, but rather which Buddhists, which issues, and for what specific Buddhist reasons.[2]

"To survey immigrant religions accurately," advises Bruce Lawrence, "one must map the limits of their potential engagement in a common American public space." In his chapter on "Civil Society and Immigrants," Lawrence profiles two religious groups, Institute of Islamic Information and Education (III&E) and Vishwa Hindu Parishad of America (VHP), both of whose contributions to American civil society Lawrence finds "compromised through their tacit networks of support," III&E to a theocratic Saudi Arabia, VHP to the Hindutva nationalist movement in India (2002, 33, 65). Clearly, not all religious groups engage American society to a significant degree, and not all that do, do so positively, according to consensus political or moral standards. As a whole, the congregations in this study have made positive contributions, while none has made a negative one.

A welcome byproduct of increased scholarly attention to the transnational context of American immigration has been a growing awareness of immigrant religions' global networks (e.g., Levitt 2001; Ebaugh and Chafetz 2002), which we included under the rubric of organizational ecology. Even so, the pendulum can swing too far in a well-meaning effort to bring international breadth and balance to the research, as when an immigrant congregation's civic networks are thickly described in the home country but only cursorily treated in the American context. We are left to wonder whether this lopsided civic engagement is indeed the case and, if so, why that might be; or whether the imbalance merely reflects the researcher's primary interest (see Guest 2005). We need systematic comparative research on the civic engagement patterns of immigrant religious groups across societies (cf. van Tubergen 2006, 1). How might these patterns differ in European versus North American contexts, for instance? A fruitful tack might be to study large, centralized religious groups in this regard, like the BAPS Swaminarayans who claim more than 600 temples and nearly 9,100 centers in forty-five countries. How might local context affect a Swaminarayan temple's interaction with civil society and various levels of government? Or is Swaminarayan sectarianism strong enough to routinize such interaction no matter what the local context?

Broadly construed, the field of American congregational studies comprises two wings, both of which can benefit from the insights of our research. First, traditional congregational studies, which tend to feature Christian congregations, would do well to pay more systematic attention to immigrant congregations in order to sort out both what is common to congregational life and experience generally and what is unique about immigrant congregations. A logical first step toward comprehensive coverage would be to include immigrant Christian churches in the research pool, since Christians probably make up approximately two-thirds of America's most recent immigration wave (Jasso et al. 2003).

Second, the growing corpus of immigrant congregational studies would do well to pay more sophisticated attention to religious distinctiveness, as we have argued throughout this book. This would avoid the still-too-common "Religion 101" descriptions that provide no specificity of religious ideas, practices, and identities. Just as all cats are not gray, all congregations within a religious tradition are not alike in their instantiation of that larger tradition. Even our three Catholic parishes are not "Catholic" in the same manner—it depends on priest, parish, and hermeneutics, to use a Christian theological term—that is, how Catholic texts and tradition are interpreted and applied to contemporary situations. The same for our other congregations, which are never merely generic representatives of their larger religious traditions. As helpful as broad comparisons are, such as the standard comparative studies of Protestants and Catholics, the devil is usually found in the local details.

Civic engagement patterns have garnered less attention from scholars of immigrant congregations than from scholars of nonimmigrant congregations, due to a preoccupation with internal organizational dynamics and ethnic identity formation issues in the immigrant case. Since congregations are not monolithic institutions, internal fault lines with regard to civic involvement should be investigated. As in the case of Naperville Church of the Brethren, notions of Brethren identity varied across theological and generational lines within the congregation. Since congregations are not static institutions either, congregational evolution should be tracked whenever possible, since a portrait in time may not reflect long-term congregational dynamics. We saw this in the cases of Islamic Foundation School's increasingly positive civic engagement, Ling Shen Ching Tze Buddhist Temple's tentative attempts at making a connection to another local Buddhist group, and in the dynamic nature of the organizational ecologies of immigrant congregations generally.

Scholars from all disciplines would do well to keep two principles in mind when researching immigrant religious groups. First, religion is a key identity factor, at times the primary one. Historian of classical American immigration, Timothy L. Smith (1978, 1169), made this point decades ago when he chided sociologists and historians for their "preoccupation . . . with the secular aspects of ethnicity and nationality." Smith corrected their perception that other factors tended to outweigh religion in immigrant associational life: "The appeal of common language, national feeling, and belief in a common descent was sufficient in only a few minor cases to outweigh the attraction of religious affiliation as an organizing principle."

Second, religion can and does act as an independent variable in immigrant contexts, yet, to date, the literature has tended to point the causality or influence arrow in the opposite direction. Religion is typically portrayed as a dependent

Immigrant congregations are, above all else, religious. Photo by Jerry Berndt.

variable (e.g., van Tubergen 2006), even as "a defensive, dependent, doomed" factor instead of "an active, independent, emergent" one as Warner argues (1998a, 202). When the arrow is reversed, new insights about immigrant religion can emerge.

Toward the end of their seminal study, *Religion and the New Immigrants,* Ebaugh and Chafetz (2000b) take stock of their findings in historical perspective, as should all researchers of recent immigrant congregations. "We are left to wonder just what is 'new' about the phenomena we have observed" (450). What they find "old" about new immigrant congregations—in other words, what both classical and post-1965 immigrant congregations share in common—has to do with organizational, polity, and leadership issues; internal conflicts over the use of English, multiethnic memberships, and intergenerational dynamics; and the congregation's key role in "reproducing the group's cultural and religious heritage while assisting immigrants in the process of adapting to a new society" (453). We believe we have at least one answer to the "newness" question posed by Ebaugh and Chafetz: specifically religious ideas, practices, and identities have always been key to immigrant congregational experience, and post-1965 immigrants have brought a host of new religious phenomena to the American scene. Attention to these should not be crowded out by other variables that researchers may deem prima facie valuable.

Much of what Ebaugh and Chafetz find new about post-1965 immigrant congregations has to do with America being a different kind of society than in the classical period of U.S. immigration. America is now more multiculturally friendly and less demanding of straight-line assimilation into the dominant culture, and American society has been transformed by the women's rights movement and postindustrialization. Moreover, the sheer variety of immigrant religious groups, both Christian and non-Christian, and the enhanced transnationalism of recent immigrants differ from the classical immigration period. This all implies opportunities for significant influence both in a new America and in a new global system. We again caution against underappreciating the role that religious ideas, practices, and identities play in this new scenario.

## Recommendations to Other Interested Parties

Academics are by no means the only ones interested in America's newest immigrant religions and their civic engagement patterns. Here we offer recommendations to parties in two other areas—government and interreligious relations—who would benefit from a nuanced understanding of the particular religious motivations and goals of immigrant religious groups they wish to engage in some way.

### Government

Civic acknowledgments and/or celebrations of America's growing religious diversity have become common in recent years at all levels of government. At the federal level, for instance, the White House hosts an annual Iftar dinner during the Muslim month of Ramadan, while the State Department has established religious roundtables on Buddhism, Islam, and Hinduism for the dual purpose of monitoring religious freedom around the world and providing a channel for "marginal religious groups in the U.S., especially recent immigrants" to share "concerns about their treatment within the U.S." (Numrich 2001, 13).

Moreover, opening prayers at the U.S. House of Representatives were given by a Hindu priest from Ohio in 2000 and a Muslim imam from Georgetown University in 2001. The Hindu priest serves the Shiva Vishnu Temple of Greater Cleveland,[3] an example of what Raymond Williams (1988, 1992) would call an ecumenical Hindu temple—that is, one that accommodates a variety of Hindu lineages and practices in an effort to draw together the diverse local immigrant

Hindu community. The Hindu Temple of Greater Chicago is also an ecumenical Hindu temple (Numrich 2000c). Such temples differ from the more sectarian Hindu temples that honor only one god or divine teacher, such as Swaminarayan temples, and thus make more suitable choices for public appearances as representatives of the entire immigrant Hindu community.

The Muslim imam who gave the prayer at the House, Mr. Yahya Hendi, serves as a chaplain at both Georgetown University and the National Naval Medical Center in Bethesda, Maryland. He is the imam of a local mosque in Maryland, the Islamic Society of Frederick,[4] and a member of the Fiqh [Islamic Jurisprudence] Council of North America, which in 2005 issued a *fatwa* (a formal Islamic legal opinion) against religious extremism, terrorism, and violence against innocent life.[5] Mr. Hendi received a master's degree from Hartford Seminary, a progressive Protestant seminary that offers a Graduate Certificate in Islamic Chaplaincy, and he is pursuing a Ph.D. in comparative religions. He advised the White House after 9/11 and is heavily involved in interfaith activities, making frequent visits to synagogues and churches "hoping to create a new positive relationship between the followers of the three Abrahamic religions."[6] In other words, Imam Hendi is a prime example of modernist Islamic brokering to the larger American community.

At the state level there is a similar growing recognition of religious diversity, sometimes accompanied by intense public debate over the place of religion and religious symbolism in the public sphere (Saldana 2005). A few state universities offer optional interfaith baccalaureate services as part of their commencement activities (White 2005). State legislatures have addressed a variety of issues, including the complicated legal definition and prosecution of hate crimes (e.g., "Sikh Beating" 2005). Effective in 2002, the Illinois General Assembly passed the Halal Food Act mandating Department of Agriculture regulation of products claiming to be prepared according to Islamic legal prescriptions (*halal*).

Municipal initiatives across the country celebrate increasing local religious diversity. These include some observations of the National Day of Prayer on the first Thursday in May, although another trend restricts this event to Christian participation (Ronald 2006). Such local events can offer some interesting insights into civic engagement dynamics affecting immigrant religious groups. Our sense is that municipal officials and offices may be generally uninformed about the complexities of religious identities in local immigrant communities. They may simply wish to represent as much diversity (ethnic/racial as well as religious) in their celebrations as possible, without much understanding of which religious groups might share their wish and which might not. For the municipal organizers, diversity represents a civic virtue, but it does not necessarily carry religious significance to immigrant (or nonimmigrant) congregations.

The city of Naperville sought to include as much diversity as possible in its Celebration 2000 commemoration of the turn of the millennium.[7] A Spiritual

Events Committee considered the question, "What common themes might persons of all faiths meet together to celebrate?" The committee planned two events, an Interfaith Prayer Breakfast where "people of diverse faith communities in the City of Naperville will join together to pray for peace and harmony in our local community, nation and world," and a Concert of Sacred Music "in celebration of our common spiritual heritage," "to glorify God," and to "[send] us joyfully into the new century strengthened in faith, hope, and love."

The Concert of Sacred Music was a distinctly mainstream Christian affair, with only one nonmainstream group, Christian Science, participating, and that not far removed from mainstream Christianity in this context. No immigrant religious groups of any kind participated in the concert. The Interfaith Prayer Breakfast, on the other hand, included far more religious and ethnic diversity: a Reconstructionist synagogue, a Unitarian Universalist church, the Latter-day Saints stake, a Science of Spirituality center, a diverse immigrant mosque, a Vietnamese Buddhist meditation group, and Truth Lutheran Church, the immigrant Chinese congregation in this study. Participation by Truth Lutheran is consistent with our understanding of its mainstream Protestant (ELCA) identity, and the involvement of the local mosque was consistent with its modernist Islamic identity. Sectarian expressions of either of these religious traditions would less likely participate in an interfaith prayer breakfast or show much interest in celebrating religious diversity per se.

The Buddhist meditation group's participation in Naperville's interfaith breakfast is more complex. On the one hand, such civic engagement is perfectly consistent with the views of the group's spiritual teacher, the Vietnamese monk Thich Nhat Hanh, a well-known international proponent of socially engaged Buddhism. On the other hand, the Naperville group, described by Numrich in another context (2000b), tends to focus on Hanh's teachings about personal transformation through meditation and practices a distinctly ethnic-Vietnamese style of Buddhism (in contrast to Hanh's convert followers). When Numrich was asked by a Naperville municipal official whether this group would participate in the interfaith activities surrounding Celebration 2000, he shared his doubts. The eventual participation of the group's leader in the prayer breakfast may reflect a personal level of civic engagement—this person is a state employee—more than the civic engagement level of the group per se or its members. Certainly, the group's leader could draw authority from Thich Nhat Hanh in deciding to participate. Naperville officials were mostly just happy to include two marks of diversity in their celebration, Vietnamese ethnicity (representing Naperville's growing Asian population) and Buddhist religious identity (the specificity of Thich Nhat Hanh's lineage was relatively unimportant).

Municipal prayer breakfasts around the country are undergoing new diversification to reflect America's changing religious landscapes. Historically diverse in Christian and Jewish representation, such events can feature awkward moments if organizers do not do their homework on the religious representatives they invite into the program. Numrich was present recently at the mayor's annual prayer breakfast in a suburb of a major midwestern city (not Chicago). The mayor had reinstated the event after some years' hiatus but now recast it in interfaith terms in light of the changing demographics of the metropolitan region.

On this particular occasion, two Muslim participants were invited to read passages from Islamic sources. Both represented what we have called modernist Islamic organizations, so it was likely that they would choose readings appropriate both to the interfaith composition of the audience and to the spiritual conviviality of the occasion. Yet one chose a reading proclaiming the supersessionist truth claims of Islam over Judaism and Christianity, while the other cited advice from the Qur'an and the Hadith stressing humility, reverence, and peaceable relations with adherents of other religions. The awkwardness created by the first reader might have been avoided with more due diligence in researching the type of Islam he himself represented, not just what his local mosque represented. (Here again we note the internal diversity of views in congregations.) Such screening of speakers has always been done to ensure the goodwill at such civic occasions, usually favoring mainstream Protestant, Catholic, and Jewish representatives. The same screening for mainstream Muslim and other non-Jewish-Christian representatives may need to be done by interfaith event planners if they wish to keep rogue sentiments from disturbing the civic peace intended for such gatherings.

### Interreligious Relations

Interreligious relations are any interactions, formal or informal, between religious groups or individuals across large religious identity boundaries. Intrareligious relations, in distinction, involve interaction between religious groups or individuals within large religious boundaries. As explored in chapter 10, both types of relations are important to a full understanding of the organizational ecologies of recent immigrant religious groups. But here we consider the implications of our research only for those engaged in interreligious relations, under the assumption that they may not be fully informed of the complexities of the religious ideas, practices, and identities of groups significantly different from their own religious tradition. Often, religious people know the complexity of their own tradition but fail to see the commonsense analogy that other traditions are comparably complex.

Interreligious relations can include everything from aggressive proselytization to casual conversation, from doctrinal debate to informational exchange, from religiously motivated bias crimes to cooperative social projects. In the United States, Christianity's dominant historical, social, and cultural position makes it an unequal partner in interreligious relations despite the de jure protections of religious freedom enshrined in the Constitution and confirmed in numerous Supreme Court rulings in recent decades.

Two significant trends in contemporary interreligious relations in the United States deserve special attention, missionary initiatives and the interfaith dialogue movement. For the most part, these two trends involve different sets of participants. Sometimes, however, the same group may hold these two emphases in tension.

Missionary initiatives originate from multiple quarters and target a variety of potential converts. We can define the basic missionary impulse as the desire to propagate religious truth claims perceived as universally salvific. A universal religious truth claim is not sufficient in and of itself. To qualify for missionary status, a religious group must also actively propagate that claim beyond its identity boundaries. Missionary groups use "religious propaganda" in pursuing their "expansionist" agenda (Antes and Waldenfels 1997). As Max Stackhouse (2005, 6070) explains, missionary religions are "going" religions; "staying" religions, in contrast, are "constitutively tied to specific sociopolitical contexts and often to ethnic particularities."

Buddhism, Christianity, and Islam are generally considered the quintessential missionary religions. However, not all subgroups within these large religious traditions act on the missionary impulse. Moreover, some groups within historically nonmissionary religions have become missionary minded in the contemporary period, often in response to, even in imitation of, Christianity. These include neo-Hindu groups like ISKCON, whose initial missionary efforts targeting the American counterculture have diminished in favor of an intrareligious appeal to Hindu immigrants (Vande Berg 2005). Swaminarayan Hinduism represents a more classically "staying" religion, to use Stackhouse's term, while the Gayatri movement combines a primarily "staying" emphasis with at least a potentially "going" one.

For many evangelical Protestants, non-Christian immigrants and refugees in America represent a new mission field. As one author explains in *The Gospel for Islam: Reaching Muslims in North America,* published by the Evangelism and Missions Information Service of the Billy Graham Center at Wheaton College, "Many workers ministering among Muslims have invested a large amount of time and effort trying in various ways to motivate God's people here in North America to get involved in sharing Christ with the six million Muslims God is bringing into our midst" (Bailey 2001, 187). Non-Christian immigrant congregations are not always aware of the underlying missionary motivation of social services offered by evangelical Christian churches and groups. They may offer the same social services as mainline Christian providers, but it is likely that when the conversation does turn to religious matters, the underlying missionary impulse of the evangelicals will surface. For many evangelical Protestant immigrants, the Gospel beckons them to preach to their non-Christian fellow immigrants. Naperville Church of the Brethren has tapped into an Indian evangelical network to accomplish such work. This congregation is not of one theological mind, however, some being conservative missionary Brethren and others being liberal Brethren.

Other congregations in the present study evidence a missionary mindedness to one degree or another. In the two Buddhist cases, this is more pronounced at HanMaUm than at Ling Shen Ching Tze, though both give less emphasis to mission work than some other immigrant Buddhist temples in the United States (e.g., Numrich 1996). Both mosques of this study include mission-minded or *da'wah* sentiments in their institutional objectives. Recall, for instance, that one of the stated goals of Islamic Foundation School is to "help our young children to get necessary training to become future Da'ees [Propagators, a variant of da'wah] of Islam." The school's parent mosque provides a description of its many da'wah activities in its informational brochure, including Islamic speakers for outside groups and a monthly forum with local Christian congregations ("Islamic Foundation: An Introduction"). The informational brochure of Islamic Cultural Center of Greater Chicago celebrates the Muslim community's contributions to America, including Islamic teachings ("The Islamic Cultural Center of Greater Chicago"): "Enjoying religious freedom and appreciating the plurality of the American society, the Muslims are making their own religio-cultural history in the United States by expanding their physical presence and spreading their spiritual values." Still, both mosques hold such missionary goals in some tension with the goals of the interfaith dialogue movement in which they also participate.

The contemporary interfaith dialogue movement in the United States is a decentralized social movement of individuals, groups, and organizations seeking to foster mutual respect and understanding across religions in order to achieve positive individual, social, cultural, and civic change. The movement's roots lie in the landmark 1893 World's Parliament of Religions in Chicago. That event's parliamentary nature fostered a measure of respect for the truth claims and spiritual heritages of the represented religions, while its goals, as stated by organizer Charles Bonney, included presenting "the substantial unity of many religions in the good deeds of the religious life" and hastening "the coming unity of mankind, in the service of God and man" (Seager 1993, 5). The interfaith dialogue movement in the United States today comprises hundreds of formal groups and organizations, plus countless informal initiatives. Little systematic analysis has been done on this movement (e.g., Lee 1992; Charaniya and Walsh 2001), although the Pluralism Project at Harvard University has sponsored important preliminary research on interfaith groups and activities in Philadelphia (researcher Cecilia Owen), Minnesota (researcher Elizabeth Varro), and nationally (researcher Joel Beversluis).[8]

Across the country, local clergy associations that have historically included Christian and Jewish religious leaders are now considering the possibilities and implications of expanding their representation to include Muslim imams, Hindu priests, Buddhist monastics, and other diverse religious leadership. Again, the lesson for everyone is to know who you're dealing with, since not all religious groups buy into the interfaith agenda.

The Niles Township Clergy Forum, which draws from the near north suburb of Skokie, had been meeting for some thirty years, but it took the events of 9/11 to open its Jewish and Christian members to the idea of expanding its representation. The forum began working with the Council for a Parliament of the World's Religions and established an interfaith Thanksgiving service that drew participation by leaders from local Baha'i, Buddhist, Muslim, and Hindu groups. Conspicuous by their absence in such interfaith activities have been the local Assemblies of God, Missouri Synod Lutheran, and Lubavitch Jewish groups, although our informant indicated that these groups sometimes cooperate in civic projects that do not jeopardize the sanctity of their religious truth claims. Another lesson here: some groups that do not buy into the ideological aspects of the interfaith agenda may nevertheless cooperate for the common civic good. Still, when all is said and done, certain groups simply pose "an altogether contrary presence in the community," as our informant described the local Jews for Jesus congregation.

In a nearby suburb, several members of the Northbrook Clergy Association released a statement in May 2003 concerning "the challenge of extremism [that] threatens us—from within our own hearts, and from others in our society." Denouncing "extreme religious views and behaviors" as "evidence of spiritual disease" and "maladies of the heart," these clergy held up instead "the shining examples of those exalted souls among us who have devoted their lives to the pursuit of true spirituality."

> It is in this spirit that we call on our congregations and our community, and commit ourselves to:
>
> – strive to transform ourselves so that our ego does not tyrannize us or others,
> – speak up within our own traditions to take responsibility for "our" extremists,
> – live and practice the principles of friendship, awareness, acceptance, and dialogue, to promote justice, peace, and welfare for all.[9]

The signatories of this statement all represent mainstream and relatively liberal religious groups whose histories and doctrines resonate with the sentiments of this statement. The Christian signatories of the statement include representatives of five mainline Protestant denominations and the Seventh-day Adventists, the latter a denomination that has mainstreamed in many ways over its history (see Albanese 1999). The two Jewish signatories represent Reform Judaism and the United Synagogue of Conservative Judaism (formerly "of America"), both relatively liberal expressions of American Judaism. A Baha'i and two signatories from Islamic Cultural Center of Greater Chicago, Imam Senad Agic and a convert to Sufi Islam, represent the new religious presence in the community. The sentiments of the above statement resonate well with the Baha'i emphasis on interfaith dialogue and the tenets of the Sufi order practiced at Islamic Cultural Center.

Muslim leaders across the country have begun to invite the interfaith community to Iftar dinners, the traditional breaking of the fast during the month of Ramadan. These events provide an opportunity for the Muslim community to educate the larger public about Islam as well as to strengthen ties of goodwill among local interfaith leadership. Both the sponsoring Muslim groups and their guests tend to fall on the mainstream end of the religious spectrum, as we would expect, and more particularly in the liberal or modernist camps of their respective traditions.

Hamid and Mazher Ahmed, cofounders of Batavia Islamic Center in the far west suburbs of Chicago, have organized an annual Iftar dinner for several years (Numrich n.d.). The congregation of Batavia Islamic Center has been hosted since 1987 by Calvary Episcopal Church. It is not unusual for Muslim groups in the United States to purchase former Christian facilities and transform them into mosques. However, at least in Chicago, this is the only case of a functioning church hosting a mosque.

" 'Interfaith' is a buzzword now," said Mazher Ahmed, who, by all accounts, is a driving force in the local interfaith movement. "You think, 'Oh my goodness, interfaith—it's a great thing,' " she continued. "But at that time [the 1980s], who knew about interfaith? I don't think people even understood what interfaith was all about. That is why I feel real proud that we have started a tradition—and not because of the necessity of 9/11." Even so, 9/11 has invigorated the interfaith connections between liberal mainstream religious groups across the country.

But interfaith dialogue initiatives can "cross over" to include nonliberal, even sectarian groups in surprising ways at times. The work of the Chicago-based Council for a Parliament of the World's Religions (CPWR) on the north side of the metropolitan region provides one example. Considering itself the direct heir to the landmark 1893 World's Parliament of Religions, CPWR seeks "to cultivate harmony between the world's religious and spiritual communities and foster their engagement with the world and its other guiding institutions in order to achieve a peaceful, just, and sustainable world."[10] In 1996 CPWR began an initiative in an area encompassing the north side of the city of Chicago and some of the near north suburbs, calling it the Creating Community Vision Project, later Pathways to Peace. Both Gayatri Pariwar Mandir and ISKCON Chicago participated in the activities of this initiative, but it took a good deal of cajoling in the latter case.

CPWR's community organizer had to "camp out at ISKCON to get them to participate," explained a CPWR official. "It was very difficult to get them involved at first," whereas there was no such hesitancy at Gayatri Pariwar Mandir. Much of ISKCON's guardedness certainly stemmed from its relatively more sectarian nature, and perhaps "especially its negative public image," as the CPWR official suggested to us. Yet ISKCON Chicago eventually deemed it a positive to join this local interfaith initiative—one year preparing food for more than nine hundred people when a major event was held at a nearby Catholic church, and chanting for a two-hour slot in a post-9/11 interfaith service held at a Muslim mosque. "They know the ground rules of interfaith interaction," our CPWR contact explained, "and do not proselytize."

We mentioned at the outset of this section that Christianity's dominant historical, social, and cultural position in the United States makes it an unequal partner in interreligious relations. Thus Christian responses to America's increasing religious diversity are crucial to the future of interreligious relations in this country. As we learned in the Church Next Door project, a study of Christian congregations in Chicago funded by the Louisville Institute (Numrich n.d.), American Christians are responding to religious diversity in a variety of ways. Robert Wuthnow (2005), for one, in his book *America and the Challenges of Religious Diversity,* thinks that "Christians of all stripes are simply not doing very well with the challenges of religious diversity" (Kniss 2005, 46).

## When Religion Doesn't Matter

At the end of a book dedicated to the proposition that religion qua religion matters at least as much in explaining the civic engagement patterns of immigrant congregations as other variables favored by scholars and observers of recent American immigration trends, we do well to keep our claims in perspective. We certainly do not wish to make too much of religion, even though we suspect that the day when this will be a problem generally is a long way off. We offer caveats along two lines.

First, we recognize that religion does not matter to all immigrants (cf. B. Lawrence 2002, 94–99). Full religious coverage, so to speak, has never characterized whole immigration waves or entire immigrant communities in this country. Even Oscar Handlin's (1951) classic treatment, *The Uprooted,* in which the author tends to argue the indispensability of religion to immigrant transition to the new America experience, recognized the "danger in the pervasive latitudinarianism of religion in the United States. Too many Americans were ready to believe that salvation could come through any faith *or none*" (128; emphasis added). Many immigrants, Handlin admitted, were "open to the temptation of falling away from the Church," and many became "apathetic and unaffiliated" (136).

The same can be said of the latest American immigrants. Fifteen percent of the total number of respondents to the New Immigrant Survey, conducted of persons admitted in 1996, indicated no religious preference, while seven sending areas—from lowest to highest, El Salvador, Canada, Vietnam, United Kingdom, the former Soviet Union, Taiwan, and mainland China—had percentages ranging from approximately 20 to more than 60 percent expressing no religious preference (Jasso et al. 2003, 221, 227). As Jasso and colleagues suggest, these data "signal the continuing attractiveness of the United States as a place of tolerance for both diversity of religious expression and freedom from religion" (221).

Second, we also recognize that as important as religion qua religion is to immigrant congregations—and we hope to have made the case that this is not as obvious to scholars as one might expect—other variables sometimes matter more than religion in explaining immigrant perspectives and behaviors. At times religion matters not at all, at other times it is part of a complex ensemble of forces, to borrow a phrase from urban studies (see Wedam 2003).

Congregational contexts and circumstances certainly matter. Mark Chaves (2004) lists the following congregational features that strongly shape congregational activities, only half of which are religious per se: "size, denomination, religious tradition, human and material resources" (43). Chaves examines the role and quality of clergy leadership under the rubric of human resources, but the point holds for congregational lay leadership as well, whether or not an immigrant congregation also has clergy. Sometimes an immigrant congregation's behavior, like any congregation's behavior, stems quite frankly from ineptness, fatigue, failure of nerve, or other leadership inadequacies or contingencies that can hardly be attributed to "religious ideas, practices, and identities."

As we heard in our very first interview with a clergy leader of one of the research sites when we asked whether there were times that this person declined to work with a leader of another organization: "I have because I'm too busy to do everything I'm asked to do. I mean I can't ever think of anything that I was asked to do that I didn't do because I thought it was questionable, but, yeah, time is a factor. So, yeah, I don't always do everything I'm asked to do." Every harried clergyperson, immigrant or not, can relate to such practical obstacles to investment of time and energy beyond the needs of the congregation. The special nature of the immigrant experience—for instance, simply a language barrier—can mitigate against certain kinds of activity that a nonimmigrant congregation from the same religious tradition might pursue.

The point is that, when an immigrant congregation is headed by quality clergy and/or lay leaders, and when it overcomes practical obstacles, whether inherent to the congregational model or peculiar to the immigrant experience, we must not underestimate how much, and in what specific ways, religion might matter to that congregation's engagement with the larger society. Religious motivations, based as they are in notions of transcendent authority, can overcome deficiencies in the mere things of this world, like size, resources, or circumstances.

The religious leader of one of our smallest, yet proportionally most actively engaged congregations, put it succinctly when we asked what was behind it all: "Ah, it's all inspiration. I was studying and learning all about my [spiritual teacher] and all of a sudden I got inspired by [him]. I mean, I had never seen him, but his inspiration—I was inspired so much by his writings and I thought, 'I have to do this,' and I joined [the movement]. He attracted me in such a way."

Drawing upon the insights of Max Weber, the charismatic authority of religious leaders, and even the more routinized authority of religious movements, institutions, and traditions, can be powerful motivators to religious individuals and congregations. Such motivations should not be discounted or underappreciated in understanding the behavior of religious immigrants and congregations, and in turn in explaining their civic engagement patterns.

# Appendix A:
# Research Sites

## Roman Catholic Christianity

*Five Holy Martyrs Roman Catholic Church*

Southwest side of Chicago, established 1908. Theologically mainstream, historic anchor parish for Polish community, serves between 1,000 and 1,500 congregants at Sunday masses. Congregants primarily Polish immigrants and descendants of Polish immigrants, with small (approximately 10 percent) Mexican constituency. Offers a few small-scale social and educational activities. Operates K–8 parochial school.

*Maternity BVM Roman Catholic Church*

West side of Chicago, established 1909. Theologically mainstream and politically progressive, serves about 1,650 congregants at weekly masses. Includes a large Catholic charismatic group that holds regular services. Congregants primarily Mexican and Puerto Rican, with a smaller group of Central Americans. Offers broad range of social and educational activities, classes, and interest groups. Operates K–8 parochial school.

*St. Lambert Roman Catholic Church*

Skokie, near north suburban Cook County, established 1951. Theologically mainstream, serves about 1,200 congregants at weekly masses. Involved in interfaith dialogue, as well as celebrating ethnic diversity within the congregation. Largest immigrant group is Filipino, in addition to Sri Lankans, Mexicans, Haitians, and several smaller immigrant groups. Operates multicultural workshops and participates in communitywide ethnic festivals. K–8 parochial school closed by archdiocese in 2003.

## Protestant Christianity

*Naperville Church of the Brethren*

Naperville, west suburban DuPage County, established 1855. Historic German American congregation, became predominantly Gujarati Indian in the 1990s. Congregation is conservative evangelical in a denomination that is theologically more liberal and mainline. Average attendance of about 100 at Sunday morning services. Primarily middle-class members.

### Truth Lutheran Church

Naperville, west suburban DuPage County, established 1985. Housed in historic building, former town library. Congregation is theologically evangelical but maintains mainline denominational affiliation with the Evangelical Lutheran Church in America. Nearly all congregants are mainland Chinese or Taiwanese, predominantly middle class. Attendance of between 100 and 150 at Sunday services. Cooperates with other Protestant churches in humanitarian and social programs.

### Victory Outreach Church

Southwest side of Chicago, established 1993. Part of an international Protestant Pentecostal organization. About 75–100 attend Sunday services. Congregants predominantly Mexican, with Puerto Rican minority. Outreach ministries target drug/alcohol abuse, prostitution, and gang activities, focusing primarily on individual rehabilitation. Mostly poor and working-class members.

## Orthodox Christianity

### Holy Virgin Protection Cathedral

Des Plaines, northwest suburban Cook County, established 1954. Affiliated with ROCOR (Russian Orthodox Church Outside of Russia), a traditionalist Russian Orthodox group that does not recognize the Moscow Patriarchate. About 80–120 attend Sunday liturgies. Parish membership is predominantly Russian; also includes Serbians, Bulgarians, Ukrainians, and small numbers of several other Eastern European ethnicities. Parish programming focuses on religious and ethnic activities.

### St. Demetrios Greek Orthodox Church

North side of Chicago, established 1928. Theologically mainstream Greek Orthodox parish, historic anchor for Greek community. Sunday attendance 200–250, up to 2,500 on major religious holidays. Congregants nearly 100 percent Greek ethnicity. Parish operates wide range of religious and social programming, including instruction in Greek language, culture, and history.

## Judaism

### Synagogue FREE

Far north side of Chicago, established 1973. Lubavitch Hasidic congregation. FREE stands for Friends of Refugees of Eastern Europe, a larger Lubavitch organization. Members are predominantly Russian, many recent immigrants. Shabbat services average about 150 in attendance, up to 1,500 on major religious holidays. Programs include religious education, Russian-language newspaper, and cooperative social programs with other Jewish (including non-Orthodox) organizations.

## Islam

### Islamic Cultural Center of Greater Chicago

Northbrook, north suburban Cook County, parent organization established 1906, first mosque established 1954, moved to Northbrook 1976. Large, modernist Sunni mosque with about 300 average attendance at Friday prayers. Also hosts Sufi prayer group. Facility includes Bosnian cultural center and museum/library. Imam and largest group of attendees are Bosnian, but membership and leadership also include significant Arab and Indo-Pakistani participation. Involved in interfaith activities and programs. Operates K–5 parochial school.

### Islamic Foundation

Villa Park, west suburban DuPage County, established 1974. Large, modernist Sunni mosque with about 2,000 average attendance at Friday prayers. Membership approximately 60 percent Indo-Pakistanis, 30 percent Arabs, the rest Africans, African Americans, Iranians, and whites; primarily middle- and upper-class members. Operates K–12 parochial school.

## Hinduism

### BAPS Shree Swaminarayan Mandir

Bartlett, west suburban DuPage County, opened first facility in west suburban Glen Ellyn 1983, presently operates multimillion-dollar complex (cultural center opened 2000, temple structure 2004). Followers of Pramukh Swami Maharaj, the spiritual descendant of Hindu holy man and founder Sahajanand Swami or Swaminarayan (d. 1830). Strong moral proscriptions, especially with regard to dietary and gender practices. Average attendance 1,000-plus at Sunday assemblies, 5,000 at monthly festivals. Participants nearly all Gujarati Indians. Offers a variety of sports, cultural, and educational programming.

### Gayatri Pariwar Mandir

Far north side of Chicago, established 1989, opened small storefront temple 1997. Devotees of the Hindu goddess Gayatri and followers of holy man and founder Pragyavtar Gurudev. Values gender equality and social action. Large celebrations and festivals held off-site, small group of regulars attend ceremonies at temple. Small operation selling literature and traditional health products and offering yoga classes. Primarily working- and middle-class participants; mostly Gujaratis, along with other Indians.

### International Society for Krishna Consciousness, Chicago

Far north side of Chicago, established 1966, moved to present facility, a former Masonic lodge, 1979. Honors the Hindu god Krishna as supreme godhead and follows holy man and founder A. C. Bhaktivedanta Swami Prabhupad (d. 1977).

Approximately 15 live-in devotees, 20 householder devotees, and 100 others who attend Sunday services. Offers classes in Bhagavad Gita and other scriptures. Primarily working- and middle-class participants; mostly Gujaratis, along with other Indians and some whites (in leadership positions).

## Buddhism

### HanMaUm Zen Center

Skokie, north suburban Cook County, established 1991. Affiliated with Chogye Order of Korean Seon (Zen) Buddhism, followers of movement headed by Korean nun Dae Haeng Kun Sunim. Local temple led by Korean Buddhist nuns. About 40–50 participants in the Sunday gatherings, predominantly Korean, with some white converts as well. Provides few social services for immigrants and does little cooperatively with other Buddhist temples.

### Ling Shen Ching Tze Temple (Chicago)

South side of Chicago, established 1994, occupies former Presbyterian church. Affiliated with True Buddha School, followers of Taiwanese Grand Master Sheng-yen Lu, now residing near Seattle, Washington. About 30 participants in Sunday gatherings, predominantly Taiwanese and mainland Chinese. Programs include Feng Shui workshops and martial arts classes.

# Appendix B:
# Sectarianism Coding for
# Research Sites

## Roman Catholic Christianity

*Five Holy Martyrs Roman Catholic Church*

*Religious.* Low tension: Mainstream theologically, twice visited by Pope John Paul II.

*Cultural.* Low tension: Anchor parish for Polish Catholic community, congregants reflect changing ethnic character of neighborhood.

*Social.* Low tension: Mainstream Catholic on gender, race, and class issues. Little political activism.

*Maternity BVM Roman Catholic Church*

*Religious.* Low tension: Mainstream theologically, inclusive of various religious expressions, including charismatic.

*Cultural.* Low tension: Anchor parish for its Hispanic neighborhood. Open to multiple ethnicities.

*Social.* Medium tension: Engages in class-based political activism, particularly on housing, labor, and immigration issues.

*St. Lambert Roman Catholic Church*

*Religious.* Low tension: Mainstream theologically, inclusive of various religious expressions.

*Cultural.* Low tension: Inclusive of multiple ethnicities in a multiethnic neighborhood.

*Social.* Low tension: Reflects the social status of its surroundings. Focuses on religious practice and celebration more than social issues.

## Protestant Christianity

*Naperville Church of the Brethren*

*Religious.* Medium tension: A mainline Protestant church, but more evangelical than most congregations in its denomination.

*Cultural.* Low tension: Open to participation of multiple ethnicities. Core group made up of mainstream, middle-class Indians.

*Social.* Low tension: Focuses on religious purposes. Avoids oppositional stances on social issues.

### *Truth Lutheran Church*

*Religious.* Medium tension: A mainline Protestant church, but more evangelical than most congregations in its denomination.

*Cultural.* Low tension: Core group of mainstream, middle-class Chinese immigrants. Reflects mainstream cultural practices of that group.

*Social.* Low tension: Focuses on religious purposes. Avoids oppositional stances on social issues.

### *Victory Outreach Church*

*Religious.* High tension: Strong Pentecostal theology that maintains strong contrasts with and distance from other religious groups. Heavy emphasis on proselytizing.

*Cultural.* Low tension: Reflects mainstream Hispanic immigrant culture. Emphasizes family values typical of mainstream conservative American culture.

*Social.* High tension: Organizes as an enclave community, particularly with regard to its drug rehabilitation program. Constructs strong boundaries between itself and outside world.

## Orthodox Christianity

### *Holy Virgin Protection Cathedral*

*Religious.* High tension: Belongs to a conservative sectarian branch of Russian Orthodox Christianity. Maintains strong oppositional stance to mainstream church.

*Cultural.* Medium tension: Serves as an ethnic enclave. Little cooperation with other groups in an ethnically diverse neighborhood, but not particularly oppositional, either.

*Social.* Medium tension: Middle- to upper-class congregation. Little concern with American social issues or political activism. Some tension exists with former Soviet Union as well as recent political developments in Russia.

### *St. Demetrios Greek Orthodox Church*

*Religious.* Low tension: Large, mainstream representative of its theological tradition.

*Cultural.* Low tension: Mono-ethnic but open to relationships with other ethnic groups. Pillar congregation of the Greek American community.

*Social.* Low tension: Little opposition or activism on social issues. Patriarchal organization typical of its tradition.

## Judaism

### *Synagogue FREE*

*Religious.* High tension: Sectarian branch of Hasidic Judaism, following messianic founder.

*Cultural.* High tension: Distinctive visible cultural practices separate congregation from mainstream culture and from other Jewish groups.

*Social.* Medium tension: Strict gender segregation but also cooperates with other Jewish groups in job training and social service organizations.

## Islam

### *Islamic Cultural Center of Greater Chicago*

*Religious.* Low tension: Mainstream, somewhat modernist Islam. Inclusive of multiple religious expressions, including Sufism.

*Cultural.* Low tension: Core group of mainstream Bosnian Americans. Inclusive of multiple ethnicities.

*Social.* Medium tension: Largely middle- to upper-class participants. Located in wealthy northern suburb. Tension exists (often imposed from outside) related to political issues.

### *Islamic Foundation*

*Religious.* Low tension: Reflects mainstream, somewhat modernist Islam. Anchor mosque for Muslim community.

*Cultural.* Low tension: Core group of mainstream South Asians. Inclusive of multiple ethnicities.

*Social.* Medium tension: Largely middle- to upper-class participants. Some tension exists around gender issues, educational programs, and externally imposed tension related to post-9/11 politics.

## Hinduism

### *BAPS Shree Swaminarayan Mandir*

*Religious.* High tension: Sectarian form of Hinduism, led by lineage of gurus. Views itself as representing pure or true Hindu religion. Attempts to proselytize other Hindus.

*Cultural.* High tension: Heavy emphasis on maintaining Gujarati culture. Dietary and other cultural restrictions create boundaries with other Indian groups and mainstream American culture.

*Social.* Medium tension: Largely middle- to upper-class participants. Maintains strong positive relationships with suburban Republican party. Some tension exists over gender issues.

### *Gayatri Pariwar Mandir*

*Religious.* High tension: Sectarian form of Hinduism, follow guru founder. Some theological emphases create distinctions regarding other Hindus.

*Cultural.* Low tension: Representative of mainstream Indian American culture. Dietary/health practices and yoga instruction typical of a particular strand of mainstream American culture.

*Social.* Medium tension: Politically active group in support of Democratic Party politics. Progressive views/practices on gender create some separation from other Hindus and other traditional American groups.

### International Society for Krishna Consciousness, Chicago

*Religious.* High tension: Sectarian form of Hinduism, led by lineage of gurus. Views itself as representing pure or true Hinduism. Strong emphasis on proselytizing other Hindus and people from non-Hindu religious backgrounds.

*Cultural.* High tension: Distinctive dress, dietary, and communal practices maintain visible differences between devotees and others, including other Hindus.

*Social.* High tension: Maintains strict gender segregation rules. Lives communally as an enclave separated from outside world.

## Buddhism

### HanMaUm Zen Center

*Religious.* Medium tension: Some distinctive religious ideas and practices based on teachings of founding nun but exists within a mainstream (Chogye) order of Korean Zen Buddhism.

*Cultural.* Low tension: Cultural practices typical of Korean Buddhists. Exists peaceably in a multiethnic community with significant Korean population.

*Social.* Medium tension: Little political or social activism. Female leadership structure places it in some tension with other Buddhist groups as well as traditional groups in U.S. society generally.

### Ling Shen Ching Tze Temple (Chicago)

*Religious.* High tension: Sectarian form of Buddhism. Follows gurulike founder. Views itself as representing true Buddhism. Proselytizes more than most Buddhist groups.

*Cultural.* Medium tension: Majority of participants are Chinese. Located near Chinatown neighborhood. Incorporation of various kinds of new age cultural practices places it in some tension with mainstream Buddhist schools.

*Social.* Low tension: Little political or social activism but open to relationships with other organizations in Chinatown neighborhood. No particular oppositional positions on gender, class, or race.

# Notes

I — INTRODUCTION

1. "Pluralism" has a variety of meanings across authors (e.g., Eck 2001; Fuchs 1990; Marger 1997, 122–132). We use it here in the sense of America's historic ideal—if not always reality—of mutual respect and accommodation of culturally diverse population groups (see Schaefer 1998, 26–27).

2. E.g., Sherkat 1999; Smith 2002. Survey data reported by Jasso et al. 2003 suggest that 65 percent of recent immigrants to the United States are Christian.

3. The term "recent" specifies post-1965 immigration, distinguishing it from the classical period of American immigration which historians divide into "old" (pre-1880) and "new" (1880–1924) waves. Following convention in current literature, we use "recent" and "new" interchangeably in this book to refer to post-1965 immigration.

4. See also http://www.newimmigrants.org.

5. We chose congregations as our unit of investigation because of the congregation's continuing central role in the organized expression of religion in the United States, including the immigrant context (e.g., Chaves 2004; Warner 1993b; Wind and Lewis 1994). Our working definition of a congregation was as follows: A local association of people who gather periodically for varied activities deemed to have religious significance. The literature no longer confines the word "congregation" to its original Jewish/Christian context, although we should remember that mosques, temples, *gurdwaras,* etc. do not always function like typical churches and synagogues. We based the 20 percent cut-off on the commonsense notion that an observer will begin to notice diversity in a group at about this level (see Emerson et al. 2003 for a theoretical basis).

2 — PURITY AND PROTEST

1. Later, he expanded his conception to seven subtypes (Wilson 1963).

2. Stark and Bainbridge themselves were highly critical of the whole typological project and proposed "cult" as an element in their larger deductive theory of religious movements. But the concept was adopted by scholars who continued in the typologizing tradition.

3. Some scholars deny the applicability of church-sect-etc. typologies to non-Western religions (e.g., Chen 2002, 220; Williams 1988, 283). Perhaps due to this largely unexamined assumption, most recent scholarship on immigrant religions ignores the

issue, with the exception of some work on Muslims (Haddad and Smith 1993; Koszegi and Melton 1992) and Buddhists (Fronsdal 1998; Nattier 1998; Numrich 2000b).

### 3 — LOCATING THE MORAL AUTHORITY OF IMMIGRANT CONGREGATIONS

1. See Harrison (1959) for a masterful analysis of the emergence of clerical authority and power in decentralized Protestant churches.

### 4 — THE MORAL PROJECTS OF IMMIGRANT CONGREGATIONS

1. For example, see Esposito and Voll (2001) for descriptions of nine different contemporary Muslim activist intellectuals who are attempting to reconcile religion, society, and the state within a modern context.

2. See Williams (1990) and Woodhead (2004) for good overviews of Orthodox Christian thought and practice, and Orthodox Christianity's historical development in Europe and the United States.

### 5 — "MAKING IT IN AMERICA"

1. It should be noted, however, that in the third edition of their book Portes and Rumbaut added an entire chapter on religion, correcting for its nearly complete absence in the first two editions, published in 1990 and 1996.

2. Available at the Vatican Web site, http://www.vatican.va.

3. Available at http://www.usccb.org/sdwp/laborday2001.htm.

4. Available at the Lubavitch Web site, http://www.obshina.com.

### 6 — RELIGION, EDUCATION, AND CIVIC TENSIONS IN IMMIGRANT CONGREGATIONS

1. We use the word "parochial" for a full-time school operated by a religious group or organization as an alternative to government-sponsored public education for grades K–12 (or some portion thereof) in the United States.

2. See http://www.islamicfoundationvp.org/school/index.html.

3. See http://www.averroesacademy.org.

4. Available lists and tallies of Islamic schools in the United States tend to be imprecise, making it difficult to distinguish immigrant from nonimmigrant schools and parochial from other types of educational programs. See, e.g., http://islamicvalley.com/prod/entitySearch.php/t/0BK; http://www.msa-natl.org/resources/Schools.html; Hasan 2002, 145; Nimer 2002, 54–55; Wormser 1994, 54; "Directory of Masjids and Muslim Organizations of North America 1994/1415."

5. http://www.ed.gov/pubs/RegPrivSchl/illinois.html.

6. http://www.ncacasi.org.

7. http://www.isbe.state.il.us/news/2003/04_recog_nonpublic_schls.pdf.

8. http://www.islamicfoundationvp.org/school/index.html.

9. http://www.averroesacademy.org/index.php?option=com_content&task=view&id=25&Itemid=1.

10. http://www.averroesacademy.org.

11. Without more research, it is difficult to assess the extent of the isolationist trend identified in this article. We feel it does not represent the mainstream Islamic parochial school movement in the United States today. Findings from the Mosque Study Project report (Bagby, Perl, and Froehle 2001, 29–30) suggest that a large majority of U.S. mosques can be classified as modernist or progressive: 71 percent make Islamic decisions by taking into account modern circumstances and the contexts of authoritative texts and traditions, whereas only 21 percent follow a "literal interpretation" of the texts and traditions and include no consideration of modern circumstances.

12. http://www.islamicfoundationvp.org/school/index.html.

13. http://www.averroesacademy.org.

14. http://www.averroesacademy.org.

15. http://www.chicagomuslimscouts.org.

16. According to spokespersons for the Boy and Girl Scouts of America, in 2003 there were fifty-eight Boy Scout units sponsored by mosques in the United States and "at least a handful" of Girl Scout units (Yates 2003).

17. http://www.muslimhomeschool.com/index.html.

18. Our thanks to Elliot Dorff for these insights shared at an authors meeting for the book *The Child in American Religions* (Browning and Miller-McLemore, forthcoming).

19. http://www2.hongwanji.or.jp/english.

20. http://www.hongwanjihawaii.com/honpa.

21. http://www.buddhistchurchesofamerica.com/index.html.

22. http://www.buddhistchurchesofamerica.com/links/index.shtml.

23. http://www.hais.org/hi_pr_schools.htm.

24. http://www.hongwanjihi.org.

25. http://www.pacificbuddhistacademy.org.

26. Mission statement, http://www.pacificbuddhistacademy.org.

27. http://www.advite.com/sf/cttb/cttbindex.html.

28. See also http://www.namastecharterschool.org.

29. The recent trend of establishing day schools in some liberal Jewish quarters deserves mention here, as it clearly contrasts to the situation during the classical period of Jewish immigration. The recent trend stems from a concern that part-time Jewish education programs are insufficient to retain students' Jewish identities. (Again our

thanks to Elliot Dorff for this insight.) We can see this either as a sectarian impulse in a historically mainstream American religious group or as a reassertion of a heretofore abandoned collectivist moral orientation found in traditional Judaism.

30. http://www.ciogc.org.

## 7 — MARRIAGE PATTERNS IN IMMIGRANT CONGREGATIONS

1. Bogardus used various designations for what came to be known as the social distance scale: social contact range index, social contact distance index, social contact quality index, ethnic distance scale, and racial distance index. The value of Park's famous race relations cycle has been thoroughly debated, and the implied significance of race has certainly changed among sociologists today. Nevertheless, Park's views on the correlation between biological "amalgamation" and social distance remain instructive for our purposes. Park (1931, 535) considered amalgamation "one of the indices, perhaps the ultimate index, of the extent to which cultural fusion in any given case has actually taken place." It does not appear that Park required amalgamation in the final stage of his race relations cycle—i.e., assimilation (see Yu 2001).

2. In rare cases immigrant parents will actively encourage exogamy to their American-born offspring. For instance, some segments of the Sri Lankan immigrant community in Los Angeles downplay the importance of preserving immigrant identity (see Numrich 1996, 104–107).

3. Islam has always held special consideration for Jews and Christians as fellow People of the Book—that is, religions whose prophets received a revealed written scripture from God.

4. We assume she was referring to the Hebrew term *sheketz*, "abomination" or "unclean creature." The derivative Yiddish terms, *shiksa* (female) and *shegetz* (male), are often used of non-Jewish marriage partners.

5. The Baha'i Faith stands out for its doctrine of racial equality, but its record on interracial marriage in the United States is uneven (Haithman 1987, 185–186). According to a source at the Baha'i national offices in Wilmette, Illinois, the Baha'i have never conducted a statistical survey of their rates of interracial marriages or cross-racial adoptions (the latter may be more common than the former, according to this source).

6. Religion is indexed only once in this important book. In that reference (260), religious factors are discounted in explaining educational achievement levels across Southeast Asian groups since the authors consider these factors too complex.

## 8 — LANGUAGE IN IMMIGRANT CONGREGATIONS

1. http://www.tbsn.org.

2. Poston uses the terms "defensive-pacifist" and "offensive-activist," which we render here as "passivist" and "activist," respectively.

3. In our discussion of the moral project in chapter 4, we place ICCGC in a middle category because of its mix of the collectivism of traditional Islam and the individualism of Sufi mysticism. Obviously, here we focus on the collectivist aspects of this mix.

## IO — ORGANIZATIONAL ENGAGEMENT

1. Sociologists of religion who make use of the ecology metaphor draw on an extensive organizational ecology literature spawned by the seminal work of Hannan and Freeman (1989).

2. Wuthnow (1998) makes a similar point in *Loose Connections,* a study of changing patterns of personal and group affiliations.

3. Ebaugh et al. (2000b) found a similar proportion in their study of eleven immigrant congregations in Houston.

## II — WHEN AND HOW RELIGION MATTERS FOR IMMIGRANT CIVIC ENGAGEMENT

1. We do not agree with Vasquez's ideological critique of the congregational approach to immigrant studies—namely, that this approach represents a thinly veiled American exceptionalism (see 230–235).

2. Five of the twenty-three parties in this amicus brief are ethnic-Asian groups with long histories in the United States (all in the Japanese Jodo Shinshu lineage), sixteen are so-called convert groups representing a variety of Buddhist lineages. It seems likely that the two Thai temples joined the amicus brief through the influence of one of the convert groups, namely A Few Simsapa Leaves Buddhist Center, which claims "a close relationship" with these Thai temples and distinguishes its practice of Buddhism from traditional Thai Buddhism in the following description: "Basically Theravada but without what a person of common sense would consider myth or superstition" (http://a.webring.com/hub?ring=wb1967; on the "two Buddhisms" of America, culture Buddhists and convert Buddhists, see Numrich 2003).

3. http://www.shivavishnutemple.org.

4. http://www.isfmd.org.

5. http://www.isna.net/index.php?id=316.

6. See profile at http://campusministry.georgetown.edu.

7. Sources for this discussion: "Interfaith Prayer Breakfast" and "Music of the Millennium" programs, and a photocopy list of "Interfaith Prayer Breakfast Benefactors."

8. http://www.pluralism.org.

9. http://www.bosnjaci.net/aktuelnosti.php?id=437&polje=aktuelno.

10. http://www.cpwr.org.

# References

Abd'l-Haleem, Khadijah. 2001. "Islamic Schooling in the Rear View Mirror." *Chicago Muslim* (newsletter of the Council of Islamic Organizations of Greater Chicago) (July): 5–6.

Abramson, Harold J. 1980. "Religion." In *Harvard Encyclopedia of American Ethnic Groups,* ed. Stephen Thernstrom, 869–875. Cambridge, Mass.: Belknap Press.

Ahmed-Ullah, Noreen S., Kim Barker, Laurie Cohen, Stephen Franklin, and Sam Roe. 2004. "Hard-Liners Won Battle for Bridgeview Mosque." *Chicago Tribune,* February 8, sec. 1.

al-Ahari, Muhammed Abdullah. 2001. "A Pioneering Muslim Scholar in America: The Achievements of Imam Kamil Avdic." In *Zivot i djelo Camila Avdica: Zbornik radova,* 50–76. Sarajevo: El-Kalem.

Albanese, Catherine L. 1999. *America: Religions and Religion.* 3d ed. Belmont, Calif.: Wadsworth Publishing Co.

Alumkal, Antony W. 2001. "Being Korean, Being Christian: Particularism and Universalism in a Second-Generation Congregation." In *Korean Americans and Their Religions: Pilgrims and Missionaries from a Different Shore,* ed. Ho-Youn Kwon, Kwang Chung Kim, and R. Stephen Warner, 181–191. University Park: Pennsylvania State University Press.

Ammerman, Nancy T. 1997. *Congregations and Community.* New Brunswick, N.J.: Rutgers University Press.

———. 2001. "Doing Good in American Communities: Congregations and Service Organizations Working Together." Hartford, Conn.: Hartford Institute for Religion Research.

———. 2005. *Pillars of Faith: American Congregations and Their Partners.* Berkeley: University of California Press.

Ammerman, Nancy T., Jackson W. Carroll, Carl S. Dudley, and William McKinney, eds. 1998. *Studying Congregations: A New Handbook.* Nashville, Tenn.: Abingdon Press.

Anand, Priya. 2004. "Hindu Diaspora and Religious Philanthropy in the United States." Paper presented at Sixth International Society for Third Sector Research, Toronto, July.

Anderson, Allan. 2004. *An Introduction to Pentecostalism.* Cambridge: Cambridge University Press.

Antes, Peter, and Hans Waldenfels. 1997. "Mission in Non-Christian Religions." In *Dictionary of Mission: Theology, History, Perspectives,* ed. Karl Muller, Theo Sundermeier, Stephen B. Bevans, and Richard H. Bliese, eds., 303–307. Maryknoll: Orbis Books.

Bagby, Ihsan, Paul M. Perl, and Bryan T. Froehle. 2001. *The Mosque in America: A National Report.* Washington, D.C.: Council on American-Islamic Relations.

Bailey, Richard P. 2001. "The Call to the Church in North America." In *The Gospel for Islam: Reaching Muslims in North America,* ed. Roy Oksnevad and Dotsey Welliver, 187–206. Wheaton, Ill.: EMIS.

Baltzell, E. Digby. 1964. *The Protestant Establishment.* New York: Random House.

———. 1979. *Puritan Boston and Quaker Philadelphia.* Boston: Beacon Press.

Bankston, Carl L., III. 1997. "Bayou Lotus: Theravada Buddhism in Southwestern Louisiana." *Sociological Spectrum* 17 (4): 453–472.

Barazangi, Nimat Hafez. 1991. "Islamic Education in the United States and Canada: Conception and Practice of the Islamic Belief System." In *The Muslims of America,* ed. Yvonne Yazbeck Haddad, 157–174. New York: Oxford University Press.

Bean, Frank D., and Gillian Stevens. 2003. *America's Newcomers and the Dynamics of Diversity.* New York: Russell Sage Foundation.

Bechert, Heinz. 1984. "Buddhist Revival in East and West." In *The World of Buddhism: Buddhist Monks and Nuns in Society and Culture,* ed. Heinz Bechert and Richard Gombrich, 273–285. New York: Facts on File.

Beck, Walter H. 1965. *Lutheran Elementary Schools in the United States: A History of the Development of Parochial Schools and Synodical Educational Policies and Programs.* 2d ed. St. Louis: Concordia Publishing House.

Becker, Howard. 1932. *Systematic Sociology.* New York: Wiley.

Becker, Penny. 1999. *Congregations in Conflict: Cultural Models of Local Religious Life.* Cambridge: Cambridge University Press.

Behlim, Saara. 1994. "The Islamic Cultural Center of Greater Chicago: A Historical Perspective." N.p., n.d.

Bellah, Robert N., Richard Madsen, William M. Sullivan, Ann Swidler, and Steven M. Tipton. 1985. *Habits of the Heart: Individualism and Commitment in American Life.* Berkeley: University of California Press.

Bloom, Stephen G. 2000. *Postville: A Clash of Cultures in Heartland America.* New York: Harcourt.

Bodnar, John. 1985. *The Transplanted: A History of Immigrants in Urban America.* Bloomington: Indiana University Press.

Bogardus, Emory S. 1925a. "Measuring Social Distances." *Journal of Applied Sociology* 9 (March–April): 299–308.

———. 1925b. "Social Distance and Its Origins." *Journal of Applied Sociology* 9 (January–February): 216–226.

———. 1968. "Comparing Racial Distance in Ethiopia, South Africa, and the United States." *Sociology and Social Research* 52 (January): 149–156.

Bosch, David J. 1980. *Witness to the World: The Christian Mission in Theological Perspective*. Atlanta: John Knox Press.

"A Bosnian Muslim Speaks Out: An Interview with Imam Senad Agic." 1995. *Christian Century* 112 (August 2): 745–747.

Browning, Dan S., and Bonnie Miller-McLemore, eds. Forthcoming. *The Child in American Religions*. New Brunswick, N.J.: Rutgers University Press.

Burns, J. A., Bernard J. Kohlbrenner, and John B. Peterson. 1937. *A History of Catholic Education in the United States: A Textbook for Normal Schools and Teachers' Colleges*. New York: Benziger Brothers.

Cainkar, Louise. 1988. "Palestinian Women in the United States: Coping with Tradition, Change, and Alienation." Ph.D. diss., Northwestern University, Evanston, Ill.

Chai, Karen J. 1998. "Competing for the Second Generation: English-Language Ministry at a Korean Protestant Church." In *Gatherings in Diaspora: Religious Communities and the New Immigration*, ed. R. Stephen Warner and Judith G. Wittner, 295–331. Philadelphia: Temple University Press.

Charaniya, Nadira K., and Janet West Walsh. 2001. "Interpreting the Experiences of Christians, Muslims, and Jews Engaged in Interreligious Dialogue: A Collaborative Research Study." *Religious Education* 96 (Summer): 351–368.

Chaves, Mark. 2004. *Congregations in America*. Cambridge, Mass.: Harvard University Press.

Chen, Carolyn. 2002. "The Religious Varieties of Ethnic Presence: A Comparison between a Taiwanese Immigrant Buddhist Temple and an Evangelical Christian Church." *Sociology of Religion* 63 (2): 215–238.

Chong, Kelly H. 1998. "What It Means to Be Christian: The Role of Religion in the Construction of Ethnic Identity and Boundary among Second-Generation Korean Americans." *Sociology of Religion* 59 (3): 259–286.

Christerson, Brad, and Michael Emerson. 2003. "The Costs of Diversity in Religious Organizations: An In-Depth Case Study." *Sociology of Religion* 64 (2):163–181.

Cieslak, Michael. 2004. "Future Educational Needs of Suburban Parishes without Catholic Schools." *Review of Religious Research* 46 (September): 105–106.

———. 2005. "The Lack of Consensus among Catholics for Establishing New Elementary Schools." *Review of Religious Research* 47 (December): 175–189.

Cnaan, Ram A. 2002. *The Invisible Caring Hand: American Congregations and the Provision of Welfare*. New York: New York University Press.

Cragg, Kenneth. 1975. *The House of Islam.* Encino, Calif.: Dickerson Publishing Co.

Curran, Francis X. 1954. *The Churches and the Schools: American Protestantism and Popular Elementary Education.* Chicago: Loyola University Press.

D'Agostino, Peter R. 2000. "Catholic Planning for a Multicultural Metropolis, 1982–1996." In *Public Religion and Urban Transformation: Faith in the City,* ed. Lowell W. Livezey, 269–291. New York: New York University Press.

Dashefsky, Arnold, Bernard Lazerwitz, and Ephraim Tabory. 2003. "A Journey of the 'Straight Way' or the 'Roundabout Path': Jewish Identity in the United States and Israel." In *Handbook of the Sociology of Religion,* ed. Michele Dillon, 240–260. Cambridge: Cambridge University Press.

"The Demand of the Times." N.d. Gayatri Pariwar Mandir booklet.

"Dharma Suffers in US Schools." 1987. *Hinduism Today,* August. http://www.hinduism-today.com/archives/1987/08/1987-08-01.shtml.

Dillon, Michele. 1999. *Catholic Identity: Balancing Reason, Faith, and Power.* Boston: Cambridge University Press.

"Directory of Masjids and Muslim Organizations of North America 1994/1415." [1994?] Fountain Valley, Calif.: Islamic Resource Institute.

Dolan, Jay P. 1975. *The Immigrant Church: New York's Irish and German Catholics, 1815–1865.* Baltimore: Johns Hopkins University Press.

———. 1985. *The American Catholic Experience: A History from Colonial Times to the Present.* Garden City, N.Y.: Doubleday.

———. 1988. "The Immigrants and Their Gods: A New Perspective in American Religious History." *Church History* 57 (March): 61–72.

Ebaugh, Helen Rose. 2002. "Return of the Sacred: Reintegrating Religion in the Social Sciences." *Journal for the Scientific Study of Religion* 41 (3): 385–395.

Ebaugh, Helen Rose, and Janet Saltzman Chafetz. 2000a. "Dilemmas of Language in Immigrant Congregations: The Tie That Binds or the Tower of Babel?" *Review of Religious Research* 41 (June): 432–452.

———. 2000b. *Religion and the New Immigrants: Continuities and Adaptations in Immigrant Congregations.* Walnut Creek, Calif.: AltaMira Press.

———, eds. 2002. *Religion across Borders: Transnational Immigrant Networks.* Walnut Creek, Calif.: AltaMira Press.

Ebaugh, Helen Rose, Jennifer O'Brien, and Janet Saltzman Chafetz. 2000. "The Social Ecology of Residential Patterns and Membership in Immigrant Churches." *Journal for the Scientific Study of Religion* 39:107–116.

Ebaugh, Helen Rose, Paula F. Pipes, Janet Saltzman Chafetz, and Martha Daniels. 2003. "Where's the Religion? Distinguishing Faith-Based from Secular Social Service Agencies." *Journal for the Scientific Study of Religion* 42 (September): 411–426.

Eck, Diana L. 2001. *A New Religious America: How a "Christian Country" Has Become the World's Most Religiously Diverse Nation*. San Francisco: Harper San Francisco.

Ecklund, Elaine Howard. 2005. "Models of Civic Responsibility: Korean Americans in Congregations with Different Ethnic Compositions." *Journal for the Scientific Study of Religion* 44 (March): 15–28.

Ehrenberg, John. 1999. *Civil Society: The Critical History of an Idea*. New York: New York University Press.

Eiesland, Nancy L. 2000. *A Particular Place: Urban Restructuring and Religious Ecology in a Southern Exurb*. New Brunswick, N.J.: Rutgers University Press.

Eiesland, Nancy L., and R. Stephen Warner. 1998. "Ecology: Seeing the Congregation in Context." In *Studying Congregations: A New Handbook,* ed. Nancy T. Ammerman, Jackson W. Carroll, Carl S. Dudley, and William McKinney, 40–77. Nashville: Abingdon Press.

Eliade, Mircea. 1958. *Patterns in Comparative Religion*. New York: Sheed & Ward.

———. 1961. *The Sacred and the Profane: The Nature of Religion*. Trans. Willard R. Trask. New York: Harper Torchbooks.

Emerson, Michael O., and Christian Smith. 2000. *Divided by Faith: Evangelical Religion and the Problem of Race in America*. New York: Oxford University Press.

Emerson, Michael O., Christian Smith., and Karen Chai Kim. 2003. "Multiracial Congregations: An Analysis of Their Development and a Typology." *Journal for the Scientific Study of Religion* 42 (2): 217–227.

Esposito, John L. 1998. *Islam: The Straight Path*. 3d ed. New York: Oxford University Press.

———. 2002. *What Everyone Needs to Know about Islam*. New York: Oxford University Press.

Esposito, John L., and John O. Voll. 2001. *Makers of Contemporary Islam*. New York: Oxford University Press.

Essoyan, Susan. 2003. "Buddhist School to Focus on Peace." *Honolulu Star-Bulletin,* February 18. http://starbulletin.com/2003/02/18/news/story1.html.

Farnsley, Arthur Emery, II. 2000. "Congregations, Local Knowledge, and Devolution." *Review of Religious Research* 42 (September): 96–110.

Fichter, Joseph H. 1958. *Parochial School: A Sociological Study*. Notre Dame: University of Notre Dame Press.

"First Hindu Temple in Wisconsin Opens." 2000. *Indian Reporter*. September 15.

Fisher, James T. 2002. *Communion of Immigrants: A History of Catholics in America*. New York: Oxford University Press.

*Five Holy Martyrs Diamond Jubilee*. 1985. Des Plaines, Ill.: King Co.

Foner, Nancy. 2000. *From Ellis Island to JFK: New York's Two Great Waves of Immigration.* New York: Russell Sage Foundation.

Franklin, Stephen. 2001. "Growing Pains: It's Not Easy Being Muslim in America, But It Is Getting Less Lonely." *Chicago Tribune Magazine,* March 18, 12–17.

Friedland, Lewis A. 2001. "Reform Judaism and Modern American Community." In *Contemporary Debates in American Reform Judaism: Conflicting Visions,* ed. Dana Evan Kaplan, 39–48. New York: Routledge.

Fronsdal, Gil. 1998. "Insight Meditation in the United States: Life, Liberty, and the Pursuit of Happiness." In *The Faces of Buddhism in America,* ed. Charles S. Prebish and Kenneth K. Tanaka, 164–180. Berkeley: University of California Press.

Fu, Vincent Kang. 2003. "Regional, Temporal, and Group Variation in US Racial and Ethnic Intermarriage." Ph.D. diss., University of California, Los Angeles.

Fuchs, Lawrence H. 1990. *The American Kaleidoscope: Race, Ethnicity, and the Civic Culture.* Hanover, N.H.: Wesleyan University Press.

Gallanis, Bess. 2004. "Chicago Board of Education Charters The Namaste School." http://www.yogachicago.com/may04/namaste-school.shtml.

Gaustad, Edwin S., and Leigh Schmidt. 2004. *The Religious History of America: The Heart of the American Story from Colonial Times to Today.* San Francisco: Harper.

Gjerde, Jon. 1986. "Conflict and Community: A Case Study of the Immigrant Church in the United States." *Journal of Social History* 19:681–697.

Gombrich, Richard F. 1988. *Theravada Buddhism: As Social History from Ancient Benares to Modern Colombo.* New York: Routledge.

Granovetter, Mark S. 1973. "The Strength of Weak Ties." *American Journal of Sociology* 78:1360–1380.

Greeley, Andrew M., and Peter H. Rossi. 1966. *The Education of Catholic Americans.* Chicago: Aldine Publishing Co.

Gross, Rita M. 1993. *Buddhism after Patriarchy: A Feminist History, Analysis, and Reconstruction of Buddhism.* Albany: SUNY Press.

————. 2005. "Buddhist Contributions to the Civic and Conscientious Public Forums." In *Taking Religious Pluralism Seriously: Spiritual Politics on America's Sacred Ground,* ed. Barbara A. McGraw and Jo Renee Formicola, 215–233. Waco: Baylor University Press.

Guest, Kenneth J. 2005. "Religion and Transnational Migration in the New Chinatown." In *Immigrant Faiths: Transforming Religious Life in America,* ed. Karen I. Leonard, Alex Stepick, Manuel A. Vasquez, and Jennifer Holdaway, 145–163. Walnut Creek, Calif.: AltaMira Press.

Hack, Chris, and Allison Hantschel. 2003. "US Investigating Mosque Foundation." *Daily Southtown,* September 21. http://www.dailysouthtown.com/southtown/dsnews/211nd1.htm.

Haddad, Yvonne Y. 1986. "A Century of Islam in America." *The Muslim World Today,* Occasional Paper No. 4. Washington, D.C.: American Institute for Islamic Affairs.

———. 1997. "Make Room for the Muslims?" In *Religious Diversity and American Religious History: Studies in Traditions and Cultures,* ed. Walter H. Conser Jr. and Sumner B. Twiss, 218–261. Athens: University of Georgia Press.

Haddad, Yvonne Y., and Adair T. Lummis. 1987. *Islamic Values in the United States: A Comparative Study.* New York: Oxford University Press.

Haddad, Yvonne Y., and Jane Idleman Smith. 1993. *Mission to America: Five Islamic Sectarian Communities in North America.* Gainesville: University Press of Florida.

Haeng, Dae. 1999. *The Inner Path of Freedom: The Teachings of Seon Master Dae Haeng Sunim.* Anyang City, Korea: HanMaUm Seon Center.

Haithman, Gloria. 1987. "On Being Black, Female, and Baha'i in America." In *Equal Circles: Women and Men in the Baha'i Community,* ed. Peggy Caton, 169–189. Los Angeles: Kalimat Press.

Hammond, Phillip E., and Kee Warner. 1993. "Religion and Ethnicity in Late-Twentieth-Century America." *Annals of the American Academy of Political and Social Science* 527 (May): 55–66.

Hannan, Michael T., and John Freeman. 1989. *Organizational Ecology.* Cambridge, Mass.: Harvard University Press.

Harrison, Paul. 1959. *Authority and Power in the Free Church Tradition: A Social Case Study of the American Baptist Convention.* Princeton, N.J.: Princeton University Press.

Hart, Stephen. 1992. *What Does the Lord Require?* New York: Oxford University Press.

Hasan, Asma Gull. 2002. *American Muslims: The New Generation.* 2d ed. New York: Continuum.

Henry, Carl F. H. 1947. *The Uneasy Conscience of Modern Fundamentalism.* Grand Rapids, Mich.: Eerdmans Press.

Herberg, Will. 1955. *Protestant-Catholic-Jew: An Essay in American Religious Sociology.* Garden City, N.Y.: Doubleday.

———. 1961. "Religion and Education in America." In *Religious Perspectives in American Culture,* ed. James Ward Smith and A. Leland Jamison, *Religion in American Life,* 2:11–51. Princeton, N.J.: Princeton University Press.

Hicks, Douglas A. 2003. *Religion and the Workplace: Pluralism, Spirituality, Leadership.* Cambridge: Cambridge University Press.

Horan, Deborah. 2002. "Put Off by Public Schools, More Muslims Home-Teach." *Chicago Tribune,* December 16, sec. 1.

"How to Quiet the Mind and How to Recite Mantras." N.d. Trans. Janny Chow. Purple Lotus Series No. 1.5. San Bruno, Calif.: Purple Lotus Society.

Hunter, James Davison. 1987. *Evangelicalism: The Coming Generation*. Chicago: University of Chicago Press.

———. 1991. *Culture Wars: The Struggle to Define America*. New York: Basic Books.

Hunter, Louise H. 1971. *Buddhism in Hawaii: Its Impact on a Yankee Community*. Honolulu: University of Hawaii Press.

Hutchison, William R. 1982. *The Modernist Impulse in American Protestantism*. New York: Oxford University Press.

Hyeseon Sunim. 2004. "Master Daehaeng's Teachings on Spiritual Practice." Paper presented at 8th Sakyadhita International Conference on Buddhist Women, Seoul, South Korea, 27 June–5 July.

"The Islamic Cultural Center of Greater Chicago." 1986. Brochure. Northbrook, Ill.: Islamic Cultural Center of Greater Chicago.

"Islamic Foundation: An Introduction." N.d. Brochure. Villa Park, Ill.: Islamic Foundation.

"Islamic Foundation School Parents and Students Handbook (Rules and Regulations) 2000–2001." 2000. In-house brochure.

Jackson, Carl T. 1994. *Vedanta for the West: The Rama Krishna Movement in the United States*. Bloomington: Indiana University Press.

Jacoby, Tamar, ed. 2004. *Reinventing the Melting Pot: The New Immigrants and What It Means to Be American*. New York: Basic Books.

Jasso, Guillermina, Douglas S. Massey, Mark R. Rosenzweig, and James P. Smith. 2003. "Exploring the Religious Preferences of Recent Immigrants to the United States: Evidence from the New Immigrant Survey Pilot." In *Religion and Immigration: Christian, Jewish, and Muslim Experiences in the United States,* ed. Yvonne Yazbeck Haddad, Jane I. Smith, and John L. Esposito, 217–253. Walnut Creek, Calif.: AltaMira Press.

Jenkins, Kathleen E. 2003. "Intimate Diversity: The Presentation of Multiculturalism and Multiracialism in a High-Boundary Religious Movement." *Journal for the Scientific Study of Religion* 42 (September): 393–409.

Jick, Leon A. 1976. *The Americanization of the Synagogue, 1820–1870*. Hanover, N.H.: University Press of New England.

Johnson, Benton. 1963. "On Church and Sect." *American Sociological Review* 28:539–549.

Jones, Maldwyn Allen. 1960. *American Immigration*. Chicago: University of Chicago Press.

Kantowicz, Edward R. 2000. "Separate but Equal: The Civic Incorporation of Chicago Catholics." Paper commissioned by the Religion, Immigration, and Civil Society in Chicago Project.

Kashima, Tetsuden. 1977. *Buddhism in America: The Social Organization of an Ethnic Religious Institution*. Westport, Conn.: Greenwood Press.

Kennedy, Ruby Jo Reeves. 1944. "Single or Triple Melting-Pot? Intermarriage Trends in New Haven, 1870–1940." *American Journal of Sociology* 49 (January): 331–339.

———. 1952. "Single or Triple Melting-Pot? Intermarriage Trends in New Haven, 1870–1950." *American Journal of Sociology* 58 (July): 56–59.

Khalidi, Omar. 1998. "Approaches to Mosque Design in North America." In *Muslims on the Americanization Path?* ed. Yvonne Yazbeck Haddad and John L. Esposito, 399–424. Atlanta: Scholars Press.

Khan, M. A. Muqtedar. 2003. "Constructing the American Muslim Community." In *Religion and Immigration: Christian, Jewish, and Muslim Experiences in the United States,* ed. Yvonne Yazbeck Haddad, Jane I. Smith, and John L. Esposito, 175–198. Walnut Creek, Calif.: AltaMira Press.

Kibria, Nazli. 2002. *Becoming Asian American: Second-Generation Chinese and Korean American Identities.* Baltimore: Johns Hopkins University Press.

Kim, Kwang Chung, and Shin Kim. 2001. "The Ethnic Roles of Korean Immigrant Churches in the United States." In *Korean Americans and Their Religions: Pilgrims and Missionaries from a Different Shore,* ed. Ho-Youn Kwon, Kwang Chung Kim, and R. Stephen Warner, 71–94. University Park: Pennsylvania State University Press.

Kim, Yong Choon. 1988. "The Nature and Destiny of Korean Churches in the United States." In *Koreans in North America: New Perspectives,* ed. Seong Hyong Lee and Tae-Hwan Kwak, 215–230. Seoul: Kyungnam University Press.

Kitagawa, Joseph, ed. 1967. *The History of Religions: Essays on the Problem of Understanding.* Chicago: University of Chicago Press.

Kivisto, Peter. 1993. "Religion and the New Immigrants." In *A Future for Religion? New Paradigms for Social Analysis,* ed. William H. Swatos Jr., 92–108. Newbury Park, Calif.: Sage Publications.

Kniss, Fred. 2005. Review of Robert Wuthnow, *America and the Challenges of Religious Diversity. Christian Century,* December 13, 46–48.

———. 1997. *Disquiet in the Land: Cultural Conflict in American Mennonite Communities.* New Brunswick, N.J.: Rutgers University Press.

———. 2003. "Mapping the Moral Order: Depicting the Terrain of Religious Conflict and Change." In *Handbook of the Sociology of Religion,* ed. Michele Dillon, 331–347. New York: Cambridge University Press.

Koszegi, Michael A., and J. Gordon Melton, eds. 1992. *Islam in North America: A Sourcebook.* New York: Garland Publishing.

Krindatch, Alexei D. 2002. "Orthodox (Eastern Christian) Churches in the United States at the Beginning of a New Millennium: Questions of Nature, Identity, and Mission." *Journal for the Scientific Study of Religion* 41 (September): 533–563.

Kurien, Prema A. 2004. "Christian by Birth or Rebirth? Generation and Difference in an Indian American Christian Church." In *Asian American Religions: The Making and*

*Remaking of Borders and Boundaries,* ed. Tony Carnes and Fenggang Yang, 160–181. New York: New York University Press.

Kwon, Ho-Youn, Kwang Chung Kim, and R. Stephen Warner, eds. 2001. *Korean Americans and Their Religions: Pilgrims and Missionaries from a Different Shore.* University Park: Pennsylvania State University Press.

Lannie, Vincent P. 1970. "Catholics, Protestants, and Public Education." In *Catholicism in America,* ed. Philip Gleason, 45–57. New York: Harper & Row.

Lawrence, Bruce B. 2002. *New Faiths, Old Fears: Muslims and Other Asian Immigrants in American Religious Life.* New York: Columbia University Press.

Lawrence, Stewart J. 1998. "Religion and Immigration in the Contemporary United States: A Bibliographic Review Essay." Unpublished manuscript commissioned by the Louisville Institute.

Lee, Jennifer, and Frank D. Bean. 2004. "America's Changing Color Lines: Immigration, Race/Ethnicity, and Multiracial Identification." *Annual Review of Sociology* 30:221–242.

Lee, Richard Wayne. 1992. "Christianity and the Other Religions: Interreligious Relations in a Shrinking World." *Sociological Analysis* 53 (Summer): 125–139.

Lee, Sharon M., and Barry Edmonston. 1994. "The Socioeconomic Status and Integration of Asian Immigrants." In *Immigration and Ethnicity: The Integration of America's Newest Arrivals,* ed. Barry Edmonston and Jeffrey S. Passel, 101–138. Washington, D.C.: Urban Institute Press.

Lee, Sharon M., Barry Edmonston, and Marilyn Fernandez. 1998. "Trends in Asian American Racial/Ethnic Intermarriage: A Comparison of 1980 and 1990 Census Data." *Sociological Perspectives* 41 (2): 323–342.

Leon, Luis. 1998: "Born Again in East LA: The Congregation as Border Space." In *Gatherings in Diaspora: Religious Communities and the New Immigration,* ed. R. Stephen Warner and Judith G. Wittner, 163–196. Philadelphia: Temple University Press.

Leonard, Karen. 2003a. "American Muslim Politics: Discourses and Practices." *Ethnicities* 3 (June): 147–181.

———. 2003b. *Muslims in the United States: The State of Research.* New York: Russell Sage Foundation.

Levitt, Peggy. 2001. *The Transnational Villagers.* Berkeley: University of California Press.

Lieberson, Stanley. 2000. *A Matter of Taste: How Names, Fashions, and Culture Change.* New Haven: Yale University Press.

Lieberson, Stanley, and Mary C. Waters. 1988. *From Many Strands: Ethnic and Racial Groups in Contemporary America.* New York: Russell Sage Foundation.

Livezey, Lowell W. 2000. "The New Context of Urban Religion." In *Public Religion and Urban Transformation: Faith in the City,* ed. Lowell W. Livezey, 3–25. New York: New York University Press.

Livezey, Lowell W., David Daniels, Paul D. Numrich, and Elfriede Wedam. Forthcoming. *Religion in the New Urban Era*. Chicago: University of Chicago Press.

Lund, Gene Jessie. 1954. "The Americanization of the Augustana Lutheran Church." Th.D. diss., Princeton Theological Seminary.

Mann, Gurinder Singh, Paul David Numrich, and Raymond B. Williams. 2001. *Buddhists, Hindus, and Sikhs in America*. New York: Oxford University Press.

Marger, Martin N. 1997. *Race and Ethnic Relations: American and Global Perspectives*. 4th ed. Belmont, Calif.: Wadsworth Publishing Co.

Marsden, George M. 1980. *Fundamentalism and American Culture: The Shaping of Twentieth-Century Evangelicalism, 1870–1925*. New York: Oxford University Press.

McGraw, Barbara A. 2005. "Introduction to America's Sacred Ground." In *Taking Religious Pluralism Seriously: Spiritual Politics on America's Sacred Ground*, ed. Barbara A. McGraw and Jo Renee Formicola, 1–25. Waco: Baylor University Press.

McGraw, Barbara A., and Jo Renee Formicola, eds. 2005. *Taking Religious Pluralism Seriously: Spirited Politics on America's Sacred Ground*. Waco: Baylor University Press.

McGreevy, John T. 1996. *Parish Boundaries: The Catholic Encounter with Race in the Twentieth-Century Urban North*. Chicago: University of Chicago Press.

McKinney, William. 2005. Review of Mark Chaves, *Congregations in America*. *Journal for the Scientific Study of Religion* 44 (September): 361.

Mead, Sidney E. 1963. *The Lively Experiment: The Shaping of Christianity in America*. New York: Harper & Row.

Metcalf, Barbara D. 1996. "Introduction: Sacred Words, Sanctioned Practice, New Communities." In *Making Muslim Space in North America and Europe*, ed. Barbara Daly Metcalf, 1–27. Berkeley: University of California Press.

Mihalopoulos, Dan. 2003. "Melting Pot Often Heated." *Chicago Tribune*, December 26, sec. 1.

Min, Pyong Gap. 2002. "A Literature Review with a Focus on Major Themes." In *Religions in Asian America: Building Faith Communities*, ed. Pyong Gap Min and Jung Ha Kim, 15–36. Walnut Creek, Calif.: AltaMira Press.

Min, Pyong Gap, and Jung Ha Kim, eds. 2002. *Religions in Asian America: Building Faith Communities*. Walnut Creek, Calif.: AltaMira Press.

Moes, Matthew. N.d. "Islamic Schools as Change Agents." http://www.isna.net/library/Papers/education/IslamicSchoolsAsAgents2.htm.

Nattier, Jan. 1998. "Who Is a Buddhist? Charting the Landscape of Buddhist America." In *The Faces of Buddhism in America*, ed. Charles S. Prebish and Kenneth K. Tanaka, 183–195. Berkeley: University of California Press.

Nelson, E. Clifford, ed. 1975. *The Lutherans in North America*. Philadelphia: Fortress Press.

Neuwien, Reginald A., ed. 1966. *Catholic Schools in Action: A Report: The Notre Dame Study of Catholic Elementary and Secondary Schools in the United States*. Notre Dame: University of Notre Dame Press.

Niebuhr, H. Richard. [1929] 1957. *The Social Sources of Denominationalism*. New York: Meridian.

Nimer, Mohamed. 2002. *The North American Muslim Resource Guide: Muslim Community Life in the United States and Canada*. New York: Routledge.

Numrich, Paul D. 1996. *Old Wisdom in the New World: Americanization in Two Immigrant Theravada Buddhist Temples*. Knoxville: University of Tennessee Press.

———. 1997. "Recent Immigrant Religions in a Restructuring Metropolis: New Religious Landscapes in Chicago." *Journal of Cultural Geography* 17:55–76.

———. 1999. "Local Inter-Buddhist Associations in North America." In *American Buddhism: Methods and Findings in Recent Scholarship*, ed. Duncan Ryuken Williams and Christopher S. Queen, 117–142. London: Curzon Press.

———. 2000a. "Change, Stress, and Congregations in an Edge-City Technoburb." In *Public Religion and Urban Transformation: Faith in the City*, ed. Lowell W. Livezey, 187–210. New York: New York University Press.

———. 2000b. "How the Swans Came to Lake Michigan: The Social Organization of Buddhist Chicago." *Journal for the Scientific Study of Religion* 39 (June): 189–203.

———. 2000c. "Recent Immigrant Religions and the Restructuring of Metropolitan Chicago." In *Public Religion and Urban Transformation: Faith in the City*, ed. Lowell W. Livezey, 239–267. New York: New York University Press.

———. 2001. "Health, Faith, and Ethics at the State Department: The Park Ridge Center Consults on a Buddhism Roundtable." *The Park Ridge Center Bulletin* (September/October): 13.

———. 2003. "Two Buddhisms Further Considered." *Contemporary Buddhism: An Interdisciplinary Journal* 4 (May): 55–78.

———. 2005. "Complementary and Alternative Medicine in America's 'Two Buddhisms.'" In *Religion and Healing in America*, ed. Linda L. Barnes and Susan S. Sered, 343–357. New York: Oxford University Press.

———. 2007. "Immigrant American Religions and the Family: New Diversity and Conservatism." In *American Religions and the Family: How Faith Traditions Cope with Modernization and Democracy*, ed. Don S. Browning and David A. Clairmont, 20–34. New York: Columbia University Press.

———. Forthcoming a. "American Lessons about Religious and Racial Liberties, with Special Reference to Asian-American Buddhists." In *Religious Pluralism in Democratic Societies: Challenges and Prospects for Southeast Asia, Europe, and the United States in the New Millennium*, ed. K. S. Nathan. Singapore: Konrad Adenauer Foundation/Kuala Lumpur: Malaysian Association for American Studies.

————. Forthcoming b. "Facing Northeast in a Midwestern Metropolis: The Growth of Islam and the Challenge of the 'Ummatic' Ideal in Chicago." In *The History of Religion and Urban America,* ed. Virginia Brereton. New York: Auburn Theological Seminary.

————. Forthcoming c. "Immigrant Parochial Schools: Religion, Morality, Citizenship." In *The Child in American Religions,* ed. Don S. Browning and Bonnie Miller-McLemore. New Brunswick, N.J.: Rutgers University Press.

————. N.d. "The Church Next Door: Local Christians Face America's New Religious Diversity." Unpublished manuscript.

Numrich, Paul D., and Fred Kniss. 2005. "Immigrant Congregational Names in Chicago: Religious and Civic Considerations." *Names* 53 (December): 275–292.

Nyholm, Paul C. 1963. *The Americanization of the Danish Lutheran Church in America.* Copenhagen: Institute for Danish Church History.

Osterman, Rachel. 2004. "Judge Upholds Ouster of 2 Monks." *Chicago Tribune,* July 20, sec. 2 (Metro Chicagoland).

Otto, Rudolf. 1950. *The Idea of the Holy: An Inquiry into the Non-Rational Factor in the Idea of the Divine and Its Relation to the Rational.* 2d ed. Trans. John W. Harvey. London: Oxford University Press.

Pagnini, Deanna L., and S. Philip Morgan. 1990. "Intermarriage and Social Distance among U.S. Immigrants at the Turn of the Century." *American Journal of Sociology* 96 (September): 405–432.

Park, Robert Ezra. 1924. "The Concept of Social Distance." *Journal of Applied Sociology* 8:339–344.

————. 1931. "Mentality of Racial Hybrids." *American Journal of Sociology* 36 (January): 534–551.

————. 1955. *Society. The Collected Papers of Robert Ezra Park.* Vol. 3. Glencoe, Ill.: Free Press.

Perl, Paul, and Jonathon L. Wiggins. 2004. "Don't Call Me Ishmael: Religious Naming among Protestants and Catholics in the United States." *Journal for the Scientific Study of Religion* 43 (2): 209–228.

Perreira, Todd LeRoy. 2004. "*Sasana Sakon* and the New Asian American: Intermarriage and Identity at a Thai Buddhist Temple in Silicon Valley." In *Asian American Religions: The Making and Remaking of Borders and Boundaries,* ed. Tony Carnes and Fenggang Yang, 313–337. New York: New York University Press.

Platvoet, Jan, and Karel van der Toorn. 1995. "Pluralism and Identity: An Epilogue." In *Pluralism and Identity: Studies in Ritual Behaviour,* ed. Jan Platvoet and Karel van der Toorn, 349–360. New York: E. J. Brill.

"Poll: American Jews Accept Intermarriage." http://www.beliefnet.com/story/49/story_4975_1.html.

Portes, Alejandro. 1995. "Economic Sociology and the Sociology of Immigration: A Conceptual Overview." In *The Economic Sociology of Immigration: Essays on Networks, Ethnicity, and Entrepreneurship,* ed. Alejandro Portes, 1–41. New York: Russell Sage Foundation.

Portes, Alejandro, and Lingxin Hao. 1998. "*E Pluribus Unum*: Bilingualism and Loss of Language in the Second Generation." *Sociology of Education* 71 (October): 269–294.

Portes, Alejandro, and Ruben G. Rumbaut. 2006. *Immigrant America: A Portrait.* 3d ed. Berkeley: University of California Press.

———. 2001. *Legacies: The Story of the Immigrant Second Generation.* Berkeley and Los Angeles: University of California Press.

Portes, Alejandro, and Min Zhou. 1993. "The New Second Generation: Segmented Assimilation and Its Variants." *Annals of the American Academy of Political and Social Science* 530:74–96.

Poston, Larry. 1992. *Islamic Da'wah in the West: Muslim Missionary Activity and the Dynamics of Conversion to Islam.* New York: Oxford University Press.

Prorok, Carolyn V. 1994. "Hindu Temples in the Western World: A Study in Social Space and Ethnic Identity." *Geographia Religionum* 8:95–108.

Queen, Christopher S. 2002. "Engaged Buddhism: Agnosticism, Interdependence, Globalization." In *Westward Dharma: Buddhism beyond Asia,* ed. Charles S. Prebish and Martin Baumann, 324–347. Berkeley: University of California Press.

"Questions and Answers on the True Buddha School." 1993. San Bruno, Calif.: Purple Lotus Society.

Rambachan, Anantanand. 2005. "The Hindu Tree on America's Sacred Ground." In *Taking Religious Pluralism Seriously: Spiritual Politics on America's Sacred Ground,* ed. Barbara A. McGraw and Jo Renee Formicola, 173–189. Waco: Baylor University Press.

Reat, N. Ross. 1983. "Insiders and Outsiders in the Study of Religious Traditions." *Journal of the American Academy of Religion* 61 (3): 459–476.

Ronald, Emily. 2006. "America's National Day of Prayer." http://www.pluralism. org/research/profiles/display.php?profile=74229.

Roozen, David A., William McKinney, and Jackson W. Carroll. 1984. *Varieties of Religious Presence: Mission in Public Life.* New York: Pilgrim Press.

Rothberg, Donald. 1998. "Responding to the Cries of the World: Socially Engaged Buddhism in North America." In *The Faces of Buddhism in America,* ed. Charles S. Prebish and Kenneth K. Tanaka, 266–286. Berkeley: University of California Press.

Sadhu Shantipriyadas. 2000. *Mandir: Traditions and Beliefs.* Amdavad, India: Swaminarayan Aksharpith.

Saenz, Rogelio, Sean-Shong Hwang, Benigno E. Aguirre, and Robert N. Anderson. 1995. "Persistence and Change in Asian Identity among Children of Intermarried Couples." *Sociological Perspectives* 38 (Summer): 175–194.

Safi, Louay M. 1999. "The Transforming Experience of American Muslims: Islamic Education and Political Maturation." In *Muslims and Islamization in North America: Problems and Prospects,* ed. Amber Haque, 33–48. Beltsville, Md.: Amana Publications.

Saldana, Stephanie. 2005. "Religious Symbols in the American Public Square." http://www.pluralism.org/research/profiles/display.php?profile=73493.

Saloutos, Theodore. 1973. "The Greek Orthodox Church in the United States and Assimilation." *International Migration Review* 7 (4): 395–407.

Samarin, William J. 1976. "The Language of Religion." In *Language in Religious Practice,* ed. William J. Samarin, 3–13. Rowley, Mass.: Newbury House Publishers.

Sanjek, Roger. 1994. "Intermarriage and the Future of Races in the United States." In *Race,* ed. Steven Gregory and Roger Sanjek, 103–130. New Brunswick, N.J.: Rutgers University Press.

Sargeant, Kimon H. 1998. "Religion and New Immigrants: A Grantmaking Agenda at The Pew Charitable Trusts."

Sarna, Jonathan D. 2003. "American Jews in the New Millennium." In *Religion and Immigration: Christian, Jewish, and Muslim Experiences in the United States,* ed. Yvonne Yazbeck Haddad, Jane I. Smith, and John L. Esposito, 117–127. Walnut Creek, Calif.: AltaMira Press.

Schaefer, Richard T. 1998. *Racial and Ethnic Groups.* 7th ed. New York: Longman.

Schmidt, Garbi. 1998. *American Medina: A Study of the Sunni Muslim Immigrant Communities in Chicago.* Lund, Sweden: University of Lund.

———. 2004a. *Islam in Urban America: Sunni Muslims in Chicago.* Philadelphia: Temple University Press.

———. 2004b. "Islamic Identity Formation among Young Muslims: The Case of Denmark, Sweden and the United States." *Journal of Muslim Affairs* 24 (April): 31–45.

Schwadel, Philip. 2005. "Individual, Congregational, and Denominational Effects on Church Members' Civic Participation." *Journal for the Scientific Study of Religion* 44 (June): 159–171.

Seager, Richard Hughes. 1993. *The Dawn of Religious Pluralism: Voices from the World's Parliament of Religions, 1893.* LaSalle, Ill: Open Court.

Selod, Saher. 2005. "The Nation of Islam and African American Churches: An Analysis of the Changing Nature of the Relationship in the Chicago Area." Paper presented at Association of Black Sociologists Annual Meeting, Philadelphia, August 13.

Shamma, Freda. 1999. "The Curriculum Challenge for Islamic Schools in America." In *Muslims and Islamization in North America: Problems and Prospects,* ed. Amber Haque, 273–295. Beltsville, Md.: Amana Publications.

Sharma, Pandit Lilapat. 1999. *Revered Gurudev: Some Touching Reminiscences.* Mathura, India: Yug Nirman Press.

Sharot, Stephen. 2001. *A Comparative Sociology of World Religions: Virtuosos, Priests, and Popular Religion.* New York: New York University Press.

Sharpe, Eric J. 1975. *Comparative Religion: A History.* London: Duckworth.

Sherkat, Darren E. 1999. "Tracking the 'Other': Dynamics and Composition of 'Other' Religions in the General Social Survey, 1973–1996." *Journal for the Scientific Study of Religion* 38 (4): 551–560.

———. 2003. "Religious Socialization: Sources of Influence and Influences of Agency." In *Handbook of the Sociology of Religion*, ed. Michele Dillon, 151–163. Cambridge: Cambridge University Press.

"Sikh Beating Shows Complications of US Hate Crime Law." 2005. http://www.sikhsangat.org/publish/article_681.shtml.

Slessarev-Jamir, Helene. 2003a. "A Place of Refuge and Sustenance: How Faith Institutions Strengthen the Families of Poor Asian Immigrants." Baltimore: Annie E. Casey Foundation.

———. 2003b. "Sustaining Hope, Creating Opportunities: The Challenge of Ministry among Hispanic Immigrants." Baltimore: Annie E. Casey Foundation.

Smart, Ninian. 1984. *The Religious Experience of Mankind.* 3d ed. New York: Charles Scribner's Sons.

———. 2000. *Worldviews: Crosscultural Explorations of Human Beliefs.* 3d ed. Englewood Cliffs, N.J.: Prentice-Hall.

Smith, Christian. 1998. *American Evangelicalism: Embattled and Thriving.* Chicago: University of Chicago Press.

Smith, James P., and Barry Edmondston, eds. 1997. *The New Americans: Economic, Demographic, and Fiscal Effects of Immigration.* Washington, D.C.: National Academy Press.

Smith, Jane I. 1999. *Islam in America.* New York: Columbia University Press.

Smith, Timothy L. 1978. "Religion and Ethnicity in America." *American Historical Review* 83:1155–1185.

Smith, Tom W. 2002. "Religious Diversity in America: The Emergence of Muslims, Buddhists, Hindus, and Others." *Journal for the Scientific Study of Religion* 41 (3): 577–585.

Snoek, Jan. 1995. "Similarity and Demarcation." In *Pluralism and Identity: Studies in Ritual Behaviour*, ed. Jan Platvoet and Karel van der Toorn, 53–67. New York: E. J. Brill.

Spickard, Paul R. 1989. *Mixed Blood: Intermarriage and Ethnic Identity in Twentieth-Century America.* Madison: University of Wisconsin Press.

Stackhouse, Max L. 2005. "Missions: Missionary Activity." In *Encyclopedia of Religion*, 2d ed., ed. Lindsay Jones, 9:6068–6076. Detroit: Macmillan Reference USA.

Stark, Rodney, and William Sims Bainbridge. 1979. "Of Churches, Sects and Cults: Preliminary Concepts for a Theory of Religious Movements." *Journal for the Scientific Study of Religion* 18:117–133.

Stevens, W. David. 2004. "Spreading the Word: Religious Beliefs and the Evolution of Immigrant Congregations." *Sociology of Religion* 65 (Summer): 121–138.

Stout, Harry S. 1975. "Ethnicity: The Vital Center of Religion in America." *Ethnicity* 2 (2): 204–224.

Suarez-Orozco, Marcelo M., Carola Suarez-Orozco, and Desiree Qin-Hilliard, eds. 2001. *The New Immigrant and Language: Interdisciplinary Perspectives on the New Immigration.* Vol. 6. New York: Routledge.

Swami Jyotirmayananda. 2001. "How to Change Your Life." *Learning Torch* (quarterly newsletter of Gayatri Pariwar Mandir, Chicago) 1 (January 28): 8–9.

Swearer, Donald K. 1970. *Buddhism in Transition.* Philadelphia: Westminster Press.

Takaki, Ronald. 1998. *Strangers from a Different Shore: A History of Asian Americans.* Rev. ed. Boston: Little, Brown and Co.

Tanaka, Kenneth K. 2001. "American Buddhism's Racial Divide." http://www.beliefnet.com/story/7/story_732.html.

Tedesco, Frank M. 2003. "Social Engagement in South Korean Buddhism." In *Action Dharma: New Studies in Engaged Buddhism,* ed. Christopher Queen, Charles Prebish, and Damien Keown, 154–182. London: Routledge Curzon.

Ternikar, Farha Bano. 2004. "Revisioning the Ethnic Family: An Analysis of Marriage Patterns among Hindu, Muslim and Christian South Asian Immigrants." Ph.D. diss., Loyola University, Chicago.

"Thoughts of Gurudev." 2001. *Learning Torch* (quarterly newsletter of Gayatri Pariwar Mandir, Chicago) 1 (January 28): 19.

Tocqueville, Alexis de. [1831] 1969. *Democracy in America.* Ed. J. P. Mayer. Trans. George Lawrence. Garden City, N.Y.: Anchor Books.

Tomasi, Silvano M. 1975. *Piety and Power: The Role of the Italian Parishes in the New York Metropolitan Area, 1880–1930.* New York: Center for Migration Studies.

Tönnies, Ferdinand. [1887] 1955. *Community and Association (Gemeinschaft und Gesellschaft).* Trans. Charles P. Loomis. London: Routledge & Kegan Paul.

Troeltsch, Ernst. [1931] 1960. *The Social Teachings of the Christian Churches.* Vols. 1 and 2. Trans. O. Wyon. New York: Harper and Row.

Tse, Lucy. 1995. "Language Brokering among Latino Adolescents: Prevalence, Attitudes, and School Performance." *Hispanic Journal of Behavioral Sciences* 17 (May): 180–193.

Tvrtkovic, Rita George. 2001. "When Muslims and Christians Marry." *America: The National Catholic Weekly* 185 (September 10). Available at http://www.americamagazine.org/gettext.cfm?articleTypeID=1&textID=1108&issueID=322.

U.S. Supreme Court. 2004 "Brief Amicus Curiae of Buddhist Temples, Centers and Organizations Representing over 300,000 Buddhist Americans in Support of

Respondents." No. 02–1624. February 12. http://pewforum.org/religion-schools/pledge/docs/BuddhistTemples.pdf.

Vande Berg, Travis. 2005. "Meaning and Identity in the New Immigration: ISKCON and Indians." Ph.D. diss., Loyola University, Chicago.

Vande Berg, Travis, and Fred Kniss. Forthcoming. "ISKCON and Immigrants: The Rise, Decline, and Rise Again of a New Religious Movement." *Sociological Quarterly.*

van der Leeuw, G. 1938. *Religion in Essence and Manifestation: A Study in Phenomenology.* Trans. J. E. Turner. London: George Allen & Unwin Ltd.

van Tubergen, Frank. 2006. "Religious Affiliation and Attendance among Immigrants in Eight Western Countries: Individual and Contextual Effects." *Journal for the Scientific Study of Religion* 45 (March): 1–22.

Vasquez, Manuel A. 2005. "Historicizing and Materializing the Study of Religion: The Contribution of Migration Studies." In *Immigrant Faiths: Transforming Religious Life in America,* ed. Karen I. Leonard, Alex Stepick, Manuel A. Vasquez, and Jennifer Holloway, 219–242. Walnut Creek, Calif.: Alta Mira Press.

Volkov, Dmitro. 2003. "Religion, Language Usage, and Opportunities for Citizenship Participation in the Eastern Orthodox and Hasidic Orthodox Communities of Immigrants from the Former Soviet Union." Paper presented at the Final Conference of the Religion, Immigration and Civil Society in Chicago Project, Loyola University, Chicago, June 13.

Waines, David. 2003. *An Introduction to Islam.* Cambridge: Cambridge University Press.

Walch, Timothy. 1996. *Parish School: American Catholic Parochial Education from Colonial Times to the Present.* New York: Crossroad Publishing Co.

Warner, R. Stephen. 1988. *New Wine in Old Wineskins: Evangelicals and Liberals in a Small-Town Church.* Berkeley: University of California Press.

———. 1993a. "Request to Lilly Endowment, Inc. for a Major Grant to Conduct a Training and Fellowship Program for Ethnographic Studies of New Ethnic and Immigrant Congregations (The New Ethnic and Immigrant Congregations Project)."

———. 1993b. "Work in Progress toward a New Paradigm for the Sociological Study of Religion in the United States." *American Journal of Sociology* 98 (5): 1044–1093.

———. 1994. "The Place of the Congregation in the Contemporary American Religious Configuration." In *American Congregations,* ed. James P. Wind and James W. Lewis, 2:54–99. Chicago: University of Chicago Press.

———. 1998a. "1997 Presidential Address: Approaching Religious Diversity: Barriers, Byways, and Beginnings." *Sociology of Religion* 59 (3): 193–215.

———. 1998b. "Introduction: Immigration and Religious Communities in the United States." In *Gatherings in Diaspora: Religious Communities and the New Immigration,* ed. R. Stephen Warner and Judith G. Wittner, 3–34. Philadelphia: Temple University Press.

———. 1998c. "Presentation Prepared for Consultation on Religion and New Immigrants, Pew Charitable Trusts."

———. 1999. "Changes in the Civic Role of Religion." In *Diversity and Its Discontents: Cultural Conflict and Common Ground in Contemporary American Society*, ed. Neil J. Smelser and Jeffrey C. Alexander, 229–243. Princeton, N.J.: Princeton University Press.

———. 2000a. "Epilogue: Building Religious Communities at the Turn of the Century." In *Public Religion and Urban Transformation: Faith in the City*, ed. Lowell W. Livezey, 295–307. New York: New York University Press.

———. 2000b. "Religion and New (Post-1965) Immigrants: Some Principles Drawn from Field Research." *American Studies* 41 (2/3): 267–286.

Warner, R. Stephen, and Judith G. Wittner, eds. 1998. *Gatherings in Diaspora: Religious Communities and the New Immigration*. Philadelphia: Temple University Press.

Waters, Mary C. 2000. "Immigration, Intermarriage, and the Challenges of Measuring Racial/Ethnic Identities." *American Journal of Public Health* 90 (November): 1735–1737.

Weber, Max. [1922] 1963. *The Sociology of Religion*. Trans. E. Fischoff. Boston: Beacon Press.

———. [1914] 1978. *Economy and Society*. Trans. E. Fischoff. Berkeley: University of California Press.

Wedam, Elfriede. 2000. "'God Doesn't Ask What Language I Pray In.'" In *Public Religion and Urban Transformation: Faith in the City*, ed. Lowell W. Livezey, 107–131. New York: New York University Press.

———. 2003. "The 'Religious District' of Elite Congregations: Reproducing Spatial Centrality and Redefining Mission." *Sociology of Religion* 64 (Spring): 47–64.

Westphal, David. 1999. "Minorities Exceed 25% of Population." *Chicago Sun-Times*, September 15.

Wheelock, Wade T. 1987. "Language: Sacred Language." In *Encyclopedia of Religion*, ed. Mircea Eliade, 8:439–446. New York: Macmillan Publishing Co.

White, Aaron. 2005. "Baccalaureate Services and Pluralism." http://www.pluralism.org/research/profiles/display.php?profile=74136.

Wiebe, Donald. 1984. "The Failure of Nerve in the Academic Study of Religion." *Studies in Religion/Sciences Religieuses* 13 (4): 401–422.

———. 1998. *The Politics of Religious Studies: The Continuing Conflict with Theology in the Academy*. New York: St. Martin's Press.

Wiegers, Gerard. 1995. "Language and Identity: Pluralism and the Use of Non-Arabic Languages in the Muslim West." In *Pluralism and Identity: Studies in Ritual Behaviour*, ed. Jan Platvoet and Karel van der Toorn, 303–326. New York: E. J. Brill.

Williams, Peter M. 1990. *America's Religions: Traditions and Cultures*. New York: Macmillan.

Williams, Raymond Brady. 1988. *Religions of Immigrants from India and Pakistan: New Threads in the American Tapestry.* New York: Cambridge University Press.

―――. 1992. "Sacred Threads of Several Textures: Strategies of Adaptation in the United States." In *A Sacred Thread: Modern Transmission of Hindu Traditions in India and Abroad,* ed. Raymond Brady Williams, 228–257. Chambersburg, Pa.: Anima.

―――. 1996. *Christian Pluralism in the United States: The Indian Immigrant Experience.* Cambridge: Cambridge University Press.

―――. 1998. *Loose Connections: Joining Together in America's Fragmented Communities.* Cambridge, Mass.: Harvard University Press.

―――. 2001. *An Introduction to Swaminarayan Hinduism.* Cambridge: Cambridge University Press.

Wilson, Bryan. 1959. "An Analysis of Sect Development." *American Sociological Review* 24:3–15.

―――. 1963. "Typologie des Sectes Dans une Perspective Dynamique et Comparative." *Archives de Sociologie des Religions* 16:49–63.

Wind, James P., and James W. Lewis, eds. 1994. *American Congregations,* 2 vols. Chicago: University of Chicago Press.

Woodhead, Linda. 2004. *An Introduction to Christianity.* Cambridge: Cambridge University Press.

Wormser, Richard. 1994. *American Islam: Growing Up Muslim in America.* New York: Walker Publishing Co.

Wuthnow, Robert. 1987. *Meaning and Moral Order: Explorations in Cultural Analysis.* Berkeley: University of California Press.

―――. 2004. "Presidential Address 2003: The Challenge of Diversity." *Journal for the Scientific Study of Religion* 43 (June):159–170.

―――. 2005. *America and the Challenges of Religious Diversity.* Princeton, N.J.: Princeton University Press.

Xenos, Peter, Herbert Barringer, and Michael J. Levin. 1989. *Asian Indians in the United States: A 1980 Census Profile.* Honolulu: East-West Population Institute.

Yang, Fenggang. 1999. *Chinese Christians in America: Conversion, Assimilation, and Adhesive Identities.* University Park: Pennsylvania University Press.

Yang, Fenggang, and Helen Rose Ebaugh. 2001. "Religion and Ethnicity among New Immigrants: The Impact of Majority/Minority Status in Home and Host Countries." *Journal for the Scientific Study of Religion* 40 (3): 367–378.

Yates, Jon. 2003. "Muslim Scouts Blazing Own Trail." *Chicago Tribune,* January 12, sec. 4 (TribWest).

"Yearbook of Immigration Statistics: 2004." Office of Immigration Statistics. Table 6. http://uscis.gov/graphics/shared/statistics/yearbook/2004/table6.xls.

Yinger, J. Milton. 1946. *Religion and the Struggle for Power*. Durham, N.C.: Duke University Press.

Yoo, David K., ed. 1999. *New Spiritual Homes: Religion and Asian Americans*. Honolulu: University of Hawaii Press.

Yu, Henry. 2001. *Thinking Orientals: Migration, Contact, and Exoticism in Modern America*. New York: Oxford University Press.

*Yuli—The Holy Book*. 1996. Trans. Jason Yum. Singapore: True Buddha Publications.

Zajac, Andrew, and Rummana Hussain. 2001. "Indian Groups Unite to Fund Quake Relief." *Chicago Tribune*, January 28, sec. 4 (Metro West).

Zelinsky, Wilbur. 2002. "The Names of Chicago's Churches: A Tale of at Least Two Cultures." *Names* 50 (2): 83–103.

Zernov, Nicolas. 1997. "Christianity: The Eastern Schism and the Eastern Orthodox Church." In *Encyclopedia of the World's Religions*, ed. R. C. Zaehner, 77–93. New York: Barnes & Noble Books.

Zvizdich, Zerina. 1988. "Imam Mustafa Ceric." In *The Islamic Cultural Center: The Center, the People and the Mission*, 10–11. Northbrook, Ill.: Islamic Cultural Center of Greater Chicago.

# Index

# About the Authors

Fred Kniss is an associate professor and chair of the Sociology Department at Loyola University Chicago and the director of the McNamara Center for the Social Study of Religion. He is the author of *Disquiet in the Land: Cultural Conflict in American Mennonite Communities* (Rutgers University Press, 1997), and has published various articles on religious conflict and change.

Paul Numrich is chair of the Program in World Religions and Inter-Religious Dialogue, Theological Consortium of Greater Columbus, and an affiliate research associate professor in the McNamara Center, Loyola. He is the author of *Old Wisdom in the New World: Americanization in Two Immigrant Theravada Buddhist Temples* (University of Tennessee Press, 1996) and other works on American religions.